M000251366

Baseball's Great Expectations

Baseball's Great Expectations

Candid Stories of Ballplayers Who Didn't Live Up to the Hype

Patrick Montgomery

ROWMAN & LITTLEFIELD

Lanham • Boulder • New York • London

Published by Rowman & Littlefield
An imprint of The Rowman & Littlefield Publishing Group, Inc.
4501 Forbes Boulevard, Suite 200, Lanham, Maryland 20706
www.rowman.com

86-90 Paul Street, London EC2A 4NE, United Kingdom

British Library Cataloguing in Publication Information Available

Library of Congress Cataloging-in-Publication Data

Names: Montgomery, Patrick, 1971– author.
Title: Baseball's great expectations : candid stories of ballplayers who Didn't live up to the hype / Patrick Montgomery.
Description: Lanham : Rowman & Littlefield, [2024] | Includes index. | Summary: "Baseball's Great Expectations features the fascinating stories of baseball players who were on the cusp of greatness, who everyone expected to be the next superstar, but never quite lived up to the hype—or through tragic circumstances, never had the chance"— Provided by publisher.
Identifiers: LCCN 2023036309 (print) | LCCN 2023036310 (ebook) | ISBN 9781538181805 (cloth) | ISBN 9781538181812 (epub)
Subjects: LCSH: Baseball players—United States—Biography. | Baseball—United States—History. | Baseball players—United States—Miscellanea.
Classification: LCC GV863.A1 M624 2024 (print) | LCC GV863.A1 (ebook) | DDC 796.3570922 [B]—dc23/eng/20230805
LC record available at https://lccn.loc.gov/2023036309
LC ebook record available at https://lccn.loc.gov/2023036310

For those who tossed the ball against the wall as a kid,
listened to baseball games through a hidden radio
below a pillow past bedtime, but most of all to
the next wave of boys and girls falling in love with the game.

Contents

Foreword

By Pat Gillick,
National Baseball Hall of Fame Baseball Executive
With Bob Elliott,
BBWAA Career Excellence Award Winner

My dear friend Elmer (Dutch) Gray was a hardworking scout who was respected by all in the business. He scouted and signed Ken Griffey to a contract with the Cincinnati Reds. You may have heard of his Hall of Fame son, Ken Griffey Jr.

Elmer once told me a story of a young bird dog scout he had in Canada in 1968. Elmer's young scout was overly excited when a promising third baseman came to an open tryout. Elmer explained to the young man how it was a scout's job to look at a teenager and project where the player would be in five years. "Would he be able to take Tony Perez's job at third base for the Cincinnati ball club in five years?" Elmer asked. The young part-timer shook his head no and said, "Mr. Gray, you must have specials eyes to be able to determine that."

In 2011, the Veteran's Committee elected me to the Hall of Fame in Cooperstown as a general manager, in tribute to my strong staff of scouting and development helping build contending teams in Toronto, Baltimore, Seattle, and Philadelphia . . . and winning three World Series Championships. But I consider myself more of a scout. That's where I started and that's what I did when I was no longer general manager of the Phillies It is what I enjoy the most.

I always admired the scouts like Paul Richards, Bobby Mattick, Hugh Alexander, Dallas Green, Wayne Morgan, Ken Madeja, Charlie Kerfeld, and many others. And of course, our former scouting director with the Blue Jays, Bob Engle, who drafted two Cy Young award winners for us—Pat Hentgen and Chris Carpenter—and signed another winner, Felix Hernandez, when he had Latin America for the Seattle Mariners.

Some of the players Patrick Montgomery details in this book were can't-miss prospects, blue chippers as the saying goes. It isn't that the scouts missed on a player. Sometimes life happens. There was evidence of greatness.

That old line about how scouting isn't an exact science is true. In the case of scouting Brian Milner, he was one of the finest catching prospects I have ever seen. He was as good as Hall of Famers Johnny Bench and Gary Carter when I scouted them. Brian showed he could hit, going 4-for-9 in his first two games in the majors, playing directly from high school. He could handle the velocity from the opposing pitcher; however, it was a difficult adjustment catching pro pitchers, many who had yet to master command or control.

In this book, Montgomery examines the career of position players Josh Booty, Brian Cole, Ben Grieve, Cale Iorg, Brian Milner, and Dan Pasqua who, combined, played in 1,896 games in the majors with 6,782 plate appearances and 235 home runs. On the mound, David Clyde, Ron Necciai, and Brien Taylor pitched in 96 games, working 471 innings, registering 19 wins.

Some days the "special eyes" are accurate and the "can't miss prospect" does not miss. Other days the "special eyes" see only glimpses and a player's career is derailed by injury. And some nights, the "special eyes" are not really in focus.

Acknowledgments

A special thank you to the many people pushing, trusting, and inspiring me along the path of this book. Jeff Pearlman, Marty Appel, Ian O'Conner, Ken Davidoff, Brad Balukjian, and Jay Horwitz are all authors way out of my stratosphere who all took time to encourage me along the way. The Rita Rosenkranz Literary Agency for fighting for me and this book. Christen Karniski of Rowman & Littlefield for bringing the book to you, and to the incredible Kate Scheinman serving as my editor and taskmaster.

The cooperation and interviews from family, players, and baseball executives, including Heath Bell, Josh Booty, David Clyde, Greg Cole, Jim Duquette, Ben Grieve, Tom Grieve, Jay Horwitz, Cale Iorg, Garth Iorg, Kevin Millar, Brian Milner, Ron Necciai, Dan Pasqua, Brian Sabean, Pat Strange, Brien Taylor, David Wright, and Jason Zillo.

The gathering of baseball statistics and biographic information on the players in this book took many paths but would not have been possible without the amazing resources of baseball-reference.com, stathead.com, Baseball America, sabr.org, and the SABR Research Collection, which contains access to the *Baseball Research Journal*, *The National Pastime*, and the SABR Digital Library.

My wife, Barbara Montgomery, deserves a plaque in the Spouse Hall of Fame.

Introduction

I am going to be brutally upfront and honest with you about this book. This is not really a baseball book about baseball players. Baseball is the essential background but not the star of the book, much like a speedy .272 hitting fifth outfielder off the bench is essential for a baseball team. The chapters in *Baseball's Great Expectations: Candid Stories of Ballplayers Who Didn't Live Up to the Hype* delve into what we thought we knew about the featured players—so painstakingly close to reaching the echelon of baseball stars—but the individuals themselves are just as remarkable as the baseball players they once were.

This book is a timely and poignant tale of loss and redemption of celebrated, disdained, or forgotten blasts from baseball's past. What were once names on old baseball cards or in dusty books can now be seen in a whole new light. The viewpoints expressed in this book are from the ballplayers themselves as well as others who know or knew them personally. The players featured in each chapter are more than their role in baseball, so baseball cannot define who they are, or what their lives became without or beyond baseball.

Baseball is the Great American Pastime. During times of fear, confusion, and division, people look for the comfort of tradition to remind themselves of the *good old days.* Baseball is timeless, able to be newly discovered again.

Baseball and accompanying nostalgia will never go away; boxes jammed with baseball cards, gameday programs, ticket stubs, and old baseballs sit in basements and attics in many homes. Tales of parents tossing boxes of priceless cards or autographs into the trash are everywhere.

Millions of boys and girls play baseball and softball into adulthood. The game runs through their veins. Anyone who played at any level, from the backyard to the major leagues, has their own great story and still tells their friends about that "one time" or "remember when."

The stories of baseball idols and heroes are spoken of near and far; they appear in all styles of books and media formats. But what about those names tucked away in the corner of your mind, names that can still conjure memories of the certain wind-up of a pitcher, the sound of spikes down cutting the baseline, or the distinct thwack of greatness heard in the bat of a player who simply never became the player you knew—you could feel in your bones—he would become?

Answers to some of these questions are revealed in the chapters of *Baseball's Great Expectations*, directly from the players themselves, or from their families, friends, or others who knew them best: What if? Could'a been . . . , and What happened to?

A few people have been fortunate enough to feel the jarring "something different" sound that causes a pit in their stomachs when a particular ball is hit so sweet, hard, and perfect. A sound that rare and special makes it easy to imagine that, if you could close your eyes, listen, and eavesdrop through time, this would be the same sweet sound heard nearly a hundred years ago from the bat of Babe Ruth or in Bernard Malamud's world of Roy Hobbs.

In 2013, I was about twenty feet behind a batting cage as Yankees were taking cuts on a backfield during spring training in Tampa, Florida. I know what I saw and heard. It was perfect. One spectacular ball hit so sweet by Austin Romine, that I heard a sound that can only be described as an axe cutting perfectly through a log with the brute strength, comfort, and smoothness of Chuck Norris daintily galloping on a unicorn into the sunset of a double rainbow toward a pot of gold he knew was there for his taking.

I could see the ball overpowered by the bat becoming a different form, even the roundness of the perfect size and shape of a baseball being compressed so hard it wobbled, then teetered on the precipice of absolute destruction, becoming the shape of a teardrop orb, and ultimately straightening to a ball that will not be denied where it wants to go. The ball itself violently crashed to the ground and then beautifully rolled to a final resting place. My eyes may have been able to deceive me into thinking it was at least five hundred-feet power, but the sound confirmed it in my memory.

The sound of a ball hit like that stays with you. It was the sound of greatness heard from the bat of a backup to a backup catcher. I never thought a player like that would be able to make his bat bellow like that on a swing. But it started me thinking about how even the backup to a backup catcher could perhaps have his own baseball stardom, his "what if." Austin Romine did not become a star, but as of 2023, he is still grinding away as a thirty-four-year-old catcher with parts of twelve Major League Baseball (MLB) seasons behind him, with fewer than five hundred games played.

As I began to think about this book—from the initial idea, to research and interviews, and finally to the keyboard—it became clear that players often have a different version of events from the ones the media, fans, and baseball stubbornly hold on to over the years. One word I expected to hear often was not used much, and not in the way I thought it would be: The lack of the word "regret" was eye-opening to me. This shifted the focus of my book to the whole person, rather than just the player, and highlighted how consumable the "product" of a player can be in the eyes of professional baseball, media, and fans, intentionally or not.

These players don't look back with melancholy or sadness about their time in the game—well usually not—but the feeling is as complicated and relatable to baseball fans as the faint memory of a kiss from unrequited love. It does not mean as much now, if anything, but it once was a powerful feeling.

The memory and the *"what if?"* can linger and then disappear as quickly as Aaron Judge turning on a 2-2 fastball or the harsh reality of the seemingly impossible rising fastball of a 1985 Dwight Gooden that you know you can't catch up with but swing anyway. The players in this book once felt the rush of success followed by failure and are now on the other side of the game they do not play anymore.

Players can be fine with how things worked out for them and be happy to remember the feel of the sun on their faces when they were on the fields of professional baseball. For some, the memories of events such as the thrill of playing in the major leagues, receiving a standing ovation, winning Rookie of the Year, making the MLB All-Star team, feeling the weight of a World Series ring, or even setting a record that is sure to be as safe as the 511 career wins set by Cy Young, are more than enough. For others, it was knowing it was time to walk away, or knowing what they were walking toward as they made their decision, or it was made for them.

For so many of us fans, we who copied their batting stance, tried to throw like them, or held the glove a certain way in a vain attempt to conjure up the same skills we knew those players possessed, it is hard to comprehend how a player being paid to play baseball would be anything but heartbroken as they moved on from baseball. They, and we too—if we dreamed hard enough—were going to be the first, or next Sandy Koufax, the next Willie Mays, Mickey Mantle, or whichever player brought an extra skip to our hearts as we peeled back the wax wrapper of a baseball card pack, revealing the guy we believed in. We believe now that it didn't quite work out the way we thought it was going to.

When I, myself, was one of those kids, I knew I was going to be just like the big-swinging image of what I thought a home-run slugger should look like, and maybe I could be. I knew Mickey Mantle was out of the question, but maybe I could be like former Yankees and Kansas City 1980s cult hero Steve Balboni? I never came anything even close to Balboni; as a child I went from super skinny, to a walking wheelbarrow like Balboni, back to the body of Phil Rizzuto through high school. But those dreams and connections to the players from my childhood still make up my baseball love to this day.

At various times as a kid growing up, I would try to imitate a certain swing, or replicate the marvelous fielding play I saw on TV from players like Rod Carew, Thurman Munson, Mike Schmidt, Steve Balboni, Dave Winfield, Cecil Cooper, Dan Pasqua, Don Mattingly, Reggie Jackson, Graig Nettles, Bucky Dent, and Willie Randolph. Fred Lynn only after he left the Boston Red Sox, and I never allowed myself to entertain an opinion that Carlton Fisk or Ted Simmons were better catchers than Munson. I only conceded on Johnny Bench because he is Johnny Bench. In my opinion, Mike Schmidt and Bench are the greatest players at their respective positions of third base and catcher in baseball history. Apologies to Munson and Nettles.

One of the players in this book felt as though he has loved baseball his whole life, but baseball did not love him back. The harsh reality is that baseball doesn't love anyone, and this is a reason it can keep going. If baseball loved players, the sport would have died of heartbreak from the brutal reality of players like Christy Matthewson, Lou Gehrig, Roberto Clemente, and Brian Cole, all being taken way too soon. We as fans, teammates, family, and friends cried, but baseball kept eyes forward as some of the next great players became great, and others sadly did not.

Is it the individual player who "failed"? Or is it our own failure for not taking the time to understand how difficult it is to be one of the top players in a game of skill, how much luck (both good and bad) occurs, the opportunities that were blocked and opened, how timing plays out, how much of a business baseball really is, and how fickle the game and life itself can be? Those players did not fail—they were outstanding players and athletes.

Often perspective, context, and achievement cannot easily be defined, and they fuel the banter, arguments, whimsy, and romanticism of the game itself. The feeling of watching, playing, and remembering the players of baseball is much like the soft whispering siren always bringing us back and asking again, what if?

- "What if Josh Booty couldn't throw a football like Peyton Manning?"
- "What if David Clyde didn't look so good in his first start for the Texas Rangers?"
- "What if Brian Cole didn't have a fender bender in a Taco Bell parking lot?"
- "What if Ben Grieve had been appreciated for the player he was?"
- "What if Cale Iorg had been able to have surgery after his injury in rookie ball?"
- "What if Brian Milner had moved to the outfield?"
- "What if Ron Necciai had not pushed his arm so hard?
- "What if Dan Pasqua wasn't expected to be Mickey Mantle or the next local kid done good?"
- "What if Brien Taylor had not gone out that night?"

The most logical answer is as simple as the phrase "what if?" To paraphrase the baseball philosopher Alex Rodriguez, "Well, that's Baseball, Suzyn."

The "no regrets" these ballplayers have and their refusal to wallow in the questions of what if makes a lot more sense to me now. I am glad the players took their chances because I would have too. If you made it this far reading my book, I have a feeling you may have or will continue to swing away at a dream. This persistence makes us as relatable as the players we admire and the individuals we are—our true selves—when people stop watching us once a dream is achieved or no longer chased.

Enjoy the stories in *Baseball's Great Expectations*. Perhaps look back on your own at some of the players you have wondered about who are not mentioned in this book. Although the players may not regret much about their choices or baseball career doesn't mean the people in these chapters never felt regret, sorrow, anger, jealousy, or bitterness in years past about professional baseball.

For the friends and family of Brian Cole left behind, the what if is the largest of all. For the other players in this book, an occasional pang may arise when remembering their baseball lives, but they are happy where they are now and for their own baseball journeys; after all, it's Baseball, Suzyn.

 JOSH BOOTY, MIAMI MARLINS, 2004–2009

Position: third baseman

Bats right, throws right

Drafted by the Florida Marlins in the first round (fifth overall) of the 1994 MLB June Amateur Draft from Evangel Christian Academy, Shreveport, Louisiana

Released by the Miami Marlins on February 26, 2013

Major League Career Totals

AVG	G	AB	R	H	2B	3B	HR	RBI	SLG	OPS
.269	13	19	3	7	1	0	0	4	.308	.674

Minor League Career Totals

AVG	G	AB	R	H	2B	3B	HR	RBI	SLG	OPS
.198	478	1745	186	346	76	7	62	252	.356	.613

Highlights

- Josh Booty played with the 18U US National Junior Olympic Team, winning the silver medal. He roomed with Alex Rodriguez.
- His $1.6 million 1994 MLB draft signing bonus was the largest in history at the time.
- Booty is Mr. All-American, with High School All-America Honors in Football and Baseball.
- He was named the Best Defensive Player in the Minor Leagues by Baseball America in 1997.
- While playing football after a five-year hiatus, he beat out two future NFL quarterbacks, winning the starting position during his first season at Louisiana State University.
- Josh Booty was drafted by the NFL Seattle Seahawks in 1999 and was with the Cleveland Browns until 2003.

experience. Rodriguez had been offered close to $1.25 million to sign and report to Rookie Ball for the Mariners but declined. Rodriguez also could have been with the Olympic National team but left the team when he would not consent to his name and likeness being used for the Topps Baseball Card. He did not want to give up his rights to his first baseball card, believing it would ultimately cost him hundreds of thousands of dollars in brand management and jeopardize future baseball card contracts. Rodriguez was also there with a $1.2 million dollar insurance policy to protect him in case of injury while he was going through difficult contract discussions with the Seattle Mariners. For Booty, it was a crash course in what big time baseball could be, both financially and in terms of popularity.

Josh Booty was from a football family, and NCAA football is practically its own religion to many from Louisiana. "I was more of a football guy, but baseball too, and here I am coming from a small school in Louisiana taking ground balls with Alex Rodriguez at shortstop. All the media were there, all the attention was on him, everyone was talking about him. I figured if I stayed at shortstop I was not going to play much. During that practice I asked to shift over to third base," laughed Booty.

Alex Rodriguez and Josh Booty became roommates and friends at the Olympic Festival and even talked about what if Alex Rodriguez really would just call the Mariners bluff and go to the University of Miami to play shortstop and quarterback. "He loved football, but I think he knew baseball was his future. I'm pretty sure he made the right decision for him," said Booty.

Booty ultimately moved to third base, Alex Rodriguez batted third, and Booty fourth, batting clean-up. "We also had Paul Konerko batting fifth," said Booty.

The 1993 Junior Olympic Team ended up with the silver medal, with Josh Booty moved back to shortstop. Alex Rodriguez suffered a freak injury when a baseball hit him in the face before the start of the third game. Rodriguez suffered a cheekbone fracture and shortly after signed with the Seattle Mariners with a $1 million dollar bonus.

With an Olympic silver medal in hand, Booty returned to Louisiana for his senior year of high school, playing both football and baseball. Although he was a football hero in Louisiana and possibly the top quarterback in high school football history, his baseball stock was rising. Booty held his own and more with and against the top young baseball players in the country, and with international players like his future teammate Cuban right-hander pitcher, Liván Hernández. Baseball also had guaranteed contracts—without the risks of injury from college football—before he would even be NFL draft-eligible. As already noted, Booty had broken his hand, and he had to miss his last four games with the football team that fall. An injury to an athlete can take away a career in a microsecond, and football is a high-contact sport with a short career window and prone to injuries.

Even as Booty committed to play football and baseball at LSU, the lights and security of professional baseball started to become a viable option for the football guy. Booty was in a nice position as an athlete looking to his future. He was known as a good baseball player who was awesome at football. As his exposure grew, and with the better baseball competition following the USA Junior National Team, Booty morphed into an athletic legend. He became known as a top quarterback, shortstop, and pitcher, with the perfect combination of height and strength to be cream of the crop at the two marquee positions of their sports. Football had his heart, but what could baseball do to make him pivot from the gridiron to the diamond? Football was basically the Booty family business and calling card. Baseball would have to come at Booty hard.

Josh Booty saw how No. 1 pick shortstops from high school could do with Alex Rodriguez selected and signed in the 1993 MLB Draft. The New York Mets held the coveted spot that year. In perhaps a nod to a dual future, he went with agents Leigh Steinberg and Jeff Moorad. Steinberg was the NFL quarterback agent, and his clients included Booty's football idol John Elway. Steinberg helped Elway with dual football and baseball professional options as well. Moorad served as Booty's baseball agent and made sure MLB teams understood Booty loved LSU, and turning down the chance to play both sports at LSU would take the highest signing bonus in baseball history.

"If the Mets didn't select me at one, my agent was pushing me hard for the Florida Marlins. Their owner was a deep-pocketed Wayne Huizenga, and he was always looking for a way to create buzz in Miami at the time," explained Booty.

The script went as Jeff Moorad hoped, and in 1994, Booty was selected by the Marlins with the fifth pick of the draft. "Jeff knew I could slot right in as the Marlins top minor league prospect, he used my football and LSU leverage to secure me a record signing bonus, kind of close to Louisiana, and language in the contract to get me to the major league level quickly," said Booty. The only catch was his contract had strict language not allowing him to play football.

There have been great football players, and there have been great baseball players. But the idea of being great at both on the professional level is one of the elusive dreams of many professional athletes. The level of athleticism, focus, and practice to be great at one sport is hard enough, never mind two. Freak athletes like Dave Winfield were drafted in the MLB, NBA, and NFL, but to make it as a quarterback and in MLB just couldn't happen, right? Dan Marino was an MLB fourth-round pick as a pitcher out of high school, but he chose to play college football and had a Hall of Fame football career. John Elway used a minor league summer with the Yankees to get to the Denver Broncos and the NFL. Elway's bluff to play baseball worked perfectly, but was he really going to try both?

As great as dual athletes like Deion Sanders and Bo Jackson were, they were both in positions with less game preparation than Josh Booty's preferred quarterback and third base. A quarterback must be the leader of the team, first in, last out of the football facility and endless game study for the week. Sanders was electric as an NFL player, and Bo was a special NFL player, but he was only able to play part of each football season and shared the ball in the Raiders backfield with NFL Hall of Famer Marcus Allen. Bo Jackson had some of the most tantalizing tools in the history of the NFL and MLB but was not able to truly capitalize on either to full potential. Bo had one Pro Bowl selection in football and one All-Star game selection in baseball. The only thing Bo knew how to lead the MLB in was strikeouts with his league leading 172 in 1989. Bo Jackson was not able to capitalize on his MLB career after blowing his hip playing football. The Bo Jackson hobbling on one leg is heartbreakingly far from the image of "Bo Diddly" and the Nike commercials showing him as perhaps the greatest athlete of our time. And Deion Sanders, amazing as he was in football, could never play more than ninety-seven games a season during his choppy nine-year career. Jackson and Sanders tried, and Josh Booty made the decision to go with baseball only.

Josh Booty was going to give baseball his first shot after coming to the largest draft signing bonus in MLB history. He now had 1.6 million reasons to play for the Marlins and put the football down. But would his heart be in it? "When I was drafted and went to third base, I thought I could be a Mike Schmidt type, hit for big power, not a great average, but lots of home runs, RBI, and play a good defense. I had a great arm, I was a good pitcher in high school, if I really worked at it, I probably could have been a good pitcher too," said Josh Booty.

In 1993, as Josh Booty was flinging touchdowns and hitting home runs for his high school while deciding which path to take, Kevin Millar was grinding away on an Independent Northern League baseball field. He was trying to be noticed. Millar was a baseball player and a winner, who had led his 1988 high school baseball team to a 3-A City Title in Los Angeles. Not selected out of high school in the MLB Draft and without scholarship offers, he went on to play for Los Angeles City College (a community college) before earning a partial scholarship to play Division 1 baseball at Lamar University in Beaumont, Texas.

Millar earned All-Sun Belt Baseball Honors and was selected to play in the prestigious Cape Cod Baseball League after the 1992 season. The Cape Cod League is for players expected to have significant interest from MLB scouts and to be showcased for those teams and scouts. Throughout his high school and college career, Millar was a winner and a player the team needed, but he was not selected for an MLB organization. Millar had the size (6'1" and 200 pounds), with good power, but was somehow overlooked.

During the fall of 1993, the Miami Marlins took a chance and offered Millar $900 to sign a contract, $1,599,100 less than offered to Booty. Millar happily signed and reported to Kane County of the Mid-West A League for the Marlins 1994 team. Millar instantly paid off for the Miami Marlins as he was selected as a Mid-West League All-Star for the 1994 season and produced solid AA seasons for 1995 and 1996, but a call-up to the Marlins still didn't come. "They offered me almost nothing, but I was happy to just have an opportunity to keep playing ball," said Kevin Millar, former MLB player and present MLB Network Radio host.

The 1994 MLB player strike—the one that infamously cancelled the 1993 World Series and took a potential .400 batting average chase from Tony Gwynn, a sixty-home run chase from Larry Walker, and a potential Montreal Expos–New York Yankees World Series—carried on into the spring of 1995. The owners of the MLB teams needed players to report to spring training, but the players on an MLB roster were not doing so as part of the player strike. Since Millar was not part of the major league roster, he came in and practiced in the open MLB spring training for the Marlins. "I didn't know if I was ever going to get a sniff at the big leagues, and it was my chance. As an undrafted free agent, with almost no investment into me by the Marlins, I figured it could be my only shot to ever play even a game as a big leaguer," said Millar.

Josh Booty was struggling in the minor leagues for his 1994 and 1995 seasons with his bat, hitting 8 home runs and 46 RBI in approximately a combined 500 at-bats with his batting average at .200. Hitting the fastball came easy, but curveballs, off-speed were a hard learning curve. One of the oldest baseball cliches of "trouble with the curve" was certainly applied to Booty. "My father always told me if you are not contributing with your bat, you better bring something extra with your glove," explained Josh.

Then in 1997, Josh Booty and Kevin Millar ended up on the same Portland AA team in the Eastern League—the Portland Sea Dogs. Even better, the older, more seasoned Millar was Booty's roommate. "It almost felt like a Bull Durham thing, he was this anointed bonus baby, and I was just trying to make a name for the big leagues," said Kevin Millar. "Josh was so much more talented than me, he had more athletic talent in one finger than I had in my whole body," explained Millar. "Josh was so different than the rest of us, he would be like let's go get dinner, he meant steak and lobster, we would all be like no way, we didn't get your signing bonus!" said Millar. "That was just Josh, I loved him and thought he was a great teammate."

With Millar holding down first base and Booty at third, they both put up numbers too big to ignore. Kevin Millar hit 32 home runs, drove in 131 RBI, and hit .343 while winning the Eastern League Most Valuable Player Award. Booty hit 20 home runs, drove in 69 RBI, and locked down the 3B side with his sparkling defense. The Portland Sea Dogs were a force to be reckoned with as they went 79-63, winning the North Division by six games. Seven players hit 10 or more home runs. The team offense was dominating, pacing the league in runs, hits, doubles, home runs, RBI, batting average, and slugging percentage.

With Josh Booty already on the 40-man roster, he was called up for the second consecutive year. He appeared in four games at the end of the year receiving 5 at-bats. Booty made his first major league start on September 24, 1997. He batted eighth, started at third base, and finished the game with 2 hits in 4 at-bats, scoring twice, and walking once.

"I played first base to Josh's third and all his throws were rockets right to my chest all season. I never saw anything like that before or after," said Millar.

"I never made a throwing error while playing baseball, not one. For me I had to focus, concentrate on my footwork and hands. The hard thing was catching it, but if I did, I was making that throw. As a quarterback every throw mattered. I did the same in baseball, and I really took pride in it," said Booty.

Booty was a magician with his glove and rocket arm at the hot corner. His glove showed more than major league potential, and although the batting average was not climbing, his power numbers were coming together with back-to-back 20 home run season in 1996 and 1997, with combined double and triple numbers of twenty or more those years. The first of his major league call-ups as per his rookie contract was 1996.

Booty was only twenty-one when he was called up to the major leagues for the first time with the Marlins on September 24, 1996. He stepped in as a pinch hitter with the Marlins ahead of the Atlanta Braves in the top of the fifth for the number nine hitter, pitcher Pat Rapp, against Kevin Lomon, and promptly hit a ball to right field for a no-doubt first major league base hit. Then after the 1997 minor league season with Kevin Millar, Booty was again called up to the Marlins to taste the big-league life for the last few games of the regular season.

According to Booty, "My first big league start in 1997 against the Montreal Expos is my favorite baseball memory. It was in their old Olympic Stadium. I played well. I kind of felt like, I can do this at the major league level. The minor leagues is such a hard road, but that really helped me believe I could succeed in the big leagues."

"I was good friends with Torii Hunter, it was a long and hard minor league road for him, he was hitting .210's .220's same as me. Suddenly with enough at-bats it clicked for him, and he just figured it out. He turned into an All-Star player, bopped twenty to thirty home runs a year. I just didn't take the time to figure it out. I just really wanted to be playing football," continued Booty.

No matter where he was it seemed like Booty couldn't shake his football past, not that he really wanted to. Baseball players would ask Booty about various football players and had questions about back when he would have been the prize of any college football recruiting class—just as Alex Rodriguez had wanted to hear all about Booty's football experience when they were roommates back at the Olympic Festival. "Baseball players just love football and football players, guys in the NFL and college teams didn't care about baseball," said Josh Booty.

The baseball player, Josh Booty, loved his football too. "My time in the minor leagues, my whole approach was still wired to football. I still moved like a football player. I missed football bad. I was a football guy. My mentality was football, not baseball. There is just so much downtime in baseball, standing in the outfield shagging balls and things like that. I didn't like it," said Booty.

As a high school senior drafted in baseball, Josh Booty was months removed from his last touchdown pass. Baseball clay and dirt were still fresh in his spikes as he was drafted. Baseball was in the forefront of his mind. "The thing is, when I signed with baseball, I thought I would never look back. I was going to play baseball forever. My baseball contract wouldn't allow me to play college football. When I signed, I thought that was it for football," said Booty.

But as strikeouts piled up and the batting kept going down, it was hard to not remember the success and feeling of the football field. Booty recalled, "When I struggled offensively, couldn't get my batting average up, it just wore on me. I already really wanted to be playing football. My brother was at LSU starting as a freshman receiver. My dad's a football coach. Everybody in the state of Louisiana was trying to get me to come back to LSU. It was always a story, if I went to the game to watch my brother, the cameras were always on me asking if was coming to play quarterback for the Tigers."

NFL teams wouldn't let go either; teams reached out to Booty to gauge if he would be willing to play overseas football during the baseball offseason. NFL Draft experts were saying he could be drafted right into the NFL without even playing college football. The bonus he received to play baseball was the obstacle keeping him from his football dreams. He could not pay back the bonus because much of it had already been spent.

After the Marlins won the 1997 World Series, Booty and Millar both went to spring training for a chance to make the team and contribute. Booty started the year at third base for the 1998 Marlins when Bobby Bonilla was not healthy enough to start the season. Booty received regular playing time until Jeromy Burnitz going first to third slid into third base and injured Booty's thumb on his glove hand. Bobby Bonilla came back, and Josh Booty was gone.

The injury took time to recover, and Booty found himself back on AA and AAA teams for the remainder of 1998, struggling to keep his batting average over .200. He was miserable and wanted to play football. Booty explained, "I really struggled in 1998, I was in AAA Charlotte for a month, and my hand hurt so bad I could hardly grip the bat. I was not feeling good. The Marlins called me at the end of the year and said they were going to remove me from the 40-man roster, and I would probably be back in AAA the next year. I finally said, listen, I'm going to go back and play football."

Booty's time in AAA allowed him to catch up with Peyton Manning while Booty's team played the AAA franchise in Indianapolis. Hurting in baseball and seeing some of his football peers now succeeding at the NFL level made it even harder for Booty to focus and see a baseball future for himself. "I saw Peyton at Tennessee become Peyton Manning the huge star, first pick in the NFL Draft," said Booty. "It just became, I was crazy to not be playing football. I was thinking of going to LSU, play with my brother, and become a first-round pick. I really do like football more. I was a baseball first rounder, received the bonus I wanted, I'd always liked baseball, too. I just had those two things going in my head," explained Booty.

Once he uttered the words, "I'm going to go back and play football" to the Marlins, Booty's agent was able to reach a compromise of only an $80,000 buyout of his contract. The owner who signed him, Wayne Huizenga, had recently sold the franchise to John Henry, and Henry had no money invested in Booty and was more amenable to the request. But the Marlins retained Josh Booty's baseball rights if he intended to play again in the future.

"I understood why he left baseball, he had so much talent, but his heart was just not into it, and he was unhappy. I was glad to see him go for what he wanted so badly," said Millar. "As his friend, I wanted the best for him, and so did his baseball teammates."

But how good could Booty have been if he had really focused on baseball?

Kevin Millar says, "If I had to compare a player from today, I would say, if Josh kept at it, he would have been a player like Joey Gallo, huge power, not a good average, but he would have that kind of power." Joey Gallo is a two-time All-Star in his first eight years in the major leagues and already has two 40 home run seasons and five of 20 home runs or more.

Booty walked away from his professional baseball career and made good on his promise to play football at LSU.

During the time Booty spent at LSU, the baseball team was a national powerhouse, winning the 2000 National Championship. "I never played on the baseball field there, but looking back now, I would have enjoyed slipping between practices and launching some balls in that stadium," recalls Booty. But he was at LSU to play football with his brother Abram, and to show the NFL he could be their franchise quarterback. It was Josh Booty time—or was it?

Abram Booty was originally leaning toward a college program known for passing the ball like Florida or Miami. But LSU is a strong pull for any high school football player, and perhaps going to LSU would open the door to play with his big brother there.

It was never a lock that Josh Booty would play college football, but it happened, and he was going to have an opportunity to toss touchdowns to his brother, Abram. But first Josh had to beat out two other quarterbacks on the LSU roster, players who would both eventually go on to play in the NFL, Craig Nall and Rohan Davey. Nall eventually won the position and started the 1999 opening game against San Jose State. However, Nall quickly gave way to Josh Booty as the starting quarterback.

Not having played football for five years and then trying to pick it up at such a high level was both courageous and foolhardy for Josh Booty. "I was foolish to try to jump right back into football," he says.

The offense at LSU with head coach Gerry DiNardo was a running offense. The I formation was far removed from the four and five wide receivers in a spread formation Josh had run in high school. "I was used to the shotgun and spread, throwing the ball everywhere," said Booty. "The offense under DiNardo felt like I was in the Stone Age."

The dream combination of the Booty-Booty hookup was not dialed in often during the 1999 season. Abram Booty did not produce at the level expected after being the Southeastern Conference's sixth leading receiver in receptions during the 1998 season. But one glorious evening in the 1999 season against Ole Miss, in Tiger Stadium under the lights with 79,940 in attendance and comfortable 70-degree weather, the Booty brothers made special memories and the on-field connection both wanted at LSU. A Josh-to-Abram connection in the first quarter produced a 27-yard pass for a touchdown putting the Tigers up 7-0. At the halfway point through the third quarter with the Tigers down 28-17, Josh repeated the heroics by throwing another 27-yard touchdown pass to Abram to bring the Tigers within striking distance at 28-23. The Ole Miss Rebels went on to rush for 2 touchdowns in the fourth quarter for a comfortable 42-23 victory.

Josh finished 22-38 in attempts and 256 yards and tossed 3 touchdowns. Abram finished the game with 5 receptions, 2 touchdowns, and 86 receiving yards. It would be the only game with the Booty-to-Booty scoring connection in 1999 and ultimately would be the last touchdowns for Abram Booty for the LSU Tigers. Josh Booty only threw for 1,830 yards, against 17 touchdowns and 19 interceptions. They were not the numbers Josh, the NFL scouts, or the draft pundits were expecting to see. So, this 1999 season was one to forget for Josh Booty and LSU fans as the team wobbled to a 3-8 (1-7 SEC) record. It would prove to be the last losing season they would have until 2021.

The Josh Booty and DiNardo marriage did not last long as DiNardo was ultimately fired with one game left in the 1999 season. Nick Saban had led his 1999 Michigan State team to a 9-2 record and ranked seventh for the season, and shockingly he jumped to be the head coach for LSU Football.

"I had no problem with Coach DiNardo, I just wasn't the right fit for the style of game he wanted to use," said Booty. "Going to LSU was a huge mistake, I was warned by a lot of people to go somewhere like Florida, Miami, or even BYU where they tossed the football around, but I was stubborn, I loved LSU, and I wanted to make it work," explained Booty. "It didn't work out like I thought it would."

The 2000 LSU Football team was much improved over the 1999 team with an 8-4 (5-3 SEC) record with a final ranking of 22nd in the country under Nick Saban. Jimbo Fisher as the offensive coordinator adapted a pro-style offense with more passing opportunity for the quarterback. But Coach Saban planned on carving playing time at quarterback for Rohan Davey. The situation created heated debates and discussions among fans and local media. The last name of Booty was another name for football excellence in Louisiana, and the already high pressure intensified.

The first game of the 2000 season was a 58-0 shellacking of Western Carolina. Booty threw 2 quick touchdowns, with only 15 pass attempts in the first quarter and a 20-0 lead. Rohan Davey came in after that throwing 3 touchdowns to complete the victory. The next game was against Houston for a 28-13 victory, but only 25 passes were attempted by Booty.

Then the season hit a huge bump for Booty as he tossed 4 interceptions in a 13-10 loss against the University of Alabama at Birmingham, considered to be an inferior team from Conference-USA. With Booty on the bench against SEC opponent Tennessee the next week, Rohan Davey threw for over 300 yards, with 4 touchdowns and 0 interceptions in a 38-31 victory.

The quarterback carousel continued as Booty and Davey both played in a 41-9 loss to Florida. Josh Booty started the next six games finishing with a 5-1 record, including the Peach Bowl against Georgia Tech and a 28-14 victory.

The Peach Bowl victory, however, came at a price for Booty. With unrelenting pressure from the blitz, Booty was not able to get into a groove in the first half, throwing for only 110 yards and no touchdowns. The Tigers were down 14-3 and pulled Booty in favor of Davey for the second half. As the blocking improved, Davey was able to orchestrate a come from behind victory as the defense shut out Georgia Tech in the second half. The final was 28-14. The Bowl victory was the first of many for Nick Saban over his illustrious NCAA coaching history.

The 2000 season ended with Booty named to the 2000 Southeastern Conference Coaches First-Team All-SEC squad after his 17 touchdown, 15 interception year. Interceptions were an Achilles heel for Booty at LSU. His 19 interceptions in 1999 were second in the NCAA to future first-round pick Patrick Ramsey of Tulane who threw 24 interceptions. But still Josh Booty's 2000 year showed continued growth with more passing yards in fewer passing attempts, and more than double his touchdowns, even with appearing in forty-four fewer plays in 2000 than 1999 while starting ten games and had victories over SEC foes Kentucky, Mississippi State, Ole Miss, and Alabama.

Then Josh Booty declared for the 2001 NFL Draft and was selected as a sixth-round pick by the Seattle Seahawks. "It was time for me to leave LSU and go for the NFL and see if I could do it," said Booty. "I couldn't be twenty-six in college and keep my NFL hopes on hold."

Booty had to be patient as the picks were called and quarterbacks were being selected before him. Booty had had conversations with teams and was expecting to be selected higher than the sixth round. "I thought I would be gone by the third round for sure," said Booty. "The Cowboys said if I was still there in the third round, they were taking me for sure, but they ended up taking Quincy Carter in the second, so I knew I wasn't going there," said Booty. "I've seen both sides of professional sport drafts. I went in the first round in baseball and near the end of the football draft."

Eleven quarterbacks were selected in the 2001 NFL Draft. An incredible ten of them made NFL rosters, with only Josh Heupel not making a regular season roster. Heupel was the 2000 Associated Press Player of the Year, All-American, and led the Oklahoma Sooners to the National Championship. Quarterbacks selected before Booty were Michael Vick, Drew Brees, Quincy Carter, Marques Tuiasosopo, Chris Weinke, Sage Rosenfels, Jesse Palmer, Mike McMahon, and A. J. Feeley.

For Josh Booty, being on the Seattle Seahawks was an uphill battle. He was the fourth-string quarterback, but it was a good place to learn. Matt Hasselbeck was to be the starter, with Brock Huard, Travis Brown, and then Booty. Brown was released as the team brought in Trent Dilfer.

Booty explained, "I was in a great spot with the Seahawks. They had Matt Hasselbeck, who was a low draft pick like me years before," said Booty. "Coach Holmgren had him in Green Bay and he was the starter. But Holmgren did not like Brock Huard as the back-up and brought in Trent Dilfer as insurance for Matt."

The NFL is a numbers game for the last roster spots; the final players are relegated to watching as their career, opportunity, and livelihood can change on a dime. "They wanted to keep me over Brock, but they could not find a trade for Brock," said Booty. "He was a high draft pick a couple of years before and didn't want to just let him go," explained Booty. "I am glad for my time with the Seahawks, I learned a lot from Matt Hasselbeck, he and I were roommates at camp, and we are still close today."

The Cleveland Browns quickly picked Booty up after he was released by the Seahawks. The next few years he was paired with head coach Butch Davis, and with offensive coordinator Bruce Arians to back up Tim Couch and Kelly Holcomb at quarterback. "Butch Davis tried to heavily recruit me to Miami back in high school, and Bruce Arians tried for Mississippi State, so I knew those guys forever," said Booty. But more and more teams started to go without a third string quarterback, and Booty was released during the 2003 season.

Then a 2007 NFL attempted comeback with the Oakland Raiders did not work out as Booty did not make the team. The Raiders had the NFL 2007 first overall pick JaMarcus Russell from LSU, Josh McCown, and Andrew Walter at QB as well. With JaMarcus Russell still not signed going into training camp, the Raiders brought in Daunte Culpepper in case Russell and his holdout dragged on. "It didn't work out, but it was wild to be there while Al Davis owned the team," said Booty.

After all is said and done, and after years of reflection, which sport means more to Josh Booty? Which would he value more, a World Series ring or a Super Bowl ring? Booty answers, "A Super Bowl ring, not even a question. I have a World Series ring, and it wouldn't compare to a Super Bowl ring for playing quarterback, that is just a whole different level."

As it turns out, Josh Booty does not even have his 1997 World Series ring anymore, and he has one of his best friends to thank for it. According to Kevin Millar, "Josh and I were at Harrah's Casino in New Orleans, for a Super Bowl event in 2002, I ended up with his ring on my hand. Josh was talking crap with Drew Bledsoe, Tim Couch, Joey Harrington about who was the best athlete. I excused myself to go to the men's room. I took off the ring to wash my hands and went back to the guys still arguing. A minute or so later Josh asked for the ring back. I reach to the finger to give the ring back and it was gone. I must have left it on the counter. I ran back and it was already gone. I came back terrified to tell Josh what happened; he was like no big deal, and said let's go hit Bourbon Street, didn't even beat on me about it. I know I wouldn't have been the same way."

A few years later, Millar tried to make it up to Booty. "When I received my World Series ring for the 2004 Red Sox team, I offered it to Josh to replace his. He told me no way; it was mine and to keep it," said Millar. After all this time, the ring has not surfaced.

Josh Booty is now the father of twin boys, and they are about to make choices for college and athletic careers. "The one plays quarterback back at my old school and the other is the receiver," said Booty. "Although they are both really good and can easily play on the next level, I think the receiver can really turn out to be special," explained Booty. "My nephew plays quarterback at Oklahoma," continued Booty. For those wondering, his name is General Booty. You read that right, and that is his actual name and may rank among the most entertaining sports names of all-time.

Talking with Josh Booty, he brings a certain confidence and sense of control to his life. This is not to be confused with arrogance, which is not part of who he is. He just has a mindset that pushes him to keep going until something is no longer viable. Nothing seems to shake him or bring him down.

This is the man who raced home from church on Sundays to glue himself to the TV to watch his idol John Elway play quarterback. Booty was senior class president, homecoming king, quarterback for the football team, shortstop for the baseball team, captain for both, and named most athletic, best looking, and more in the high school yearbook. All-State selections are not large enough, it was All-American for Booty.

He dated cheerleaders in high school, and later, he dated supermodels. His mom and dad are an American dream romance, actual high school sweethearts approaching fifty years of marriage. If we could make athletes in a lab, the Booty Brothers would be the outcome. Even as other people see Josh as having fallen short in his dream of being a two-sport superstar, bigger than anyone, he is more than happy for all of his life experiences. This is not a man full of regret or bitterness at the end of his athletic career.

The closest thing to a tinge of sorrow for Booty was not having achieved the highest levels of the NFL and MLB. "I guess my biggest disappointment is that I was not able to be a Hall-of-Famer in two sports," said Booty. "I have not lost any sleep over it though."

Josh Booty is past his athletic days, although at times he swears he could still go out and compete for a spot on an NFL roster. "I see Tom Brady and Aaron Rodgers out there and I can still feel football in my blood, I just love to compete," insists Booty. When a fabulous athlete thinks about going for both baseball and football like Josh did, Booty has become the "been there and done that" symbol who the media compare to, or they ask his opinion about. Tim Tebow, Kyler Murray, and Jameis Winston all sunk their foot into the dual sport pool to an extent.

But Booty thinks if he had a time machine and could go back to his senior year of high school and make the choice again, he would have changed his decision—not necessarily in trying both sports, but in how it was done. "I know now it is about putting yourself into the best possible situation for you to succeed. I would have played college football first, not at LSU, but somewhere best suited for my strengths. I would have probably been a high draft pick and played for a long time in the NFL. If that didn't work out, or if I could balance baseball with the NFL, I still would be young enough to give baseball a good go," explained Booty.

His time in the sports world serves Booty well today as he has cultivated friendships and relationships in what he calls a "fraternity" from sports. It is not just baseball and football; he also is close to athletes in golf and basketball. "I am even friends with Karl Malone, it's crazy," said Booty.

"I am thankful for everything I was able to do, I played Major League Baseball, big time college football, and the NFL, I was lucky enough to see and experience more than anyone could ever wish for. I am thankful and blessed," said Booty.

 DAVID CLYDE, TEXAS RANGERS, CLEVELAND INDIANS, AND HOUSTON ASTROS, 1973–1979, 1981

Position: pitcher

Bats left, throws left

Drafted by the Texas Rangers in the first round (first pick overall) of the 1973 MLB June Amateur Draft from Westchester High School in Houston

Traded by the Texas Rangers to Cleveland Indians with Willie Horton for Tom Buskey and John Lowenstein, February 28, 1978

Traded by the Cleveland Indians with Jim Norris to the Texas Rangers for Mike Bucci, Gary Gray, and Larry McCall, January 4, 1980

Released by the Texas Rangers, March 31, 1980

Major League Career Totals

W	L	IP	SO	WHIP	ERA
18	33	416.1	228	1.530	4.63

Minor League Career Totals

W	L	IP	SO	WHIP	ERA
27	29	484	352	1.727	4.69

Highlights

- David Clyde is only one of four players to jump from high school to the major leagues since the amateur draft began in 1965. The others are Mike Morgan, Tim Conroy, and Brian Milner, all of whom debuted in 1978.
- Clyde is one of just three high school pitchers drafted first overall, along with Brien Taylor and Brady Aiken. Clyde is the only one of the three to play in the major leagues.
- Clyde started a major league game three weeks after throwing his last high school pitch.
- During his first major league start, Clyde walked his first two batters before striking the next three batters out in succession.
- Clyde started his 1974 season by going 3-0 with a 2.43 record through six starts. He ended the season appearing in 28 games, starting 21 of them, but failed to earn another win the rest of the season finishing 3-9 with a 4.38 ERA in 117 innings.

CHAPTER 2

David Clyde

The Phenomenal Cautionary Tale

David Clyde was born on April 22, 1955, in Kansas City, Kansas. His family moved several times before settling into the Houston, Texas area, just in time for David to play high school baseball as a freshman. As a young teenager approaching the practice field for baseball tryouts, nobody knew they were about to turn away the most impressive and accomplished high school pitcher of all time, not just in Texas, but in the world.

Clyde was used to being the new kid and moving from town to town. He and his three younger brothers, Michael, Steve, and Henry, were a tight-knit unit and played sports together. Professional baseball players often must move at a moment's notice as they are traded or on the search for the next playing opportunity, and Clyde was introduced to one of the most difficult challenges a young player faces, trying to fit in during frequent changes.

"It seemed like we were always a magnet when it came to sports. I played football, basketball, and baseball," said Clyde. Other sports were okay, but baseball was his love. "For me it was always about baseball, I always loved it, I still do." Even today Clyde clings to the romanticism and traditions of baseball. "When baseball is played right, it is beautiful, just a poetry in motion," he explains.

For the young David, playing sports was about being friends with your teammates, being together, and feeling like part of a group. "Sports is a great way to bring people together, such a unifying experience. Athletes understand other athletes. There is proving ground, but if you have it, you're accepted," explained Clyde. A boy using sports as a built-in social network is not uncommon, but Clyde's skill on the mound was special, even if nobody at his new high school was aware of that yet. "With all the social media and Internet stuff going on today, I would have walked in with the high school baseball coach knowing about me beforehand, but I was just another kid, and under the radar," said David.

Moving into a new school district is hard, especially during freshman year. But for Clyde, it was especially challenging because it was winter break. He was just another new kid who the baseball coach had never heard of and didn't know possessed a golden arm. The coach wouldn't even look at David as he tried to walk on late for the team after finishing basketball as his winter sport. "I showed up hoping to have a tryout, and the coach told me, nope, team is full, sorry," said Clyde.

His father Gene was David's baseball tutor and taught David how to pitch, but most importantly, he was also being taught how to grow into a respectful adult. David learned not to argue and not to question a coach or teacher. Rather, he was urged to show them what he was capable of. "I didn't argue, tell him that I was good," said David. Gene Clyde did what many dads do each day. He broke out the gloves and a baseball.

As the baseball team practiced, father and son played catch along the fence of the baseball field. As they tossed the baseball, David and his arm began to warm up, and he transitioned to his smooth and effortless pitching stance and delivered his typical blazing results and resounding smack of the leather. "The sound of my throws turned [the coach's] head, and he quickly found the room on the team for me," laughed David.

David was an incredible athlete at several sports during high school, making All-State and All-American in Baseball, All-State in Basketball, and All-State in Football too. He was even offered a scholarship to play football at Notre Dame. Clyde was wrapped in a perfect sports cocoon, and he was happy; surely his life after high school would be golden like always, either in college or professional sports.

Being the best Texas high school pitcher of all time would place a person high on the MaxPreps Top-50 List of All-Time High School Baseball Players, but with high school baseball phenoms like Alex Rodriguez, Ken Griffey, Joe Mauer, and Derek Jeter spread across the country, how would Texas pitchers rank? Well, seven Texas high school pitchers are on the list, with no positional players. Baseball in Texas *is* pitching, and David Clyde was considered the best. The list goes from 1965 to 2022, and only covers Nolan Ryan for his senior year in high school in 1965. Roger Clemens did not make the list, but he quickly proved himself as a community college player to earn a spot with the University of Texas, eventually leading the Longhorns to the 1983 College World Series Championship and becoming the first player to have their number retired at the university. The NCAA began to give out the Roger Clemens Award in 2004 to the NCAA Division One Pitcher of the Year. Neither of those MLB legends most often associated with the image of a Texas hurler as a gunslinger blazing their own paths with knockdown fastballs even made the list.

Four of the players in the top ten are Texas pitchers, and most baseball fans can easily recall three of them: Kerry Wood, Josh Beckett, and Clayton Kershaw. The fourth is less well-known to fans, but all baseball evaluators, scouts, and player development personnel know the tale of David Clyde. It is a tale of the good, the bad, and the ugly, and there is more to Clyde than most people know.

Clyde was a left-handed pitcher from Westchester High School in Houston. His senior year in 1973 is still the best for a high school pitcher. Clyde went 18-0 and struck out 328 batters in 148 innings pitched to 0.18 ERA. But his ERA was worse than the year before when he held batters to just an 0.16 ERA. His record as a junior was 17-1, with 248 strikeouts in 121 innings pitched. Fifty years later, Clyde still holds national high school records for career shutouts at 29 and career strikeouts of 842, and he is ranked 1 and 2 for consecutive innings pitched without an earned run of 115 and 95. To put this into context, Orel Hershiser holds the MLB record at 59.

David knew he was a great pitcher as he was playing in high school and that he could probably sign a professional contract after high school graduation. He remained low-key and humble, even as word got around to him that he probably would have been selected with the top pick in the 1972 draft as a junior, and it was assured that he would go at the top of the draft in 1973. "I didn't actually see a lot of scouts or talk to many of them," Clyde said. But he knew teams liked him and following his freshman year, he received mail from a major league team expressing their interest.

The 1972 Texas Rangers were not a good team, and by virtue of the worst record for that year, they held the top pick in the 1973 MLB Draft. The Texas Rangers smelled an opportunity to get an early peek at their potential new player during the Texas State Baseball Tournament. The owner Bob Short, General Manager Joe Burke, Manager

Whitey Herzog, and pitching coach Chuck Estrada all watched as Clyde tossed another high school no-hitter. There was no chance they were going to let this Texas prodigy go to the Philadelphia Phillies with the No. 2 pick.

"My senior year we went to Dallas for our playoffs, and the Texas Rangers kidnapped mom and dad and wined and dined them," said Clyde. He was on the bus back from the playoffs with no idea that Gene and Amy Clyde were having a night on the town with his future employer. "I came home that night, and they weren't home yet, they came home the next morning. They loved it, the Rangers showed them a great time," recalls David.

David loved the Kansas City/Oakland A's, idolized Dodger Sandy Koufax, and didn't know anything about the Texas Rangers. Clyde says, "If you told me you would shoot me at the time if I didn't know a damn thing about the Rangers, I would be dead." His hometown of Houston was a National League town, and the sports section was all about the Houston Astros, nothing about the Washington Senators who moved to Texas and became the Texas Rangers in 1972.

Clyde does not remember anything much about being drafted on June 5, 1973. He still had his high school baseball team on his mind until a semi-final loss a few days later. Television trucks ascended on his neighborhood as news arrived of the young man from Houston being picked for the other side of the state. "My father handled all the contract talks for me with the Texas Rangers and their owner Bob Short," explained Clyde.

There have been players who have gone straight to the major leagues without playing Minor League Baseball since the MLB Draft began in 1965. When this happens, it is usually with players from the top college programs who were drafted after several years of playing and training in an almost minor league environment and proving ground. High school pitchers were taken as raw projects, able to grow, mature, and refine their game as minor leaguers before being called up to the MLB team. But there has been only one player drafted who went directly from high school to the majors and stayed the whole season.

Over the years, stories about David Clyde were tinged with, "He shot himself in the foot" by DEMANDING to go straight to the major leagues, not playing minor league ball at all. "It is simply not true," continues David. "I am not sure how all the confusion is still there about that, what I wanted, and my dad asked for just a major league contract."

Tom Grieve, a future Texas teammate (and the father of Ben Grieve, the focus of another chapter in this book), is not sure what happened during Clyde's contract talks but believes the result did not do David any favors in the long run and was not a baseball decision by the Rangers.

Grieve does not pull any punches as he discusses what he believes happened to Clyde. "The Rangers moved from Washington because of low attendance and were drawing even worse in Texas. Bob Short, the owner, was on his way to bankruptcy and having to sell the team. He decided to bring David to the big leagues for his first start without any minor league indoctrination, which was completely unfair to the kid. He hadn't pitched in a month since the end of the high school season, and to bring him to the big leagues was absurd," said Grieve.

Absurd or not, that's what happened to Clyde, who says, "The demand to start in the major leagues was from them, not us. We cared about just being on the 40-man roster." He did not think he would be forced to deal with everything thrown his way the first year or two in baseball.

Clyde had a major league contract, a \$65,000 bonus, \$22,500 salary, and \$7,500 roster bonus. Only a week after signing the contract, he would join the Texas Rangers on the road and was slated to start his first game in Texas shortly thereafter. Such a deal in hand would be hard for any family or player to turn down. Especially for a player who had dominated so easily and for so long at the high school level.

"David Clyde and his family probably had confidence that it wasn't a huge risk, and he would translate his success in the majors," said Grieve, who continued, "It would have taken a rare kind of family to turn down that contract, with that money at the time. I think Bob Short took a calculated risk that in the end led to him sacrificing this kid. I believe at first, he thought there is a chance he develops, thrives, and becomes a tremendous player over a long period of time, he would be considered a genius for doing it. I don't think he looked at it as doomed right from the start. Short had to know the risk and the owner made the call taking the chances. In the end it is his fault."

With the owner pushing to make the young pitcher a media and marketing sensation, what power—other than not signing or asking for a trade—would the player and family have? Saying no to the Rangers on starting in the major leagues would have been a huge risk. Tom Grieve notes, "I wish David and his family would have said, 'Thank you very much for the opportunity to play, but David's not ready for this. I don't want to put him into that situation. I insist that he go to the minor league and develop at his own pace the way he should.' I would find it hard to believe a family would take that stand with all the circumstances." So with an unbelievable contract in hand and the understanding that he would be taking the bump in a couple of weeks against the Twins at home, Clyde was sent off to be part of the team.

The harsh reality of the major leagues hit David as soon as he joined the team on their road trip, and it was not even on the ballfield with baseball. "I had one teammate on my very first day with the team that let me know quite clearly, he didn't care for me. I hadn't done anything to him at all, but he hated me. I found out years later his best friend on the team was sent down to the minor leagues to make room for me. I now understand, but he never told me where his problem with me was coming from," explained Clyde, who continued, "For me coming from my high school baseball team just a few weeks before, it was a protected environment, everything is the team, and you are all friends. Before I even put the uniform on, I was immediately made aware it was not like that in the major leagues."

As Clyde was learning life as big leaguer and throwing a few bullpen sessions, the Texas Rangers were turning his first start into a carnival sideshow, with little thought as to what would be best for the young player himself. The expectations for Clyde would be so large and unrealistic that he was sure to disappoint by the time he hit his post-game shower.

What really happened during Clyde's first MLB game on June 27, 1973? Tom Grieve was expecting to see a frightened young boy go out to the mound and be quickly blown up by a really good hitting Minnesota Twins team that included Tony Oliva, Larry Hisle, and Rod Carew, the AL Batting Champion for 1973. However, Grieve was wrong and happy to be so. "It was exciting as a player to be in that game. I wanted to know the answer to the question of how the best high school pitcher could do against a major league team. I figured a high school pitcher going against a team like the Twins—they could really handle the bat—would get bombed, give up 15 runs in the first inning, Clyde wouldn't have a chance. This kid can't shut them down. David answered the question, all while being under crushing weight of pressure, scrutiny, expectations, and still able to keep his composure. It was incredible," said Grieve.

The pregame and game were loud, energetic, and filled with hope that the Rangers would have their Texan prodigy leading them for many years to come. Belly dancers, lion cubs, and even a theme park giraffe model were part of the festivities. As the game was about to start, many were still not in the stadium because the first traffic jam for a home game occurred. So many fans were stuck in traffic that the start of the game was delayed, and approximately ten thousand fans were turned away from the first ever stadium sell-out!

The year 1973 was a time well before the Internet, but had it existed, Clyde would have broken it, just like he broke the infrastructure surrounding the stadium that evening. Fans overwhelmed the roads, parking lots, and stadium. "Have you ever heard of a ballgame being delayed because of a traffic jam of fans wanting to see one player?" asked Clyde.

"The game was supposed to start, they had a toll road, and the cars were so backed up on the toll road trying to get to the stadium. He already started to warm-up, news cameras on him the whole time, the adrenaline rush of ready to go and then had to sit down and wait, and do it again, before taking the field. That is almost an impossible ask for a pitcher," said Grieve.

"My first pitch was a ball," said Clyde. "I think I was squeezed. It should have been called a strike," explained Clyde, still showing a dose of the confidence he displayed that Texas night.

"The first two batters including Rod Carew walked. David then struck out the side, it was just incredible," said Grieve, who clarified that the players on the field that night were not envious but struck by the immense moment in time the game was to become too many. "The feeling I had then, and I still hold now, was how incredible it was to place this kid in this position. It wasn't fair to him to have those expectations placed on him. I thought to myself during the game that there is no possible way when I was eighteen that I ever would have the poise and the ability to block the noise and perform like that. Every single teammate, everyone on that field, and most of the fans had to be feeling the same thing, how in the world could that kid come up big with this pressure?" said Grieve. "I knew myself and no one else on that field could have done the same thing, it was unbelievable to watch that."

Grieve continued, "He went five innings, not pitching since a few weeks earlier at his last high school game. It is mind boggling what he was able to accomplish. What I took away that night was how proud I was to see him perform like that. It's on the list of my favorite things I witnessed in baseball."

Tom Grieve has played with many first-round picks; he was one himself and even picked them each year as a general manager. He admits that sometimes after a selection, it's not always clear why the player was taken so early in the draft, but Clyde was not that guy, he LOOKED like he belonged. "David Clyde wasn't some guy drafted high and when you see him and think how in the world did this kid ever end up the No. 1 pick? When this kid went out there, it was wow, this kid looks like a big leaguer right now. He wasn't a 96 or 97 miles per hour guy, probably 93 or 94, but he had a big curveball. Sandy Koufax was his idol and had a huge curveball. They both had a great delivery. Clyde looked like not just a big leaguer, but a polished big leaguer," said Grieve.

As mentioned above, Clyde idolized Sandy Koufax, another left-handed pitcher with an easy delivery, a fastball that could explode, and a curveball to make kneecaps buckle. Clyde even wore number 32, like Koufax did. And although the two players never met, the idol reached out to the rookie just thirty minutes before the game was to start—with a telegram from Sandy Koufax to David Clyde, congratulating him on the huge step he was about to take.

Sandy Koufax also never played Minor League Baseball before his MLB debut, and he well knew how hard it would be to accomplish what Clyde was attempting to do.

Koufax went from being an unknown walk-on to the basketball team as a freshman at the University of Cincinnati, to earning a partial scholarship and trying out and making the varsity baseball team a year later. After one year of college baseball, he signed with the Brooklyn Dodgers for a bonus of $14,000 (about $150,000 in 2023 dollars). The $14,000 was above the $4,000 signing bonus threshold making him a "Bonus Baby," and requiring the Dodgers to keep Koufax on their major league roster for two years and ineligible to play in the minor leagues.

Like Clyde, a seasoned player on the parent team would be sent down to make room for the green rookie, and future Hall of Fame Dodger Manager Tommy Lasorda was the player sent down to the Montreal Royals.

Over the next five years, Koufax would struggle to learn how to be a pitcher at the major league level on the fly. The initial version of Sandy Koufax was a mediocre pitcher with too many walks, finishing with more games lost than won at 36-40, with an unsightly 4.10 ERA. After the 1960 season, Koufax was ready to call it quits, even tossing his gloves and spikes into the trash after the last game of the season and walking out of the locker room. Koufax decided to give it one last try in 1961. It all came together for him as he made the All-Star game the next six years, winning three Cy Young Awards and an MVP. Sandy Koufax is considered one of the greatest pitchers of all time and is a Hall of Famer solely on his incredible performance of his six final seasons before retiring young due to arthritis in the elbow.

"When I was a kid I got a hold of old film of Sandy Koufax pitching, he was a lefty like me, big curveball like me, I wanted to be just like him. Our deliveries were the same. That telegram meant everything to me at the time, and still does. It is one of the only pieces of my pro baseball memorabilia I have displayed at home. Even almost fifty years later, I cherish the telegram that he took the time to send it, and he followed my story," explained Clyde.

During that first game, Clyde appeared to toss aside the pressure, static, and hoopla to pitch 5 strong innings, allowing 1 hit, 2 runs, and struck out eight batters. All were great numbers but were balanced with a 2-run home run and 8 walks. Clyde was able to hold the great Twins hitters of Rod Carew and Larry Hisle hitless but gave up the home run to Mike Adams in the second inning. This was a first for both David Clyde and Mike Adams: the first MLB home run hit off Clyde and the first of only 3 MLB home runs hit by Mike Adams.

Number 32 on the Rangers mound that night was like an early version of Koufax, good enough to effectively hold the Twins down to allow the Rangers to win the game. The Texas Ranger fans were happy, and the publicity (both written and broadcast) about Clyde and the Rangers left owner Bob Short overjoyed, wanting more, and seeing green.

For the young player himself, the good outing was followed by an even better next start on July 2, with Clyde pitching 6 innings, striking out 6 and allowing only 4 base hits, 1 earned run, and more importantly, just 2 walks and no home runs. This time he went up against the Chicago White Sox with pitcher Steve Stone, who became a great pitcher later in his career. Clyde battled Stone pitching 6 innings, leaving the game to the bullpen with the Rangers up 4-3. Clyde did his job to keep the Rangers in the game, before the White

Sox were able to score the winning runs against the bullpen in the eighth and ninth innings.

But pitching a strong first game followed by another may have ruined Clyde's chances to develop into one of the best pitchers of his generation. According to Clyde, "We thought it would only be a couple of starts and off to the minors, that is what the manager thought was best, but the owner said no, it was more important to keep me selling tickets. The Rangers front office overruled [Manager Whitey Herzog] and insisted I stay up." So a real baseball education was put on hold, like Sandy Koufax before him, and with even less experience, Clyde was expected to pick it up, keep up, and produce.

The young player's goal was to produce on the mound, but for the Rangers front office, it was about producing fans in the seats. "I was on the team just to make the team money. The Rangers made a fortune off me. I paid my bonus back probably if not in the first start, in the first two starts," explained Clyde on the ticket and concessions bump with him pitching in 1973.

Attendance for the 1973 Texas Rangers was abysmally low, at 686,085, putting them in eleventh of twelfth place for the American League. But when Clyde started in home games, average attendance would triple. So Clyde started eighteen games, twelve of which were at home. During those twelve games, the crowd averaged 18,369. Without Clyde on the mound, the crowd averaged 6,748. More fans equaled more money for the owner and a spot for Clyde in the big leagues.

Now that Clyde was in the big leagues for 1973, the eighteen-year-old had to try to blend in with an older veteran team with the next youngest player seven years older than David. It was a huge gap not only in age, but in life experiences, shared bonds (such as having played in the minor leagues), and many players were married with children. Clyde was once again the new kid in town, but this time (and without his brothers around), the "other kids" were not as welcoming to him.

"The best high school pitcher was able to pitch effectively and earn a win in a major league start. Now, was it the best thing for him to be a big leaguer? No. He's eighteen years old. We had a veteran team. You know, guys are taking him out drinking after the game. He was trying to fit in with guys who were, you know, fifteen years older than he was. It was just a totally unfair environment for an eighteen-year-old to be in," explained Tom Grieve on Clyde trying to be one of the guys on the team.

Clyde was now in a whole different hemisphere, and it showed. "Who wants to hang out with some eighteen-year-old snot nose kid? I don't necessarily think I was being pressured to go out with the guys drinking and hanging out on the road. I still don't know to this day if those guys were having me go out with them to befriend me or try to sabotage me," explained Clyde of his early experience as a player.

"I think many of them were jealous of me. I didn't pay my dues. But I didn't ask for any of that. I never said anything to them about it, I didn't think I had to say anything about it, nor did I, and I still don't," explained Clyde flatly. He is not a tattletale and still lives by an unwritten baseball code to protect his teammates, then and now. Clyde is a man of baseball loyalty who has not received the same courtesy from others over the years.

"The Rangers were hurting for money. I showed I could put money in the bag, put fans in the seats, without me I don't think Bob Short could have sold the team," explained Clyde on his importance to the 1973 team bottom line, making it possible for a 1974 sale.

In 1973, the Texas Rangers were losing games, when unexpectedly a proven winner—both as a player and manager—became available. Billy Martin was famous for his passion for winning, drinking, turning losing teams into winners quickly, and burning bridges. Owner Bob Short had worked with Detroit Manager Billy Martin when Martin managed the Twins, and Short had been part of their front office before he became the owner of the Texas Rangers. It was known that Short "would fire his grandmother" to get a shot at Martin managing the Rangers. When Whitey Herzog heard that he was being replaced by Martin, Herzog wryly noted that, "I must be Bob Short's Grandmother."

Billy Martin replaced Whitey Herzog as manager during the last gasp of twenty-three games ending the year. As the season went on, the promise of Clyde's strong starts faltered, and the low attendance spread to the final games he started at home.

Martin saw young pitchers differently than Herzog and managed them differently. Gone was the "let's keep it simple and natural" attitude for handling Clyde, replaced with intense pressure to win, a hard-to-approach manager, and missed turns in the rotation. With Herzog, Clyde regularly had three or four days of rest between starts, and he was limited to approximately 7 innings or 110 pitches. Now with Martin at the helm, it was eight or nine days of rest and no inning or pitch limits for Clyde. It became clear that Martin and his pitching coach Art Fowler did not have an interest in player development at the major league level; they only expected MLB results from Clyde.

The 1973 season was full of highs and lows for David, including an MLB career starting and winning a game just weeks after his last high school pitch. His season ended on the wrong end of a 7-1 score to the Kansas City Royals. The eighteen-year-old pitched 148 innings of high school ball and another 93.1 innings in the major leagues. Since Clyde finished 4-8 for the Rangers with an astronomically high 5.01 ERA, his spot on the major league roster was in question for the 1974 season.

The 1974 season would prove to be more challenging and less enjoyable for David Clyde. Billy Martin was coming back to manage, and he was given the duties of general manager with all player decisions, including the future of David Clyde. But Billy Short sold the team just before the start of spring training, and the new owner took away the general manager duties and the roster decisions from Martin. Despite the objection to Clyde by Martin, Clyde was a member of the 1974 Texas Rangers, and Martin did not appreciate having to carry a player on the field he didn't want in the first place. "Billy Martin wanted to win now and didn't want David in the big leagues. I don't think he put him in positions to succeed. It was doomed right from the start. No matter how poised and how talented David was, he couldn't thrive in that environment. Nobody would have, and he didn't," explained Tom Grieve.

Clyde understood that he was not going to have a smooth relationship with Martin, but he always hoped it would improve. "We had a new manager that came into play the end of my first year. And that was Billy Martin. I am not going to go too in-depth because unfortunately Billy is not around anymore to defend himself. Strike one, he didn't like young players. Strike two, he was not a pitcher and didn't know how to handle them. Strike three, believe me, I did not ask to be the center of attention, and by virtue of what happened, I was. The Rangers really wanted me to be the star of the show. But Billy wanted to be the star of the show, bigger than the players, owner, whoever, and I got caught in the crossfire," explained Clyde on the pattern that followed Martin throughout his managing career.

The Rangers had a huge turnaround from 1973, going from chump to looking like a champ for much of the season under Billy Martin in 1974. "The Rangers were one of the worst teams in baseball in 73. [But in 74, we] were winning, on the verge of going worst to first. We were in the race with Oakland up until like the last couple weeks of the season," explained Clyde. "Billy wanted me in the minor leagues that year, the front office told him no, and I was forced on him to be on the team, and that wasn't good for me and receiving consistent innings."

"With his personality the way it was," continued Clyde, "he wanted nothing to do with me after the front office kept me on the roster, that is just the way Billy was. His pitching coach Art Fowler was useless. This is God's honest truth, the only pitching advice I received from that pitching coach was, 'I'll kiss your a** if you throw it over home plate and let them hit it.'"

By the time players make the major leagues, they have their routines, swings, pitches, and delivery ready to contribute at that level. But David Clyde needed help to develop his. "I was looking for guidance, I needed instruction. I was not getting any better, and that was all I got from my manager, and pitching coach. I just couldn't trust Billy Martin, he would talk to me one way in front of me, and then turn around behind my back and say awful things about me," said Clyde on Martin and Fowler.

"Techniques are learned in the minor leagues. There is one instruction given in the big leagues, you are there to perform. You are out there and will learn and evolve. You're not given instruction, you got to the big leagues already, you should be ready. Coaches were there to keep you headed down the same path you were already on. If you start to fall off, they will try to bring you back to where you were before," explained Clyde.

David started in the back end of the rotation behind Hall of Famer Ferguson Jenkins who was in his first year with the team, Jim Bibby, and Steve Hargan. Clyde was proving Martin wrong about him and pitched well to start the season during his first six starts of the season going 3-0, with three complete games and a sparkling 2.34 ERA. Then the inconsistent nature of a young pitcher showed up, and David had a rough next eight starts.

Billy Martin wanted to have Clyde go down to the minors for a short time, to boost his confidence, but Martin was overruled again by the front office. So Martin put Clyde on the bench for the next ten days, perhaps making the delicate situation worse with Clyde, the team, coaches, and front office. Now he was just clogging the roster, leaving the team a player short during a season in which the Rangers were in contention in the AL West. This was certainly an uncomfortable place for Clyde, and for the rest of the season, he was used sparingly as a starting pitcher and called upon as a reliever from time to time. His season ended with a 3-9 record with 4.38 ERA.

However, under Martin, the 1974 Rangers did really well. They finished second in the AL West Division with a record of 84-76-1. When a team wins, the fans come out, and the 1974 Rangers finished with a fan attendance of 1,193,902, good for fourth in the American League.

Despite everything, Clyde is thankful to Martin for helping him in one way: "Billy made me the outgoing person I am today. I'm very opinionated. I'm not afraid to speak my opinion and I'm not afraid to get in your face. My time with him showed me it was important for me to do that," explained Clyde.

In time, Clyde learned to be more direct, so why didn't he press Martin on how he was being treated? "I was brought up to respect my elders. I never had a teammate take me under their wing, show me, teach, and look out for me either. The closest I ever had with the Rangers was Ferguson Jenkins. We wouldn't talk about baseball, but he was good to me," reflected David.

Looking back at his mindset before the 1975 season, Clyde says, "As a nineteen-year-old, you think your major league manager and coaches are all looking out for you and your best interests because you can help the team. They are not though. As I was getting ready for spring training in 1975, I told my dad I would never go through a year like that again. I would not let it happen. I would kick in the door to find out what was going on."

David Clyde was taking the 1975 season by the horns. He spent part of that offseason in the Florida Instructional League working with a pitching coach developing an off-speed pitch to compensate for his diminished curve ball. He also played in the Venezuelan Winter Baseball League. Unfortunately, David then had to have his tonsils removed. Recovery took three weeks and twenty-one pounds off him. His fight for a spot in rotation or the MLB roster didn't even happen.

The surgery and lost weight could be seen as a blessing in disguise. Clyde was going to be able to build off the valuable hands-on learning he received in the recent winter instructional league and Venezuelan experience. Also, during this time, he was coping with his recent divorce from his high school sweetheart, Cheryl. The time in AA and the instruction worked as Clyde went 12-8 in 22 starts with a 3.07 ERA and developed a change-up to go with his fastball. Those are great numbers for a twenty-year-old pitcher in AA and would have any organization excited about his baseball future.

Clyde was called up to the Rangers in September, and he made a solid start going seven innings and giving up two earned runs. Things were looking up for David in 1976—Billy Martin was fired halfway through the season, David received valuable baseball instruction time (perhaps earning his call-up at the end of 1975 purely on his value between the lines from the mound), and he was only twenty. This had been a long and strange roller coaster ride for Clyde since he had been expected to be the savior of a baseball franchise three years before. The "sure thing" earned his way back from the brink and stood poised for a long and productive career ahead of him for the Texas Rangers. But Clyde ended up having to wait longer than expected to start his 1976 spring training. MLB owners instituted a lockout of team facilities as Major League Baseball and the Major League Baseball Players Association agreement expired. The players were held in a holding pattern from March 1 to March 17 until the team owners lifted the lockout to allow the players back to the team facilities and start an abbreviated spring training. The original date of April 8 remained the opening day for the season, leaving less than three weeks for spring training. Everyone was rushing, pushing through to be ready for the opener.

An injury to another pitcher in a spring training game pressed Clyde to warm up too quickly. Back in the summer of 1973 during his debut with the Rangers, he was able to get warmed up, sit, and warm up again. This time after his pitching appearance, his arm and shoulder rebelled for the first time during his career. At the tender age of twenty-one, just when he thought he was ready as a major league pitcher, the road for Clyde to baseball stardom began the turn into baseball oblivion.

Rest and cortisone shots were prescribed for a pinched nerve near the shoulder blade with David going to the Texas Rangers AAA team to build up for a return to the Rangers. His shoulder and once magic arm were not the same, however. His once 95-mph fastball was gone, and he performed poorly during four starts with an 8.76 ERA. It was decided that David would be shut down for the rest of the 1976 season to have surgery and hopefully be ready for 1977 spring training. But this time there was a chance it could be for the Seattle Mariners or Toronto Blue Jays. The Rangers had once envisioned Clyde as the nucleus of their future. But now he was left unprotected in the expansion draft that Fall after the 1976 season to help supply two incoming MLB teams. By the age of twenty-two, it was clear to the Texas Rangers that Clyde would not be the player they thought he would be, and at least two other teams believed the same. The Blue Jays and Mariners both passed on him in the draft, and Clyde reported to the Texas Rangers 1977 Training Camp.

David Clyde was there, but he now had his eyes wide open as to the ugly underbelly of the Texas Rangers and Major League Baseball. He even allowed himself to entertain the thought of giving up baseball and going to college. At twenty-two, Clyde was still young enough to go pre-med at Stanford and do the work to become a doctor. But baseball was his first love, and he was not quite ready to leave it, even after finding out baseball did not love him back.

"This part really hurts, after I was operated on for the first time in 1976, would you think they would reach out to the player they took top of the draft and was once counting on? Wouldn't you think they would call and check on me? No, they didn't and none of my teammates called either. I was forgotten about, just discarded. To this very day I hear from none of them," explained a still disappointed David Clyde.

During 1977 spring training, Clyde was not able to display the former zip, movement, or control on his pitches and was sent down to the AAA team. He struggled mightily between the starting rotation and working out of the bullpen in relief. Then following the 1977 season, he again went to the Winter Instructional League and the Venezuelan Winter League attempting to recapture his fastball and command, and be ready for the Rangers and the 1978 season. But before Clyde could get his chance to battle back with the Rangers, he was traded to the Cleveland Indians and had the chance to kick-start his career with a new team.

David Clyde always credited his father for being the best pitching coach he had had, noting that the Rangers did very little to provide good pitching coaches to the players. In Cleveland, however, David felt the coaches were willing and able to coach. "I learned more in

Cleveland with Jeff Torborg and Harvey Haddix that spring training than my whole time with the Rangers combined," said Clyde.

Making the team as a reliever, Clyde worked his way into the starting rotation early in May, and he finished the season with an 8-11 record, an improved 4.28 ERA, and more importantly a career-high 153.1 innings pitched. Coming off a long delay and against the odds, Clyde was able to be a serviceable member of a team. It was a solid return to getting his career back on track.

Unfortunately, Clyde was not able to build off the success of his 1978 season. Injury and health conditions piled on all season as gastritis, stomach ulcer, and back injury curtailed his performance and limited his season to 45.2 innings pitched, going 3-4 with a 5.91 ERA. Then on August 7, 1979, Clyde started his last major league game and ultimately faced his last batter. David Clyde gave up six runs in 5.1, including home runs by future Hall of Famers Jim Rice and Carlton Fisk.

With one out in the bottom of the sixth, Clyde faced another future Hall of Famer, Carl Yastrzemski. This future Red Sox Hall of Famer would not smack a home run. Yastrzemski was hit by the pitch and took first base to load the bases and become the MLB batter unceremoniously ending the career of the mega-prospect once projected to be the next Sandy Koufax. In a further kick to Clyde's kneecap, the reliver came in and promptly gave up a triple to Butch Hobson, charging each of the runs to Clyde and his final MLB statistics.

Clyde's major league career was over, but he didn't know it yet. The Cleveland Indians traded Clyde back to the Rangers in time to go to their 1980 spring training. His homecoming was cut short as shoulder pain sidelined him and the team told him to rest his shoulder. Then during this rest period, the Rangers showed the loyalty and patience Clyde came to expect from them and released him from the team. Clyde underwent another season-ending surgery, this time as a free agent. He had to pay for his own surgery, and only later, after escalations from his agent and the Baseball Union, did the Rangers reimburse Clyde for half of the cost of the surgery, for which they should have paid all.

Clyde was able to rehabilitate himself during the 1980 season and earned a contract with his hometown team the Houston Astros for 1981. Just before his twenty-sixth birthday, the Astros sent Clyde to the minor leagues to see if he could make it all the way back to Major League Baseball. Clyde slayed AA over ten appearances with six starts. His 0.76 ERA earned a promotion to AAA, and Clyde was just one notch below making it all the way back. But a 4-10 record with a huge ERA took its toll on Clyde, and he would not make it back.

After the 1981 season and not making it past AAA for the Houston Astros, Clyde went to the Fall Instructional League to try to improve for the 1982 season. But the twenty-six-year-old pitcher didn't have his heart in the game anymore and was about to walk off the mound and out of baseball. "I was in instructional league that fall, and the manager came out to the mound to talk with me. I just kind of woke up on the mound that day. All I could think was what in the world am I doing? I said that to myself under my breath and walked off the mound," said Clyde. But even as he told the Astros he didn't want to play baseball anymore, the Astros did not want him to walk away. "The Astros said, 'Well, go home and think about it and let us know what you decide this spring.' True to their word they called me a week before spring training to ask me if I was going to come back. I said no, I lost my desire to keep playing baseball," explained Clyde. "The Astros still wanted me. I could have kept playing." Clyde is happy he walked away while baseball still wanted him and it was his choice to retire from the game.

Clyde did something few ballplayers were able to do after retirement. He walked away without regrets or wanting to play. With his official retirement in 1982, however, Clyde unknowingly was thirty-seven days short of qualifying for the required four years for an MLB player pension. "I walked away; I didn't look back for almost ten years. I went cold turkey from baseball. I only picked up a baseball again about nine years later when I began coaching my son and his youth teams," recalls Clyde.

So what happened that kept David from being the pitcher he was supposed to be for the Rangers? How good could he have really been? Tom Grieve believes that Clyde was robbed of his chance to be a very good pitcher for a long major league career. "I've always felt if David had been allowed a standard rookie contract, his career would have had a much different ending. He should have gone to the rookie league with other players who were eighteen years old, working his way through the minor leagues with 400 to 500 innings under his belt. He would have arrived in the majors when he was only twenty-one or twenty-two with a great chance to pitch for fifteen years. He could have won 150 to 200 games, maybe more, been someone who had a fantastic career."

"I think most Texas Rangers fans have an innate understanding of what happened to David was not his fault, and that he did not become a big-time pitcher because of the way the Texas Rangers handled him. Let's face it, if you had to select the five greatest Rangers game, his first start is one of them," concluded Grieve.

Clyde seems to accept his career as it was. "Everything that's happened in my life is for a reason. We can't change things. We can learn from them. We move forward. That's what I'm trying to help young men hopefully learn from my past mistakes," said Clyde looking back on his baseball career.

With knowing what he does about his career and how it should have gone, David does clarify one thing. "I don't want anyone to take this the wrong way, but if I could do it again, knowing now how the Rangers handled their young pitchers, I would have asked the Rangers to not draft me or ask to trade me to allow another team to develop me properly instead of what happened. I would have wanted the 40-man major league contract, but I could have gone right to the rookie league, A-Ball, whatever and worked my way up to maybe make a start or two with the Rangers at the end of the year."

David Clyde explains how he felt unprepared for the job of a major league pitcher immediately out of high school. He was an eighteen-year-old pitcher on an MLB mound for the first time and calling his own pitches to a veteran catcher. "It felt like sitting in a high school biology class straight into being told I was a doctor and told to perform an open-heart surgery. In the grand scheme of things, baseball is not that critical. But the gap of skills needed were the same. From dissecting a frog to opening somebody's heart up. Just one tiniest slip and they are dead. Would it be fair to the doctor or patient to not ensure the doctor could be accurate with the knife?" explained Clyde.

Even as Clyde would see he was not properly equipped to be playing at the major league level, he kept pressuring himself to deliver what the Rangers, baseball, and fans wanted him to be. "I put too much pressure on myself when I was playing, I knew I had to be perfect against these hitters when I was just a kid, and I tried too hard physically and mentally to try to force it to happen," said Clyde. "I was always trying to be better than I was even physically able to be, I wanted to be perfect."

And even as he put pressure on himself, he was not going to back down from any situation or hitter in baseball. Clyde is a lifelong, passionate, and old-school player and fan, respecting the game and opponent. "I was never intimidated. Never scared. I respected the players I played against. But I didn't notice or care who the batter was. I just had to know how to pitch to them. The only thing I would notice was the catcher and his glove," explained Clyde.

The David Clyde who threw all those perfect high school games and no-hitters believed he could match that success in the major leagues if he could just try hard enough. "I was overthrowing all my pitches. Trying to go past my max each pitch. There were times I was able to be in the zone, be nice and relaxed and just let my natural abilities flow. When I did that, I had some very good ball games."

The thought of easing up a little like Sandy Koufax was urged to do halfway through his career and helping to dominate baseball would have been difficult for Clyde to do. Maybe the advice from pitching coach Art Fowler to Clyde was the piece of coaching he needed after all. "The concept of easing up on your pitches is a difficult concept to grasp when you're eighteen years old. I am not sure I could make myself throw Reggie Jackson a batting practice fastball, but believe it or not, you get a lot of hitters out that way because they can get out on their front foot too early," pondered Clyde.

When Clyde eventually realized that he was just thirty-seven days short of a major league pension, he secured recommendations and updated/submitted his resume to every major league team looking for a way back into the game. That was almost twenty years ago, and he is still waiting for a response. "I tried to get back in, I had recommendations including Hall of Fame manager Whitey Herzog urging teams to hire me. I was even told by Tom Hicks when he owned the Rangers face-to-face. If he could help, to call him personally. I called him and never got a return phone call. I am not sure what the deal is, but I am persona non grata in Major League Baseball."

So Clyde took matters into his own hands to secure some sort of solution for players like him. There were about 1,650 players who did not fall under the reformed baseball pension system, created in 1980, although under the changes to this system, those players would qualify for the pension. Clyde notes, "I was part of a group about ten years ago going after the Union and Major League Baseball to make it right. Marvin Miller even admitted in his dying days that it is, that it was one of his biggest regrets not making the pension system retroactive for all of us. Through a lot of determination, we finally got something."

The solution is not perfect, and it is not exactly a pension: When a player dies, the payments are not directed to the spouse. Every day the group gets smaller and now includes approximately six hundred players. This group is not provided for by the Players Union; rather, there is an operating fund taken out of the Competitive Balance Tax from the owners. Nothing is taken from the players; it is from the owner's pockets. "It is not a pension for us, it is more like an annuity, but I am very grateful for the $8,000 or so I receive each year from baseball," explained Clyde.

"Nobody in the group of players begrudges what the players of today get. Good for them, but it was players like us who made it possible for them to be paid like they are today. There must be a way today's players can help the players like us a little more that fell through the cracks," explained Clyde. For example, Gerrit Cole and other top paid players of today receive more for each pitch played than Clyde receives a year.

Clyde has never been asked to be a guest instructor or speaker during spring training like many other former players are typically asked to do. Neither has he been added to the roster of a Fantasy Camp team of former MLB players to teach and play baseball with people paying thousands of dollars to feel like a big-league player for the week. "In some ways I haven't given up. But it's still very much a good old boy system. I understand a manager would want people that they are comfortable with and trust. I don't have anybody that I'm buddy-buddy with. Even the Texas Rangers do not acknowledge me. I don't know if this comes back to the pension thing," said Clyde on his chance to get back into baseball even as he approaches the age of seventy.

"I am the cautionary tale for how not to handle a young player out of high school. I don't think what happened to me can happen again. I am happy young players will not go through what I went through. I am proud to have that effect on how baseball player development changed due to the David Clyde cautionary tale," said Clyde. This may not be the legacy David Clyde wanted, but it is perhaps more meaningful and lasting than anyone could have imagined.

BRIAN COLE, NEW YORK METS, 1998–2000

Position: outfielder

Bats right, throws right

MLB thirty-sixth-round pick by the Detroit Tigers from Meridian High School, 1997

MLB eighteenth-round pick by the New York Mets from Navarro College, Texas, 1998

Died March 31, 2001, in Marianna, Florida

Minor League Career Totals

AVG	G	AB	R	H	2B	3B	HR	RBI	SLG	OPS
.306	320	1289	237	395	90	19	42	192	.504	.809

Highlights

- Brian Cole played in three minor league seasons before he died in a traffic accident before the start of the 2001 baseball season.
- Cole and his minor league numbers over his seasons compare favorably at .306 with 42 home runs, 90 doubles, 193 RBI, and 135 stolen bases, to Mike Trout and his three-plus years in the minors with .341, 23 home runs, 58 doubles, 134 RBI, and 108 stolen bases.
- Cole won the Baseball America Junior College Player of the Year Award after the 1998 college baseball season.
- Cole was named to the 1998 Appalachian League All-Star Team after his first year in MiLB.
- In 1999, Brian batted .316 for the Single-A Capital City Bombers with 97 runs, 41 doubles, 18 home runs, 71 RBI and 50 steals. Cole led all Met MiLB players in runs, total bases, doubles, and stolen bases.
- Cole was named a starting outfielder for the 1999 South Atlantic League All-Star Team.
- Cole was named Mets 2000 MiLB Player of the Year.
- In 2000, Brian batted .301 with 104 runs, 19 home runs, 86 RBI, and 69 stolen bases in 138 games.
- In 2000, Cole led Mets MiLB players in hits, total bases, triples, and steals.
- Cole was named to the Florida State League 2000 All-Star Team as an outfielder.
- After the 2000 season, Brian Cole was named as the Most Exciting Player in the Florida State League.

CHAPTER 3

Brian Cole

A Sad Story of a Great Player Taken Too Soon

As a baseball player, Brian Cole had so much skill and talent that even thirty years after his death, fans aren't sure if they could believe their own eyes or trust their own memories. As time steals away some details of Cole for those who played with him, his marvelous grace, speed, and power still have a place in their memories. Anger and confusion at his death have mostly been replaced with a warm sorrow and nagging thoughts of "what if?" What if he hadn't been in that fender bender at a Taco Bell? What if he had been just a few seconds faster or slower on the night he died on that Florida road? What if he had been a few inches taller?

Brian Cole—a baseball prodigy with the personality and will to win designed for the big lights of New York City—was only twenty-two when he died. Some say he could have been one of the best players ever. Cole possessed the skills of Rickey Henderson, Mickey Mantle, and Willie Mays. All those great players were rather diminutive in stature by today's gargantuan size. Henderson, Mantle, and Mays were all below two hundred pounds and under six-foot. Mickey Mantle was arguably the fastest baseball player to put spikes on the diamond. Rickey Henderson was so fast he helped to define a generation of baseball before analytics shaped a different brand of baseball that didn't prioritize stolen bases or even stretching a double into a triple. Willie Mays, perhaps the best player of all time with Hank Aaron, stood a rather pedestrian 5'10" and at a Super-Middleweight 175 pounds.

Cole was shorter and lighter than all those Hall of Fame outfielders, but Cole's speed and strength would have had him swing for swing in a Home Run Derby or step for step in a sprint down the line against those baseball legends. But fate was cruel to Cole. He never had a chance to prove his talents, even in an era when a player's size seemed to matter more than speed and strength. On March 31, 2001, his Ford Explorer flipped and killed the best baseball player many never heard of.

Brian Cole was born on September 28, 1978, in the small town of Meridian, Mississippi, with the nearest city of Jackson almost one hundred miles away. No matter how good he was on the baseball field, Cole would not be seen often enough for scouts to see what kind of athlete he was. A quick glance at his height, weight, and statistics couldn't encapsulate the "baseball player" or his raw athletic grace. Cole could never meet the initial filters of what the scouts thought was needed for the style of the 1990s, and early 2000s game without their eyes seeing what checks in a scouting report could capture. The evolving major league landscape of the late 1990s—especially the outfield template of what an outfielder should look like—did not bode well for Cole, and his size and weight would be a hurdle to overcome.

The Mets front office used a short Hall of Fame outfielder, Kirby Puckett, who had to retire in 1995 due to medical conditions, as the ceiling for Cole. Puckett possessed a much different body type as an outfielder than Cole. Puckett's 5'8" and 178 pounds looked much different than Cole's 5'8", 165-pound frame. One was stocky, the other looked like he could be the batboy, but the height of 5'8" was the start of the player comparison. Puckett averaged close to 20 home runs a year, 100 RBI, and a .318 batting average while providing Gold Glove defense and double-digit stolen bases each year. Kirby Puckett packed ten All-Star teams in his twelve-year career. It was a high ceiling for Cole, and he had to fight twice as hard to be seen by the major league organizations.

Cole's size did not hold his performance back on the playing field. He was All-State in football and baseball. Cole set the football season state record for touchdowns at 22 at Meridian High School. Even with his low academic standing and uninspiring size, the best NCAA Division 1 football programs lined up to promise him scholarships: Florida State, LSU, Tennessee, and many more came calling. High school baseball fields could not contain his power either, as he slugged 4 home runs in one game, 10 home runs in a six-game stretch, and he set a Mississippi High School state record of 22 home runs for the season.

Major League Baseball did notice his gaudy stats, but they had a hard time looking past his small stature. Division 1 baseball schools noticed also, but issues more than size stopped him from an athletic scholarship at the best programs; Cole's athletic gifts could not outweigh his grade point average or test scores. No D1 athletic scholarships were going to happen until he could qualify academically.

A great hitter is a great hitter, but Cole was backed into a corner. He had the choice of being a low draft pick and playing Minor League Baseball at a minimal signing bonus or to gut it out and attend a junior or community college to showcase his skills, qualify academically for D1 programs, and increase his draft spot for professional sports scouts.

Before Cole considered going to college after his high school graduation, the Detroit Tigers offered him a chance to play baseball. The Tigers selected Cole as a thirty-sixth-round pick in the 1997 MLB draft and offered him $5,000 to sign. It was a foot in a door, but Brian's older brothers knew it was one foot in the front door, but his other foot would already be at the back door. A player with a low bonus has little room for mistakes, and an early batting slump could end a career.

The elder Cole brothers saw the business side of baseball from the D1 and minor league levels. Greg Cole played baseball at The University of Southern Mississippi and Robert, the eldest brother, was the first African American baseball player on scholarship at Ole Miss. Robert played up to AA for the Atlanta Braves in the 1980s. Greg turned down professional offers because he wanted to finish college and pursue other interests.

Big brothers often know the truth about little brothers, and Robert and Greg were no different. The older Cole brothers knew Brian was special, and they convinced him to bet on himself. For a poor kid from Mississippi to turn down any opportunity to play pro baseball was probably unexpected, but Brian and the Cole family turned the Tigers down.

Brian set his eyes on Texas for the opportunity to show he was better—much better—and that his size would not hold him back. He enrolled at Navarro College in Corsicana, Texas, where he diligently studied to earn his way to D1 eligibility and scorched the gridiron with his speed.

In his only season of college football, Cole was All-Conference for the Navarro Bulldogs as a wide receiver and kick returner. The baseball field was close by, however, and after a late season football practice, the football coach walked Brian over to the baseball field for an impromptu baseball tryout with the baseball coach. Cole took a spot in the outfield to attempt to field his first fly ball and fell flat on his face, but not missing a beat and utilizing his blazing speed, he got up and caught the ball.

Cole made the baseball team; the switch from football cleats to baseball spikes worked well for the Navarro Bulldog baseball team as well as for Cole. In 1998, he was named Baseball America's Junior College Baseball Player of the Year. He batted .524, with 27 home runs and 82 RBI. Cole also scored 95 runs and swiped 49 bases during his sixty-game season, and in 2019, he became a member of the Navarro College Bulldog Athletic Hall of Fame.

Cole had made his case for Major League Baseball teams to draft him or for D1 football or baseball schools to offer him an athletic scholarship. Louisiana State University offered Cole the chance to play baseball and football. The 1999 LSU Tigers football team featured three quarterbacks, including Josh Booty (featured in another chapter in this book), who all went on to the NFL and two starting wide receivers who later played in the NFL. That same year, Gerry DiNardo lost his head coaching job and was replaced by the legendary Nick Saban. Cole was seriously considering LSU but wanted to see where he would be drafted in the 1998 MLB draft.

Football players often dabble in baseball, and sometimes the threat of playing baseball can be a negotiation ploy. John Elway, Dan Marino, Russell Wilson, Jameis Winston, Rickey Williams, and many other outstanding athletes played more than one sport growing up and had multisport options out of high school and during college. Kyler Murray was a first-round pick for both the NFL and MLB. Tom Brady was drafted as a catcher by the Montreal Expos out of high school as an 18th rounder in the 1995 draft. But Brian Cole's first love was baseball.

One often repeated and true tale was when older brother Greg bought Brian to a pick-up game in Meridian, where a major league pitcher was throwing to keep in shape during the 1994–1995 MLB lockout. The fifteen-year-old, 5'5", 140-pound Brian turned a nasty slider around for an estimated 500-foot home run. The pitcher later measured the mound and found it to be five feet closer than a regulation mound. This reduced distance of the mound made Brian's home run even more impressive and likely added at least 5 mph to his slider normally coming in at 92 mph. Stories like this are hard to believe, but they happened, and that is the Brian Cole standard.

The Cole family heard rumors that Brian would probably be a third rounder heading into the 1998 MLB draft. Jim Duquette of the Mets asked Dave Lottsfeldt, the scout watching Cole, what it would take to sign him, a million or so? The answer was, "5'8"—$100,000," reflecting both the shrewd and business side of baseball and a skewed formula for seemingly undersized players.

In the 1998 draft, the New York Mets took Cole in the 18th round, after taking Jason Tyner in the first round. Tyner was 6'1" and received a $1,000,000 signing bonus. The 17-round difference between Tyner and Cole was one digit less—Cole's signing bonus was $100,000. The Mets knew they were getting a player who should have gone before the 18th round. "We were willing to go to $150,000 at the time for Cole, but he took our first offer," said Jim Duquette.

Cole shortly found himself batting clean-up for the Kingsport Mets in the minor leagues. One of the pitchers he was about to face was a first-round pick, standing a foot taller, throwing a 98 mph heater and a 92 mph slider, all from the wicked left side. The young pitcher, CC Sabathia, would eventually become a six-time All-Star and World Series Champion while winning over 250 games and striking out over three thousand batters.

Sabathia made his first professional start on August 4, 1998. Members of the Cleveland Indians (Guardians) eagerly watched as their first-round prize took the bump against the Kingsport Mets. The Kingsport Mets Manager, Tim Foli, offered Cole the option to sit the game out, but Cole would not be scared off by the competition. The clean-up batter is traditionally a Steve Balboni-like bruiser, not a Brian Cole type, but the overlooked underdog dug in.

Sabathia reared back to release the bread and butter of a young flamethrower. But power collided with power as the ball clanked off the left-center field wall from Cole's bat to start what would become a 2-hit, 2-run, 1 stolen base, and 1-RBI night for Cole. Sabathia later said that Brian Cole convinced him he needed to develop an off-speed pitch. In fact, Cole dominated with each team he played for as he was trying to make it to Major League Baseball.

1998 Season Rookie and Low-A: In fifty-eight games with the Mets' Kingsport and Pittsfield farm teams, Cole hit .298/.315/.487, slugging 5 home runs and stealing 16 bases in 24 attempts.

1999 A Ball: In 125 games with the Mets' Columbia and Capital City Bombers farm teams, the twenty-year-old hit .316/.362/.522, slugging 18 home runs and stealing 50 bases in 66 attempts. The 1999 season was Cole's first full season in the minor leagues. He led all Mets farmhands in runs, total bases, doubles, and stolen bases while playing in the South Atlantic League, and he was named one the SAL's three All-Star outfielders. After the 1999 season, Baseball America named Cole the "Most Exciting" player in the organization.

2000 Season High-A and AA: In ninety-one games with the St. Lucie Mets, Cole hit .312/.356/.528, slugging 15 homers and stealing 54 bases in 65 attempts. In forty-six games with the AA Binghamton Mets, Cole hit .278/.326/.420, with 4 homers and 15 stolen bases. Cole went a combined .301/.347/.494 in 137 games for St. Lucie and Binghamton, with 19 home runs and stealing 69 bases in 84 attempts. Then in September 2000, Cole was honored at a pregame ceremony at Shea Stadium as the Mets' Minor League Player of the Year. During that fall, he was selected to play in the prestigious Arizona Fall League, reserved for MLB's best baseball prospects. Cole was named as the New York Mets third-best prospect and as the 64th-best prospect in baseball by Baseball America.

The Mets front office knew it was only a matter of time before Cole would make his MLB debut. There is a time-honored routine of bringing the best prospects to spring training to ease the transition from the minor leagues to the parent club and its veterans. Cole received an invite to the New York Met's 2001 Spring Training Camp, cementing his status as a player to watch. He went to the Met's big-league camp as a nonroster invitee. While there, he created a stir with superstars like Mike Piazza and Mookie Wilson, and with Jay Horwitz, the longtime media relations director.

The New York Mets were flying high in the Spring of 2001. The 2000 New York Mets won the National League Pennant for the first time since 1986, and better yet, they challenged the crosstown New York Yankees in the "Subway" World Series. The 2000 Mets went to the postseason and wrapped up the San Francisco Giants in four games of the best-of-five National League Divisional Series and took only five games to knock out the Saint Louis Cardinals during the National League Championship Series.

The 2000 World Series was a deceptive World Series. The Yankees won the Series in only five games to seemingly dominate the best-of-seven series. But the New York Mets lost the four games to the Yankees by only a combined 5 runs. For the Series, the Yankees only scored 3 more runs overall than the Mets for a 19-16 advantage. The Mets won ninety-four games to the Yankees eighty-seven in 2000. Going into 2001, the Mets and their fans had reason to think they were about to take over the sports landscape from the Yankees who had ruled supreme for so long with yet another dynasty from 1996–2000 with four World Series Trophy's in five years.

The door was open for the Mets, and prospects like Cole were going to bring fresh life and legs to a veteran, star-studded lineup stacked with Hall of Famer Piazza: All-Star players Todd Zeile, Edgardo Alfonzo, Robin Ventura, and the former first rounder from 1994, Jay Payton, a center fielder who finished third for the 2000 NL Rookie of the Year at a relatively old rookie age of twenty-seven. The Mets were there on the edge like they were in 1984–1985, and if history could repeat itself, 2001 was going to be the new 1986 for the Mets.

The year 2001 threw many curves at the New York Mets, at New York City, and at our world, but it did start out with the beautiful Florida sunshine for the New York Mets. The 2001 Mets spring training was joyful and full of hope as a young Cole impressed the Met's front office and players alike. Mike Piazza even pulled aside the legendary sportswriter, Peter Gammons, during a batting practice to tell him that Cole was a kid to watch. Mookie Wilson raved about Cole and his willingness to work hard, learn, and do whatever it takes to become a New York Met.

Brian Cole was rising quickly. To General Manager Steve Phillips, Jim Duquette, and the rest of the front office, it was *when*, not *if*, Cole would be patrolling the outfield, stealing bases, and exciting fans at Shea Stadium with tape-measure home runs.

The Mets had a great young crop of outfielders charging up the internal organizational bulletin boards used at the time. This was an actual physical board with all the players in scouting shorthand to show "hot or not," those rising or falling, basically like a stock board showing commodity and risk. Heralded prospects like Rob Stratton, 1996 first-round pick and 13th overall, Alex Escobar, Terrence Long, Jay Payton, and Jason Tyner were all there along with Cole.

A player picked highly in the draft would be a major disappointment if he did not rise to the top of the board. Long and Payton had both been selected by the Mets in the first round of the 1994 draft, and in their careers, both finished in the top three of Rookie of the Year voting. Escobar was a highly regarded International Free Agent. But the eighteenth-rounder Cole kept rising and making some of the more recognized prospects look expendable.

The outfielders on all levels of the Mets knew that Cole was climbing the ladder and pushing good players out of the Mets major league. Endy Chavez and Rob Stratton were some of those players keeping a close watch on Cole.

Pitcher Pat Strange shared, "I still remember the conversations with Endy. We were much better friends earlier on than I was with Brian. The level of his [Endy's] unhappiness, the frustration he had because he couldn't get on the field; he liked Brian, but he wanted to be out there in center field. We had Brian and he was the natural center fielder. [Endy] just couldn't get out there with Brian there."

Another player watching Cole was the 6'4", 250-pound hulking presence of Rob Stratton. The blue chip prospect with a few seasons of minor league ball under his belt was expected to outshine draft picks like Cole. Stratton had big-time power, smashing home run totals of 21, 29, and 30 across the 1999–2001 seasons while playing for the Mets A, A+, AA, and AAA teams. All those home runs came with 112, 180, and 203 strikeouts, with correlating on-base percentages (OBPs) going the wrong way of .374, .344, and .329 and a paltry season high of just 9 stolen bases. "Rob Stratton had Cole power. He might get a home run when he came up or just as likely to strike out. Brian was going to hit the ball hard somewhere every single time up," said pitcher Heath Bell.

Professional athletes are mostly extremely hard-working and competitive, with healthy egos. Although baseball is a team sport, each position has distinct roles and individual functions, and each player can be territorial about their place in the hierarchy. Baseball players are always comparing themselves to one another, just as general managers and scouts are always watching and ranking. Players need to believe they can outplay those around them.

For Stratton, watching the young, small centerfielder Cole, it had to be like looking into a baseball crystal ball and not seeing Stratton's own Major League Baseball future in it. Guys like Cole should only come off the bench to provide a walk, a stolen base, or a late inning defensive replacement. But this "little guy" had the power upgrade too. A multidimensional player like Cole could easily bump a one-dimensional player to the bench and therefore one step closer to being out of professional baseball.

"I thought Rob Stratton was going to be a surefire big leaguer by 2001. Stratton was standing out there with me during pregame warm-ups, saying, 'This little dude, this kid, I can't believe this, how?'" said Pat Strange. Stratton had amazing power, but Cole had even more, along with other baseball skills. "He was like openly admitting that Brian was better than him and he couldn't believe it would ever happen to him in the minor leagues anywhere," said Strange.

Endy Chavez and Rob Stratton were hardly the only players amazed by Cole and understanding that their Met's major league careers were becoming less likely with every at-bat Cole would take. Terrence Long was another player Cole was surpassing. "Long was an excellent prospect. We discussed and debated our minor league outfielders; Brian Cole and his trajectory stood out and helped shape our strategy well before we expected him to the major leagues in 2002," said Jim Duquette, the New York Met's assistant general manager at the time of Brian's career. "We felt comfortable trading away a really talented player [Long], who later placed second in the 2000 Rookie of the Year voting in the American League, to the Oakland A's, because we knew what Cole could become for us," continued Duquette.

The July 1999 trade of Long resulted in Kenny Rogers pitching for the Mets with a 5-1 win-loss record down the stretch, which helped to lead the Mets to the League Championship Series against the Atlanta Braves. The gamble ultimately didn't pay off as Rogers ended up walking in a run for a humiliating game and series walk-off loss, with the Braves going to the 1999 World Series. The Braves denied the Mets a Subway Series, as they went on to play the Yankees and to lose in a four-game sweep. However, with Cole playing into a future with the Mets, it made it possible to trade Long and to land Rogers who helped put the Mets over the top in 2000 for the last National League playoff position, by just one game over the Cincinnati Reds. It took the Reds ten more years until they made the postseason in 2010.

Jason Tyner managed to make it to the Mets in 2000 as they were on the way to the National League Pennant. The June call-up was an opportunity for Tyner to show he belonged with the Mets and could be the major league player for them they hoped for with their first pick of the 1998 draft. But Cole was making a habit of forcing the Met's front office to trade away MLB first-round outfielders. "Tyner got an opportunity in June of 2000, Cole was behind him at the time in AA, we saw Tyner at the MLB level, and with Cole having the year he was having, we were able to trade Tyner away that July," said Duquette. "Jason Tyner was a nice player, but he was what he was when the Mets drafted him, he didn't have the upside of Brian," said Heath Bell.

As noted earlier, Brian Cole had a huge year in 2000 between the High-A Port St. Lucie Mets and the AA Binghamton Mets. He led all Met farmhands that year in runs, hits, total bases, triples (tied at seven with Escobar), and steals. Cole had three seasons of Minor League Baseball at three different levels and was named to the end of year All-Star Team each year. Baseball America named Cole the "Most exciting player" in the Florida State League.

Cole could do it with the Mets in the minor leagues, but how would he do against the best young players brought together in the 2000 Arizona Fall League? The AFL is the place where the best prospects in all of baseball are invited to play and are placed on AFL teams regardless of their team affiliation. Bell was one of those players and saw first-hand how Cole stood out that fall. Cole played on a team with Albert Pujols, and even to this day, Pujols says Cole is one of the best players he played with or against.

It was now either sink or swim for players like Cole, but Brian's legend only grew in the hot Arizona sun. According to Bell, "We went to Arizona Fall League. We all saw him just mashing the ball. He was Altuve, before Altuve, but with more power. I am not going to say he had Aaron Judge power, but it was something like that. Everybody was saying it, he's going to the big leagues next year, he's probably going to get called up in the first month or two. That was the year he was heading to the big camp with the Mets. Me, other teammates in the minors were rooting for him, like one of our brothers was going to go to the big leagues first."

But even Cole could struggle on the field. "At AA, Brian struggled for a handful of days. I was giving him crap. I told him to just try to hit grounders and use his speed to get on base, he told me to concentrate on my pitching and punched me in the ribs and ran away, he did that sort of thing all the time. He started to hit, and we started to win, I think we won 16 in a row and were first place. Including sweeping three straight double headers," said Pat Strange on the 2000 season with Cole.

Strange still marvels at some of the things he saw Brian Cole do on the field, but one remarkable memory stands out: "There was an at-bat, I've never seen anything like it. We were facing a nasty, very tall, lanky, left-handed pitcher. Really good slider. He got Brian 0-2 and threw a backfoot slider trying to strike him out. It would have finished with either hitting him in the leg or been behind him. Brian jumped up in the air to not be hit by the ball. While he was in the air, he decided to swing, and so his body, if you can picture this, his body was in the air, his feet were way off the ground and his body was parallel in the air. He took a swipe and hit down the left line for a double. He was a great player, and he would do things outside of the scope of what you've seen or can even imagine."

"We were expecting Cole up with the big club probably at some point in 2001 and ready to take over centerfield in 2002," explained Duquette. "It is a shame we never saw a team of David Wright, Brian Cole, and Jose Reyes," Duquette also said. Could Cole have helped a good team like the 2001 Mets? According to Bell, "Brian Cole could have joined the team even as a rookie in and dominate baseball. He could really have done it, make a difference on that team. He could turn a good team into a World Series type of team."

Pat Strange played with all of them—Brian Cole, Jose Reyes, and David Wright—at various times across the minor and major leagues with the Mets. Strange does not believe in computers telling him who the best ball players are. "Computers can't see what you can with your own eyes and feel inside," explained Strange on how he knew Cole stood out. "Reyes was a nice talent, a good player, but he didn't have the 'IT' factor that Cole had. Wright was a really good player—as solid a player as Cole. But Cole had all the talent, if not more, than both Reyes and Wright combined, and he had the flair that needs to go with it. Derek Jeter had an 'IT' factor, for sure, and Cole had that kind of 'IT' factor," explained Strange of how Cole compared to some of the best players in New York City when Brian Cole should have also been thrilling the New York fans.

Players can wilt under the bright lights of New York and the demanding fans, but it seems that Cole would have loved the challenge. "He looked at everything as a challenge and was able to conquer it almost immediately. I remember a Mets coach saying good hitters adjust by the second or third at-bat. Great hitters adjust within the at-bat. Each pitch they are getting better. They are setting the pitcher up with every pitch. That was Brian," explained Strange, who believes Cole was a great hitter, which would have translated to Major League Baseball. But how high was his potential?

"He never even scratched the surface physically of what he could do. We don't know how much stronger he would've become and with his speed, and in that era, he was a 50-plus stolen base guy. A 30-30 guy, and I would still say quite a bit upside still left in that," explained Strange. "If he was able to stay healthy, and everything went according to plan, he absolutely would have been a Hall of Famer. If not beyond that, possibly one of the best all-time," explained Strange of the upside of Cole.

But Brian never had his Major League Baseball debut. His ending began simply, with nothing more than a slight bump to his car in late March of 2001. This was a minor fender bender, which ultimately put him on a dark Florida road with bad luck sideswiping him.

"Brian loved home. He loved his family. Brian was a homebody. I tell people this all the time. If he called and his first words were 'What you doing?' it was because he was homesick and wanted to talk. And that was the thing that drew him home before he died. He'd been gone from home for six weeks and the AA season was about to start. He didn't think he would be able to get home until September or maybe October. He was hoping to be called up to the big leagues," explained his brother Greg.

The world was changing for Brian, and this could have been the last time to be seen in his hometown as a "normal guy," without a target on his back. Greg continued, "I don't think he would have lived here once he made the big leagues. He loved when he played in the Arizona Fall League in Scottsdale. He told me he really loved Arizona and wanted to live there."

But Cole never saw his family in Mississippi again. A traffic accident stole his life during a trip home from Port St. Lucie, Florida, on the night of March 31, 2001. To this day the circumstances of Cole's death are shrouded in mystery along with blame, guilt, and anger. But still, the legacy of Cole keeps going, and some still smile at the thought of him.

As the Mets were about to start the 2002 season, their team dinner began as a jovial event before suddenly grinding to a halt from the echoes of a flipped SUV in Florida. Jay Horwitz, the Mets' longtime Media Relations Director, observed how the death of Brian Cole—a player who never actually played a game on the major league level—slammed players, coaches, and executives alike. "I was sitting there next to General Manager Steve Phillips as he got the call that Brian Cole was killed. A tremendous hush came over the room and the air escaped the room." Even the players who were often loud and full of jokes, joined in a stunned silence, which led to hushed tones and somber exits. The 2001 team dipped from back-to-back seasons of ninety plus victories to a barely above .500 season of 82 wins.

The players in the minors were the ones who had known Brian best in the Mets organization, and his death cast a heavy fog over some on the AA Binghamton Mets team. Cole finished his 2000 season there and hoped his 2001 stint would be brief before AAA and an eventual rise to New York. His Binghamton locker was already in place with his bats and uniform waiting for Cole to complete his trip from Florida with just a quick detour planned to drop off his SUV in Mississippi before hopping on a brief flight to upstate New York. As his teammates began to arrive in Binghamton for the season, the news of Cole's death was made even more real by his untouched locker, which remained in place for the entire 2002 season.

"It was a shock to all of us on the team. We never, wouldn't, didn't touch his locker after he passed. It was like what happened? One of our best guys is gone and he's not traded or anything. He's just gone," explained Heath Bell.

Sometimes grief and respect compel us to want to remember the person, and Bell is no different. "I got to Binghamton the day after he died. His bats were in his locker, and I grabbed one of them to remember him," said Bell.

Bell is proud of the many autographed baseball bats in his collection and the memories of those players who signed the bats for him. But the first bat was from not wanting to let go of Cole, and grief eventually brought the Cole baseball bat to a display in the Bell home. "That kind of started my bat collection. I have over two hundred bats of big-league guys and each one is signed. The only one that is not signed is Brian Cole. People ask me all the time why his bat is not signed; I tell them Brian Cole never had the chance to," said Bell. "He was one of the best players nobody will ever know, a stud, and on the way to the big leagues before he died in a car accident," Bell explains to those wanting to know more about Cole.

Bell has been on the mound many times with David Wright and with Jose Reyes behind him. How did Bell compare Cole to two of the most celebrated Mets position players in their franchise history? Bell, like Pat Strange, saw a player on his way to baseball superstardom.

"Brian was way better. David Wright, I think David is a borderline Hall of Famer and he played hurt toward the end, but Brian had more power, and smiled more than David. It is hard to say, because I like David a lot. I think Brian was faster than Jose Reyes and knew the game better. The Mets would have had a trio with those three guys. They would have ruled the city, and the Mets would probably have a couple more championships," explained Heath Bell on the potential of Wright, Reyes, and Cole for the New York Mets.

Bell saw the special power and speed of Cole. Bell explains, "As pitchers we were taught what runners were trying to do. I think Brian was at his top speed after his first step. He had quick and fast. Some players have a quick take-off, but they're not super-fast. There's quick and there's just guys that are fast. You don't see both quick and fast together often. Ricky Henderson had it and Cole was that type of player too."

Cole seemed to be such an athletic freak of nature possessing rare confidence in his abilities, but also not afraid to keep trying to unlock even more of his game to help his team win. "One day before a game, Brian said he was left-handed for the game today, we saw ugly swings, just horrible during BP," explained Bell. The relievers eagerly took their vantage point from the bullpen and were not expecting much. "We were all laughing, this is going to be bad. That first at-bat he hit a bomb, just crushed the ball," said Bell. "We were all like, seriously, is there anything this guy can't do?"

Bell saw Cole and saw how good he was and how easily the game could be for him. After a particular game, Cole was mad that the Mets called to tell him to go to instructional ball to learn switch-hitting during the offseason. Cole was upset because he wanted to be home in Mississippi after the season. Words like, "I'm done, I'm not going" were used. Suddenly Brian realized he still had a couple of weeks to the season. He was batting over .300 from the right side; what if he showed the Mets that he could also bat .300 on the left side? Would they change their minds about sending him to the instructional league? Brian dashed to the phone and asked them, and they answer was sure, go ahead and try. There was audible laughter in the Mets' response to Cole, but once again, Brian bet on himself.

Bell marveled at the competitiveness Cole had as he willed himself to be home that Fall and prove the Mets wrong. "Left-handers have beautiful swings, but for Brian his swing looked like a right-handed batter in the wrong box. His ugly left-handed swing crushed it, and he ended up over .400 from that side the rest of the season," said Bell.

The next year Cole was in High-A. When the Mets had a roving scout in attendance, he would do at-bats left-handed and continue to mash the ball. According to Bell, "Every time he hit the ball it was hard, even his outs were hard-hit. He never had any duck-fart hits, nothing soft. There was two weeks where he didn't have a hit, but he was crushing the ball, hitting the ball on the screws, but it was always right at somebody. Even as a pitcher I felt bad for Brian. We found out later, that during the last game of that unlucky streak he went into the locker room and took every one of his bats in his locker and destroyed them. The Mets only gave us two bats. You had to buy your other bats in the minor leagues back then. He broke his ten, twelve bats over his knee after his third at-bat of the game. The Mets fined him $100 for each bat he broke, even the ones that he had paid for."

Bell is talking quick, excited about the opportunity to share stories about an old friend who is not asked about much anymore, and he stops himself from making Brian sound like Babe Ruth, Willie Mays, or Mickey Mantle. But Bell knows what he saw and what he believes to be true. A shorter, but just as strong Paul Bunyan with a baseball bat. "I'm not trying to portray a story or an image that's not true, I'm a realist, I can honestly say Brian was that good, probably one the best players I ever saw, and I got to play on teams with a lot of Hall of Famers or Future Hall of Famers. I played with Pedro Martinez, I played with Mike Piazza, David Wright, Trevor Hoffman, Greg Maddux. Brian was one of them," said Bell as he placed Cole shoulder to shoulder with Hall of Famers and with David Wright, who is a Mets legend.

Mets Media Director Jay Horwitz was asked if a player like Cole could have changed the trajectory of the Mets putting them over the top during the good years, but not the great years of 2005 and 2006. A Mets fan could allow their imaginations to conjure what could have been for the team with a young Wright at the hot corner dropping bombs, driving in runs, and Gold Glove defense; Reyes locking down shortstop winning batting titles; and a young Cole patrolling centerfield with speed, power, and the grit of player who was once a 36th rounder.

But Horwitz was focused on the loss of Cole, the person. "Brian had the great physique, the speed, the hitting, fielding, all the tools to be a good player for us," explained Horwitz. "It is sad to look back at what could've been, what never became of Brian Cole; he lost his life at such a young age, with so much life ahead of him. His death was shocking and made me remember every day can be our last."

According to the Cole family, the Mets were there for them offering support after Brian died. Duquette, Horwitz, and others from the Mets made their way to the Meridian High School gymnasium, the only place in Meridian large enough to hold a funeral for Cole. "They were remarkable. Everything from setting up a scholarship fund at our high school, having team officials at the funeral. Flying the family to spring training for like five or six years to take in games. I grew up a Cincinnati Reds fan, and I am now a New York Mets fan. Big time," said Greg Cole.

The loss of Brian hit the Mets, the world of baseball, and the people of Mississippi hard. We still encounter Brian's legacy as we now live in the world of social media, like Twitter, that can shape the news and sometimes force traditional media outlets to reassess.

Journalism and newsrooms have changed—and are not necessarily better—since the early 2000s. The standard news cycle used to be a local TV broadcast at 6 p.m., followed by the national news at 6:30 p.m., with a repeat of the local news at 11:00 p.m. and then more time to devote to the accuracy of the news and original content by reporters and journalists. Newspapers were just starting their online editions and were still printed on paper that had to be "put to bed" late at night. The paper was a physical product to be distributed to newsstands, businesses, and homes in time to read over breakfast. The term "stop the press" was rarely used and with only breaking news of such impact that the newspaper was willing to scrap the previous edition and eat the time and cost of additional news gathering, writing, and printing of the newspaper, and of course getting it out to the readers.

Over the years, however, the twenty-four-hour news cycle crept in, bringing a constant stream of stories from news outlets. The need to fill the 24-7 news cycle and the internal pressure to be the first to report often blurs the lines between news and entertainment. Accuracy can be fixed later by updating electronically or virtually.

On September 2, 2010, a Mississippi judge from the Circuit Court of the First Judicial District of Jasper County could finally make a ruling in the case of Cole vs. Ford. It was the third trial in a highly charged lawsuit with testimony from Ford Motor Company, the New York Mets, and the family and friends of Brian Cole, the dead superstar baseball player. However, not one national media outlet was there. Zero. Why not?

A tweetstorm emerged asking why news media were not interested in the story involving the family of a dead athlete going against a multibillion-dollar company like Ford. This was a David versus Goliath story, with the former Met's General Manager Jim Duquette testifying in support of the Cole family. Soon members of the media noticed the stream of tweets. They began to write about the case, using information from the tweets, and in interacting themselves with the tweets, they began to use the tweets as a credited news source, which brought credibility to social media as a news source and created a new form of hybrid news.

The truth of what happened to Brian Cole is still not clear, and questions abound:

- Was a tire stolen from the Ford Explorer by two men from Ford in black suits?
- Did a county medical examiner prepare an autopsy report and quickly change key details to benefit Ford?
- Was a judge offered a federal courtship if the ruling went Ford's way?
- Did the Florida Highway Patrol investigate with a conclusion already in mind?
- Was evidence tampered with or was it just gross negligence?
- How could the speed of Brian's vehicle vary so differently among Ford's expert, the Cole family consultant, and the Florida Highway Patrol?
- Did a judge from an earlier trial try to sway a judge before a later trial?
- Could nobody find witnesses to verify what Brian Cole's cousin, Ryan Cole (as a passenger in the SUV), claimed caused the chain reaction leading to the rollover?
- Were there attempts to bully, threaten, intimidate, and sully the memory of Brian Cole and his poor African American family by law enforcement, big corporations, and the legal system?
- Is it over?

As mentioned earlier in this chapter, about a week before Cole died, an elderly woman backing her car up at a Taco Bell drive-through in Port St. Lucie, Florida, caused about $1,400 worth of damage to Cole's vehicle. "Just a fender bender at Taco Bell kind of set things in motion," said Greg. "He [Brian] and I argued over it, my dad and I wanted to go there and get the truck and have him just fly from Florida to Binghamton. We would bring it back to Mississippi, have it fixed, and figure out how to get it to Brian eventually. We did that before. It just boiled down that he wanted to come home for a day or two," continued Greg Cole.

Newspapers at the time never reported what the Cole family said led to the accident that night. The story of a one-car accident on a dark, lonely Florida road was going to be the one told. But why?

"Ford wanted to pin that accident on Brian," explained Greg. In our discussions for this book, I started to really hear what he was saying. I could feel his anger, sadness, disbelief, and relief to talk about it. "This is what happened. A vehicle with a trailer moved into the right lane. Brian is like the third or fourth vehicle behind this truck and trailer. Everybody goes to pass on the left lane, as Brian is going past, he is the third vehicle. The truck with the big trailer pulls over into the passing lane. Brian pulls in the median to avoid hitting the trailer. When he tried to come back on, that's when the vehicle started to roll."

According to later reports, Brian wasn't wearing a seat belt. He was ejected through the windshield causing brain, chest, lung damage, and his death. But according to Greg, "Here is the thing that people don't know. He *was* wearing a seat belt. The county medical examiner noted in his first report that Brian had a bruise on the left shoulder coming across where the seat belt would be. The report changed after someone from Ford talked to the medical examiner's office. They did the autopsy before we even got there. Ford was already there before we even arrived at the hospital. There was a little black box, kind of like an airplane, and it recorded Brian's seat belt was engaged at the time of the accident. At the first trial, we had an expert testify the Explorer was going 58 mph at the time of the accident. Ford had their expert say he was at 64 mph. The Florida Highway Patrol had him at 89.75 mph," explained an increasingly agitated Greg.

The judge went with the Ford expert on the speed of 64 mph. How could two of the accident reconstruction experts be in relative agreement (58 and 64 mph), both at least 25 mph lower than the Florida Highway Patrol's estimate? How would Ford know about a fatality in a Ford Explorer and be at the hospital within mere hours, ahead of the grieving Cole family?

"They went through great lengths to place blame on Brian. There were reconstruction engineers, experts that do this for a living saying 58 and 64, compared to people that went to a weekend school saying an extremely precise 89.75 mph," said Greg Cole as he explained his confusion on how he felt the expert testimony was pushed aside in favor of less qualified opinions. "What happened is they used an inaccurate formula to calculate the speed, several curves at the end of the route they didn't take into consideration. They considered it a straight shot so they could come up with 89.75 mph," explained Greg on how he believes the Florida Highway Patrol inaccurately came up with the 90-mph estimate of the speed at the crash.

Greg and the Cole family still have valid concerns and questions more than twenty years after Brian's death. Did the Florida Highway Patrol predetermine the speed and fill in the blanks to make it work? What about the seat belt the medical examiner had Cole wearing based upon physical evidence and later changing?

"The final thing really turning the first trial around was this, the engineer that designed that vehicle said doing rollovers the seat belt would spool out. At the trial you could see in the accident picture the seat belt spooled out. In the very top of that picture, you can see an index finger. The very next frame it is pulled tight. You could hear a big gasp in the courtroom when the jury saw that," explained Greg on why he still believes the investigation was not properly performed.

Greg Cole is not sure if it was evidence tampering or just forcefully doing whatever they could to make their theory stick. Either way suspicions linger. "We just couldn't go down late that night after we found out about Brian's death, we were not ready for Saturday, or Sunday either. Monday, our high school baseball coach drove us to Florida," said Greg.

As most families would probably would, they found their way to the facility holding Brian's battered SUV. "The guy at the wrecker yard said that Sunday morning two people showed up from Ford Motor Company to look at the vehicle, and now a front tire is gone," explained Greg.

I paused, waited, and let the silence overtake me. Greg's words still resonating in my head, then my chest, I stammered out, "What do you mean gone? Like gone?" The moment felt like forever as Greg Cole responded, "They came to look at it, and it was gone. There's was no front tire. The guy there said two guys in suits and a briefcase identifying themselves from the Ford Motor Company came down here to look at the SUV and now the tire was missing. We asked Ford where it was, and they said they were never there, they don't have it and we must have taken it. I think they knew where it was."

The man who had taken the SUV from the scene of the accident to the holding yard knew the tires had been on it and promised to look at the vehicle for the Cole family and let them know what he thought had happened. According to Greg Cole, this man said, "'Whatever happened was on the front driver side. I've seen these SUVs do it before.' He said, 'The insurance company looks for impact. But I look for the exit. I tell you what, if Ford is still looking for that tire, they're going to bury and destroy it.'"

Does Greg believe in a conspiracy theory with Ford stealing parts of the SUV? "You got the truck tire missing. Nobody's been there except the wrecker guy and two guys from Ford Motor Company. You do your own math now," said Greg. "Ford wanted to drag Firestone into the lawsuit as well, it makes me wonder if they wanted to blame Firestone and the tire, but couldn't prove it, so the tire simply disappeared."

"Some of the things Ford did were disgusting. I understand corporations doing things, but they didn't just try to win their case against us, it felt like more. Trying to save Brian's life, he was given ketamine, which is to treat traumatic brain injuries. Ford wanted to use the toxicology reports showing the ketamine to portray Brian as a kid high on drugs. They were going to kill him again. I had to keep that from my family; they still don't know about that to this day," said Greg.

Brian's teammates also followed the court cases. "I heard Ford tried to intimidate them and tried to say things that weren't true. It was crappy, big corporation stuff," said Heath Bell.

According to Greg Cole, the first trial in 2004 ended in a mistrial when the judge decided that he had made errors on handling both sides and some things went too far. A new trial and jury would be needed for him to decide the ruling. "The judge was really against us. There were some assertions by our lawyers that Ford may have promised him something. Maybe some help to be a federal judge. We were maybe two days from the end of the trial and our attorneys push for mistrial. I wasn't satisfied with their defense anyway, the judge concedes and said, 'You know what, I probably let things go on both sides I shouldn't have done. I'm going to declare mistrial,'" explained Greg about the first trial.

The Cole family is not afraid nor intimidated easily. Greg was close to opening a huge can of possible corruption concerns fitting for a Hollywood courtroom drama. "After the mistrial, I was about to send a complaint to the Judicial Commission in Mississippi about what I thought was going on, but he [the judge from the first trial] recused himself from the second trial," said Greg. However, interference from the first judge was still going to be felt after the Mississippi Supreme Court appointed another judge in 2004.

"We had to wait six years before we go to trial again. The second trial was in 2010. The old judge that recused himself wrote a note saying the Cole family should not be able to present any new evidence. Ford gave the new judge the letter. The new judge said it was his trial and threw out the note," said Greg.

The second trial ended with a hung jury, and a third trial began six months later in September 2011. "That was the trial with the jury awarding $130 million, we settled for quite a bit less. The Mississippi Supreme Court at that point was not approving any large judgments," explained Greg. "Ten years and three trials later, there is not an issue with Ford and their payments; the only issue is we still have a sum of money being held up," continued Greg.

Attorneys from the first trial fired by the Cole family are trying to get a piece of the settlement money from Ford and the Cole family. "Ford is going to get the money to the family, but these guys are holding it up. They are going after the confidence agreement of the settlement. Now they're trying to get it unsealed and things like that. Ford is working with new attorneys to keep it underground," explained Greg.

All these years later an official apology still has never come from Ford, and the Cole family understands that the settlement does not admit responsibility or guilt, nor will it bring back Brian.

As I talked to Greg, it was clear that the hurt and grief from his brother's death are still close to the surface decades later. "We are fine with Ford now, but nobody in our family will own or drive a Ford vehicle to this day," said Greg.

The story of Brian Cole cannot only be about tragically bad luck. All these years later, some still remember him as a player who could have defined a generation of baseball. More importantly, he is also remembered as a special human being.

Pat Strange has seen Brian thousands of times since Cole's death in 2002. "I just have to look at my son, and I am reminded of Brian Cole," said Strange, who named his son after Brian. His son is a baseball player at a community college, just like his namesake before him. Brian Cole Strange is knocking on the door of professional baseball.

Although Brian Cole Strange is not actually Brian Cole, I am pulling for him to find his baseball dreams. I am sure Brian Cole is also.

 BEN GRIEVE, OAKLAND A'S, TAMPA BAY RAYS, BREWERS, AND CUBS, 1994–2005

Position: outfielder

Bats left, throws right

Drafted by Oakland Athletics in the1994 MLB June Amateur Draft (second pick overall) from James W. Martin High School, Arlington, Texas. Player signed June 9, 1994.

Granted Free Agency after playing the 2005 season with the Chicago Cubs, October 6, 2005

Major League Career Totals

AVG	G	AB	R	H	2B	3B	HR	RBI	SLG	OPS
.269	976	3215	471	864	192	5	118	492	.442	.809

Minor League Career Totals

AVG	G	AB	R	H	2B	3B	HR	RBI	SLG	OPS
.302	550	2016	380	609	121	7	77	396	.484	.891

Highlights

- Ben Grieve is the son of former MLB player, Texas Rangers General Manager, and longtime Ranger's broadcaster, Tom Grieve.
- Grieve was given nicknames like "The Natural" and "The Franchise" during his career.
- Tom and Ben are the first father-son combination to both be selected in the first round of the amateur draft. Tom was the sixth pick overall of the Washington Senators in the 1996 MLB draft.
- Ben's brother, Tim, was drafted in the same year as Ben, 1994, by the Kansas City Royals.
- Ben's recognitions include
  - named Baseball America High School All-American in 1994
  - named The Sporting News Minor League Player of the Year in 1997
  - voted Minor League Baseball Player of the Year (*USA TODAY*) in 1997
  - named Player of the Year Southern League in 1997
  - voted the AL Rookie of the Year in 1998
  - voted to the Topps All-Star Rookie Team in 1998
  - named to AL All-Star in 1998
  - voted Outstanding Rookie of the Year (Player's Choice) in 1998
  - received the Sporting News Rookie Player of the Year Award in 1998

CHAPTER 4

Ben Grieve

The Underrated Player

Hype is part of baseball, and for some players it is easier to understand why expectations and potential do not algin. The gamesmanship of posturing certain players to appear better than they are is part of baseball.

On the other hand, team-building strategies may include selling the fans on a player who fits well in a particular market, or building up a player to flip in a trade, or—and this is the best case scenario—when a team has an embarrassment of riches and knows a player is going to be everything projected, but there is simply no place on the team for him, and making a trade to address a weakness, which is a rare win-win for the teams involved.

Players on the up may be derailed by issues such as physical injury, mental disorders, putting too much pressure on themselves, self-sabotage, listening to the wrong people, ego, drugs (including performance enhancing), alcohol, injury, family complications, and loss of interest. It seems that Ben Grieve and his promising career were none of those, and that is what makes his story worth telling. This is not about a blown elbow, exploded labrum, wanting to play football, using drugs or alcohol, or any other vice.

The answer is simple and logical. Nothing went wrong; Grieve had a wonderful baseball career. There may not be a "what if?" as much as a "hmmm."

Ben and his brother Tim Grieve come from a baseball family. Eventually they both went on to play professional baseball; Tim made it as high as AA, and Ben was in the big leagues for almost nine years. Their father Tom was a first-round pick of the Washington Senators/

Texas Rangers and played for them for several seasons, later finishing his career with the New York Mets and the St. Louis Cardinals. Tom has the nickname of "Mr. Ranger" and is a member of the Texas Ranger Hall of Fame. He went on to serve as the general manager of the Rangers from 1984 until 1994, before taking over in their broadcast booth until 2022.

Tom Grieve knows baseball, and Ben was raised with every possible advantage helping to ensure he would be a major league ballplayer. His 6'4" baseball frame and sweet left-handed swing was refined through thousands of hours around the game. From a young age, Ben absorbed it all like a sponge. For both Ben and Tim, baseball was a way of life, and they had front row seats to the Baseball 101 class of how to become a professional ballplayer.

"I would get lessons from the Texas Rangers batting coach, he also worked with players Juan Gonzalez and Rafael Palmeiro; I had pretty good hitters to be around and to learn from," said Ben. He also had the chance to play catch with his favorite player when the team was at home. "One of my jobs was to warm up Ruben Sierra in right field. I wanted him to get a hit every at-bat so that when he came out to the field, he wouldn't be mad and fire the ball as hard as he could with each throw," explained Ben. The Texas Rangers were Ben's favorite team growing up, but it may be for ulterior motives. "I definitely wanted the Rangers to win each game because my father was always in a better mood if they won."

At times, both Grieve brothers served as bat boys and ball boys, helping in the bullpen and whatever it took to help the team. The brothers were able to see behind the major league curtain and the schedule and pace that could feel hectic, monumental, and mundane all at the same time.

Tom credits his year with the 1978 Mets and manager Joe Torre with the start of getting Ben and Tim on a major league field. The Mets' thirty-year-old outfielder Tom was close to the end of his nine-year career, which gave the boys the opportunity to see their father play as frequently as they could.

"The year I played with the Mets, Joe Torre let kids their age come to the ballpark with their player dads. Jerry Koosman had two kids there, Ed Kranepool had a son, and our kids could come to the ballpark. The kids spent time shagging balls in the outfield and then stayed in the clubhouse during the game or had free reign around the stadium during a game. It might be one of the few times in baseball history players' kids were allowed to do that," explained Tom.

As a child, Ben went on a road trip with former major league pitcher Tom House to Boston and Detroit and was able to do what most baseball fans would give up an arm or a leg for. "Tom took them out into center field before anyone got there and pitched to them and let them hit home runs into the upper deck of the bleachers at Tiger Stadium. At Fenway they went to left field to bang balls off the Green Monster," said Tom Grieve on some of the experiences Ben had growing up.

Being the sons of a former Major League Baseball player can be loaded with expectations to play baseball. However, Tom believed that if the boys wanted to play, they would, and he would do everything he could if they asked. "Both the boys pushed me to work with them more, throw to them more, and be at the ballpark more. I never had to say let's go guys, you need to work. They both were self-motivated to become as good as they could be," explained Tom.

Nolan Ryan, forty-six, was into the last season of his career as a pitcher while with the Texas Rangers in 1993 and needed to get some pitches in on the way back from an injury. It was difficult to find batters to stand in to take hacks against him. Seventeen-year-old Ben dug in and took the legend deep, and although Tom knew Ryan was not throwing his fastball as if in a real game, it was still exciting for him to see. "It was just batting practice, and I knew Ben could hit the ball that far, but it was still a thrill to see him do it against Nolan Ryan. I also knew Ben would not show any emotion and risk any retaliation," explained Tom.

The idea of Nolan Ryan throwing at a seventeen-year-old kid is not as crazy as one would think, and the kid who grew up in major league clubhouses understood not to revel in the moment. Ryan is to Texas what Bruce Springsteen is to New Jersey, and is synonymous with the image of a strong Texas cowboy for the twenty-first century.

"I did not even look where the ball went, I just heard it hit the bleachers. Neither he nor I even acknowledged it went over the fence," said Ben. "After that they took the protective screen away from the mound and he threw all his pitches in simulated at-bats. I don't think I got a ball in play after that."

In the summer of 1994, Ben was about to start his senior year of high school—the last months before a baseball decision had to be made that could alter the course of his life. He was going to enjoy that time as a normal kid.

Ben went to Martin High School in Arlington, Texas, and played both baseball and basketball. He loved playing basketball and took the game seriously, even allowing it to cut into his baseball time. "They always had a really good basketball team, and Ben loved playing basketball and his baseball season would often start later because of it," said his father. In fact, Ben would often trade in the basketball jersey for his baseball jersey with no ramp-up practice time, and in his senior year he missed a chunk of the baseball season to keep playing on the basketball team for as long as he could. It was a move displaying his confidence in his baseball skills.

Ben was seen as one of the best high school baseball players in the country during his senior year. As ballplayers are prone to do, however, he initially went into a batting slump after returning. Each strikeout or weak contact could equate to a slipping draft position and potential loss of hundreds of thousands of dollars in a draft signing bonus. "A couple days spent with the Rangers batting coach, Tom Robson, put Ben back on track with three quick home runs," said Tom. And with this practice, Ben ended up drafted with the second overall pick of the 1994 draft by the Oakland A's.

"I was able to listen on a speakerphone with my father at the stadium as I was selected by the A's," said Ben. Imagine a bunch of people huddled around a single speaker phone with static hissing and burping the names of the next crop of baseball talent. This was not a glamourous sight for Ben as he became a future millionaire and an MLB first-round pick.

For Tom Grieve it was his last year as the general manager of the Texas Rangers before an eventual shift to a decade's-long tenure as the team broadcaster. Both of his sons were potentially going to be drafted in the 1994 MLB draft. "I knew Ben would go at or near the top of the draft; we had no chance to get him. Tim was coming out from college as a pitcher and I expected him to go later in the draft, but I couldn't be sure," said Tom. Tim went to the Kansas City Royals in the twenty-third round. The 5'11" right-handed relief pitcher won 22 games, lost only 8, and kept a miniscule 2.54 ERA, striking out 252 batters with only 154 hits allowed in 219 innings over four minor league seasons.

Having two sons drafted in the same MLB draft was special, but Ben's selection made it historic. As the second pick in the draft, Ben joined his father, Tom, as a first-round pick, making them the first father and son to both be first-rounders.

The eighteen-year-old, 6'4", 200-pound, right-handed-throwing-but-lefty-swinging Ben Grieve was positioned to be a special baseball player and expected to rise quickly through the A's minor league system. Baseball scouts considered Grieve to be the best pure hitter in the draft. A quick contract negotiation resulted in a $1,200,000 signing bonus. In fact, the Oakland A's were so confident in the skills and maturity of Ben that they assigned him to the A's Single-A team, the Southwest Oregon Ducks in the Northwest League.

Ben bypassed their rookie league team in the Arizona League where most drafted high school players are sent. Grieve was going to be tested right out of the gate against the more challenging Northwest League, stocked with players coming from college baseball and their extra years of advanced baseball training. This gap can be hard to navigate for young players.

"The first couple of weeks in Oregon were a challenge for me," recounts Ben. "I was used to seeing velocity of 83 or 84 mph. I was facing 93–94 from full-grown men. After some games it clicked for me, and I was able to make the change to it." At only eighteen, Grieve was the youngest player on the team, and he batted .329 with an incredible .456 on-base percentage (OBP). Grieve tied for the team lead in home runs at 7 and led in RBI with 50.

For the Grieve brothers, the 1994 minor league season came with an interesting twist. As they were signed to their respective teams and assigned to their separate organizational minor league teams, it appeared they would be in the same league and compete against each other. With one a starting outfielder and the other a relief pitcher, it was uncertain if this would actually happen. The long-running show *This Week in Baseball,* hosted by Mel Allen, circled a date on the schedule when the brothers could possibly play against each other and brought in a production crew to document the possible event.

Peggy Grieve, the boys' mother, was in the stands rooting on her children. "She wasn't sure who to cheer for, nervous about if it would happen, but she decided everyone should root for the underdog. She wanted Ben to make an out against Tim, maybe even a loud out, but not a strikeout," said Tom.

No one knew if or when the boys would face each other, but when the Eugene Emerald's manager Brian Poldberg placed Tim Grieve in the game to face his first professional batter, it would be Ben. "I am not sure what the manager wanted to do. I didn't know if he was messing with us or what, but it was pretty cool," said Ben. The drama ended as Ben hit a flyball for an out, with a relieved mother and an elated camera crew.

Ben cherishes that moment and all the at-bats against his brother that year. "The manager did that to us all year. I think I went 1 for 10 against him, but the one was at least a home run, so I can always say I got him. As a pitcher he would say, but what about all the other at-bats? But it doesn't matter, I got a home run against him," said Ben.

By the end of the 1994 season, Baseball America named Ben as the top prospect in the Oakland A's Farm System and the tenth overall in all Minor League Baseball going into the 1995 season.

The 1995 season was not as productive for Ben. He started in the Midwest League with the West Michigan Whitecaps and hit .262 with four home runs, 62 RBI, and a .371 on-base average over 102 games and 371 at-bats. Grieve was promoted to the Modesto A's (the High-A California League team) to finish the year ending the season with a combined .262 batting average, 6 home runs, 76 RBI with a .366 OBP over 130 games, and 478 at-bats. "I struggled during my second year in Grand Rapids, Michigan. I think they wanted to get me out of there and have a change of scenery. Every level after that I did pretty well," said Grieve.

Ben went into the 1996 season for the Modesto A's with his star slightly tarnished, but he was still the number thirty-seventh best prospect in all of baseball. He spent his first half of the year in Modesto before being promoted to the AA team in the Southern League. This Huntsville team was stacked with sixteen of thirty-two players who would go on to the major leagues.

Ben flashed the kind of numbers that would become his calling card. Good power, able to hit the ball into the gaps, and patience with his bat. His 1996 totals were solid, hitting .302, slugging 19 home runs, driving in 83 RBI, with a .388 OBP over 514 at-bats in 135 games. It was also the second year in a row with 20 or more doubles as he hit 28 for the season.

Then going into his 1997 season, Ben Grieve bounced back as the eighteenth-best prospect in the Baseball America ranking. His 1996 season was good, but he was about to put down a spectacular 1997 season making the baseball world stop and take notice. It took only 100 games at the AA level to convince the Oakland A's that Grieve was ready for a dress rehearsal with their AAA team in Edmonton of the Pacific Coast League. Between the two minor league levels that year, Grieve hit .350, slugged 31 home runs, drove in 136 RBI with a .461 OBP in 480 at-bats across 127 games. He was only twenty-one and making it impossible for the Oakland A's to not call-up the young outfielder in September. Grieve became the 17,157th player to be a major leaguer as he started a game in right field at the Oakland-Alameda County Coliseum.

The September 3, 1997, game on a Wednesday evening had a higher-than-normal attendance with 32,408 fans to see the Oakland A's battle their across-the-bay rival, the San Francisco Giants. Barry Bonds and Ben were batting in the third spot for their respective teams. Both hard-hitting lefties, Bonds was in the heart of a twenty-two-year career of legendary and infamous proportions, with 762 home runs and 7 MVP Awards. Bonds, at thirty-two, was on his way to another 40 home run season and still years from an unbelievable 73 home run season. Bonds was a slugger and only getting better as he got older.

As the best player in the minor leagues that year, Ben had gone from being a prospect on the rise to a superstar of the future. It therefore seemed fitting to have him mirror Bonds in the lineup; this could be seen as a "changing of the guard" story with Grieve as an ascending superstar and the older Bonds who would *eventually* start to decline.

"At the time I obviously knew he [Bonds] was a great ballplayer when I first saw him and watching him play against us in those interleague games, but watching videos of his days in Pittsburgh, he seemed so much more intimidating now as a Giant. Just looking at pictures of him you were just scared of this guy. He was a sight to behold. Hands down the most intimidating presence than anyone else we played against, and it really wasn't even close," explained Grieve about Bonds.

"The A's were not very good at the time, and just the fact they were playing the Giants brought in a large crowd for the home game," said Grieve of his MLB debut. The starting pitcher for the Giants was Danny Darwin. He may not be a household to name to many fans, but he was well-known in the Grieve household. "Danny Darwin was starting for the Giants, who I grew up watching all the time on the Rangers. Barry Bonds was their left fielder; I just remember being really nervous," explained Grieve.

"Just before my MLB debut, I had a really good run that year leading into the call-up. I was about as hot of a hitter as I could ever be, felt as good at the plate as I have in my entire life. Looking back, it was a perfect time to be called up, I was ready," continued Grieve.

His first at-bat came in the first inning as he stared at the mound as a major league batter for the first time and saw Danny Darwin, a player he had previously shagged fly balls with, had sat in the dugout with, and had hung around in the bullpen with. Darwin made quick work of the A's, sending them down 1-2-3, ending the inning as Grieve just missed a 2-2 pitch and hit a flyball deep into the waiting glove of left fielder Bonds.

The bottom of the fourth brought up Grieve to lead-off the inning. He managed to let a 3-2 pitch go by and draw a walk. Two plate appearances so far for Grieve against Darwin with no base hits.

The score in the bottom of the sixth had the A's clinging to a 2-1 lead and about to face Darwin again. But the game was about to change for the A's and Grieve. With Dave Madagan drawing a walk, Grieve was about to start something. A 3-1 pitch by Darwin was met with a sharp line drive to center field finding the gap and bringing Madagan in for a 3-1 lead. This was Grieve's first MLB hit, RBI, and extra base hit. It also knocked Giants pitcher Darwin from the game. "I got a double my third time-up, and I remember just standing at second base with relief and joy; it was a great feeling," recalled Grieve.

In the bottom of the seventh, Grieve came up to bat with the bases loaded in a 6-3 game favoring the A's. A base hit could break the game open for the A's. Grieve took a 2-0 pitch from Giants pitcher Jim Poole and pulled a ground ball into right field to clear the bases. It was now a 9-3 lead, and another double for Grieve. Two doubles and 4 RBI were more than any fan, or Grieve himself, could have expected that night from the young slugger. It was already a career night for many MLB players, but Ben Grieve pressed for more.

With an 11-3 lead in the bottom of the eighth, Grieve once again stared down the Giants pitcher, this time hitting a line drive to deep center field for a double and driving in Madagan for the game's twelfth and final run in a 12-3 victory over the feared San Francisco Giants. Grieve hit 3 doubles, each against a different pitcher, and drove in 5 runs in just 4 at-bats. The mega-prospect outperformed one of the all-time best hitters in Barry Bonds that night. Bonds went an uncharacteristic 0-4 with 2 strike outs. "Over the years I never talked with Barry Bonds, I didn't know him at all. During a postgame interview that night a reporter asked him about my good night with 5 RBI and 3 doubles. The Barry Bonds quote in the paper the next was basically like, 'Oh yeah, I didn't even notice' or something like that," laughed Ben on his lack of making an impression on Bonds.

Even if Bonds wasn't watching, the fans were. Grieve announced himself to baseball with fireworks. His 3 doubles were an Oakland A's franchise record for an MLB debut, and his 5 RBI tied an MLB record for most RBI in an MLB debut.

Grieve started twenty-three of the remaining twenty-four games for the Oakland A's in 1997, and he appeared in all twenty-four games. His .312 batting average, 3 home runs, and 24 RBI for the A's predicted greatness and a spot in the 1998 lineup. Across AA, AAA, and the major leagues in 1997, Grieve hit .345, slugged 35 home runs, drove in 160 runs, and had a .445 OBP and an OPS of close to 1.100. All this across 154 games and 573 at-bats. Going into the 1998 season, Baseball America named him as Major League Baseball's No. 1 Prospect. Grieve was done as a prospect; he was sticking with the Oakland A's.

In 1997, the team still had a link to the great Oakland teams of late 1980s and early 1990s. Jose Canseco returned to briefly bring the Bash Brothers back. Mark McGwire was having another massive season to follow his 52-home run outburst the year before. McGwire with his 34 home runs was traded to the Saint Louis Cardinals on July 31. McGwire hit 24 the rest of the season falling just short with 58 to the all-time season record of 61 home runs set by Roger Maris in 1961. The next year McGwire and Sammy Sosa each trampled past 61, and shortly thereafter, in 2001, Barry Bonds surpassed them all with 73.

At the start of the twenty-first century, baseball was changing; players with eye-popping physiques appeared as if from a magic lamp. The Oakland A's—and probably every MLB team—had players suspected of using performance-enhancing drugs (PED). Ben Grieve was not one of them, even after being called out in a tell-all book by Jose Canseco in 2005, which opened the door to MLB and the many players he suspected of steroid use.

Canseco believed Ben was a player who should have used steroids. The long and lean body with a 6'4" frame would be primed for muscle stacking, and only if he would have done it, he could have been a huge superstar. "It never even crossed my mind to try steroids, I was never even tempted," said Grieve.

"I totally agree with Jose Canseco. If I did do steroids, I would have put up better statistics. It is crazy to be called out during that time for NOT doing steroids. Maybe if I wasn't a top prospect, not having a fast track to the big leagues, maybe I would have had to," pondered Grieve on the reality of steroids in 1990s and early 2000s baseball.

Being named by Canseco did enough to Grieve to throw him off his course. "I remember driving to Pirates Spring Training in Bradenton in 2005, the book had just come out and someone said, oh yeah, you're in it. I'm like, what? My first thought was he accused me of taking steroids. All I knew at that moment was being named in a book where he named players he thought used steroids. I stopped at a bookstore in Mississippi, went in and found it. Just to see what it said in there about me. It was a big sigh of relief seeing it. I just didn't want him to accuse me of something I didn't do," explained Grieve on why he hunted down what Canseco said.

Grieve did not witness the administration of steroids, not in the locker room, in homes, anywhere. He never saw players inject or even openly discuss they were doing steroids. "I never saw players doing it, going into the bathroom stall to inject each other, that stuff Jose talked about. The guys in the locker room knew who was doing them, and who wasn't. But nobody ever talked about that. It is not hard to see who is barely lifting in the weight room but is getting all bulked up quickly," explained Grieve.

Close to twenty years after his last major league at-bat, Grieve still feels inner conflict between players he liked, was even friends with, who may have done steroids. "They are still my friends, but I don't have to agree with everything they did," explained Grieve.

"Looking back at it now, steroid use does bother me. I am not going to say names, but we all know about the players named in the Mitchell Report, but there were a lot of others, different kinds of players that never would have made the major leagues and kept a job without them. Some players who didn't do them never played in the major leagues because of them. It is not fair, and looking back all these years later it makes me kind of mad," said Grieve. "Steroids may have helped players in the short term, but in the long run it would cause injuries," continued Grieve. However, another thing Canseco said about Grieve may even be worse to him than the steroids nonallegation, one that he knows makes some people mad.

"The comments Jose made about the Oakland A's only drafting me as a favor to my father is just total nonsense. Sure, the second pick, your division rival, I mean come on Jose," said Grieve.

As a player, general manager, and most of all as a father, Tom Grieve is offended by Canseco's comments but chalks it up to Jose being Jose. "All we need to know is that Jose Canseco has become a cartoon character. He was a caricature of himself even while he was playing. It is the most ridiculous statement. If he was drafted in the fortieth round by the A's, that might have been a favor. No team is going to pick the second pick of the draft as a favor to a father."

Tom believes it's not just insulting to Ben and to him, but it also insults the Oakland A's. "It insinuates that Ben wasn't a player they wanted. Do me a favor? The general manager of a rival team in the American League West? It is so ridiculous to say, it almost doesn't even deserve a comment other than to say look at the moron that said it," said Tom.

"[But] I liked Canseco," continued Tom. "I even traded for him to be on the Rangers. If I bumped into Jose Canseco, I'd be friendly with him. He just himself looks like a fool for saying that [and] it takes away the modest amount of confidence anyone would have in that book and his credibility."

Could Tom, with a lifetime in the game, be reasonable with his scouting report on his own son? What would his assessment be for Ben over the next five to ten years in the game after his 1997 MLB debut? This is his general manager assessment: A chance to be between a .280–300 hitter. Could hit 30 home runs, probably 25 to 30 each year and depending on the team and the players around them, knock in 80 to 100 runs and 30–40 doubles. More slightly prone to striking out at a time when a lot of guys were striking out, but patient enough at the plate to draw 65 to 80 walks per year. An on-base percentage above the league average, maybe .360 to .380. Not blessed with above average speed. Has to work to be an average outfielder. If he were able to play that long, first base might come into play. There was also, in the American League, the chance to be a designated hitter. "You know, for five or six of his years in the big leagues, that's pretty much exactly what he was," explained Tom.

The amazing website baseball-reference.com takes the guesswork out of it. The statistic of 162-Game Average condenses each batter's career into a single season's worth of statistics. For a batter, take the career games played and divide by 162, and then divide their career totals by that factor.

Ben Grieve played for nine years. His 162 game average was a .269 batting average, 20 home runs, 82 RBI, a .367 OBP, 30 doubles, and 77 walks. The only statistic Tom missed was the projection of a .280 to .300 batting average.

The 1997 season placed Grieve on the highway to becoming a baseball superstar. His 1998 season gave him the credibility that any young baseball player would want. "I knew coming into the 1998 season I was the starting right-fielder unless I messed something up really bad," said Grieve. Rather than worry about making the team, he could focus on baseball without the added stress of camp positional battles, and the team had older more established players like Jason Giambi, Matt Stairs, and the immortal Rickey Henderson to surround him in the lineup.

"Jason Giambi was so much fun to be around, he was so outgoing, and loud. I am still great friends with him," said Grieve. Henderson throughout his Hall of Fame career was known as one of the most eccentric, almost unbelievable personalities in baseball. It is often said that Ricky couldn't be bothered to remember the names of his teammates, so it was a big deal for Rickey to know Ben's name. "I don't think he really had a choice but to remember it. I started almost every game next to him in the outfield that year, but I am convinced there were players that he had no idea of who they were, especially the guys out in the bullpen," laughed Ben.

Ben Grieve led the 1998 Oakland A's in games started at 155. He batted .288, slugged 18 home runs, drove in 89 runs, with an OBP of .386 across 583 at-bats. Even so, an All-Star selection was not reasonably expected for such a young star, but when the July 7 All-Star Game took place at Coors Field in Colorado, Grieve found himself on the roster, looking around in awe at the talent of the players. In fact, Ben was the only Oakland A's player to be on the 1998 All-Star roster, and the only position player besides Mark McGwire since Grieve's old warm-up toss buddy Ruben Sierra was selected in 1994.

"I wasn't expecting to go. Other guys on our team were doing pretty good, but I had some good games against the Indians and the All-Star Game manager was their manager Mark Hargrove; it might have helped me get there," said Ben. As he looked around, he took in the moments to appreciate he was on the field with so many all-time great players. "I was on the same team as Alex Rodriguez, Derek Jeter,

Sandy Alomar, Roberto Alomar, Cal Ripken, Roger Clemens, Pedro Martinez; it was incredible. McGwire, Gwynn, Bonds, Piazza, it had to be one of the best teams put together," said Grieve.

When the 1998 season ended, Grieve was voted the AL Rookie of the Year with twenty-three of the twenty-eight first-place votes. Cubs' pitcher Kerry Wood narrowly beat out Todd Helton of the Rockies for the NL Rookie of the Year. It would be another connection between the two Texas-raised players. Grieve once took Wood deep during a Texas high school game. The young Wood opened the eyes of Grieve as the first pitcher he faced who he realized was throwing really hard.

With an All-Star game and a lifelong defining award as Rookie of the Year, it would be easy for everyone to believe that 1999 was going to be another year in what could become a Hall of Fame career. Grieve said, "I probably thought after being an All-Star my first year I was going to have more All-Star games in my future. Why wouldn't I be? But baseball is a humbling game. You think you have it figured out, dialed in, and then you go 0 for 10, and think you will never get a base hit again."

But Grieve did have many more base hits for the Oakland A's, his numbers in 1999 and 2000 getting better each year. The 1998 team improved by nine games, and by 1999, they were a serious contender in the AL West, finishing second to Grieve's "playground," the Texas Rangers. The Oakland A's effectively put Major League Baseball on notice that they were a team ready to make noise.

The A's had a core of young players on the precipice of All-Star game appearances, Most Valuable Player Awards, Cy Young Awards, and most importantly, four postseason appearances with three Divisional titles from 2000 through 2003. Grieve hit a career-high 28 home runs in only 486 at-bats in 1999, and his 2000 season would perhaps be his best. The 2000 team included dynamic hitters like Jason Giambi, Miguel Tejada, Ramon Hernandez, John Jaha, Eric Chavez, and Matt Stairs putting up huge numbers during that run, and a pitching staff of Tim Hudson, Jason Isringhausen, Barry Zito, and Mark Mulder, among the best in baseball.

Leading into the 2000 season, Grieve signed an off-season extension of four years at $13 million. It was considered a good deal from the perspective of both sides. Ben had the security of not having to play for a yearly contract, going through the brutal and often personal arbitration process. The extension would cover him until he could test Free Agency after his seventh year. For the Oakland A's, it provided financial security and set the price for a rising ballplayer.

For the same reasons the Oakland A's liked the extension, other teams did as well and that made Ben Grieve a valuable trade chip. "I thought it was a good deal. My agent was doing their job to get the best offer, but I would have signed anyway, if it was close to the number I wanted. I wasn't the kind of player that could leave a big offer on the table and play the whole year to just hope for more. It was a good contract, and I was happy to be on such a good team and with those guys," explained Grieve.

Billy Beane, the revolutionary mastermind of the budding analytical movement in baseball, understood the importance of retaining Grieve going into the 2000 season. "The last thing I wanted to do in my tenure here is to have drafted Ben with the second overall pick and see him walk after three years. It is not just the cost predictability but what it represents. This is a sign that ownership is committed to keeping the corps of young players here that we drafted and developed," said Beane at the time, justifying the four-year extension.

The 2000 team, with Grieve as one of the three players to drive in one hundred or more runs that year, took first place in the AL West and punched their ticket to play the defending World Series Champion New York Yankees in the AL Divisional Series. The New York Yankees did not look like their 1999 team going into the playoffs that year.

The Yankees made it eight losses in a row as they lost the first game of the five-game series. The Yankees rebounded with two consecutive victories pushing the Oakland team to the brink of a Game 4 elimination at Yankees Stadium. Grieve and the A's dominated on way to an 11-1 victory. Ben had 2 base hits against Roger Clemens and knocked the Texas legend out of the game in the top of the sixth with a 2-run single to right field.

For Grieve and the A's, a victory would be a huge leap of faith in the last game of the series. The Yankees were starting Andy Pettitte. He was another big, strong pitcher from Texas, at 6'5" and 240 pounds, a lefty, and could shut down any team in baseball, especially in a playoff game.

The name Andy Pettitte is in bold across many of the career postseason records from his World Series runs with the New York Yankees and Houston Astros. His 19 wins and 276 innings pitched are the most for a pitcher in postseason history. Pettitte was simply dominating in the postseason with the fourth best Win Probability Added for all pitchers, only behind Mariano Rivera, Curt Schilling, and John Smoltz. "Andy Pettitte was tough the first couple years I played against him, but that year he began to throw a two-seamer that would come in on a lefty. He was even tougher for me to hit after that," said Grieve.

But nothing is a sure thing, and Pettitte was knocked out of the game in the bottom of the fourth giving up 10 base hits and 5 earned runs in only 3.2 innings pitched. "Looking back on that game, if I knew we would get to Pettitte like that, I would have thought we would win," said Grieve. It turns out that as bad as things were for Pettitte over 3.2 innings, the Oakland A's and their starter Gil Heredia did even worse. Heredia was only able to record 1 out while allowing 4 base hits, walking 2 and charged with 6 earned runs.

The Yankees effectively came out delivering a throat punch to Grieve and the A's. The resilient A's team fought back to scrape up 5 runs through 4 innings to make it a tight game going into the top of the fifth down only 7-5 at home. Baseball-Reference.com placed the chance for the A's to win the game at that point at a reasonable 32 percent chance.

The Oakland A's combination of relievers of Kevin Appier, Jim Mecir, and Jason Isringhausen did their job and did not allow the New York Yankees to score another run the entire game. But a huge piece of the Yankees 1990s to early 2000s was their formidable bullpen. The Yankees combination of Mike Stanton, Jeff Nelson, and Orlando Hernandez allowed the best closer in baseball history to come in and shut the door for the last 1.2 innings, leading to an Oakland A's loss while punching their ticket to another AL Championship Series and eventually a World Series Championship against New York Mets.

This was a game to forget for Grieve as he struck out in each of his 4 at-bats including his last career playoff at-bat, against Orlando "El-Duque" Hernandez in the bottom of the eighth. "That game left a bad taste in my mouth. I had a nice season with 27 home runs and 104 RBI, but that game had me feeling down about the whole season," explained Grieve. Like his All-Star game at-bat in 1998, it would be hard to believe this at-bat would be his last in the postseason.

The 2001 Oakland A's played even better than they had in 2000. They won 102 games in the regular season and reached a commanding 2-0 lead against the New York Yankees in a five-game series. The eventual charging ahead of the Yankees and Derek Jeter—including the "Flip Game"—was too much for the A's, resulting in a heartbreaking playoff loss to the Yankees in five games.

But where was Ben Grieve? Even with the contract extension he signed in 2000, Ben was being traded to the Tampa Bay Devil Rays. This trade did not compare with the "Midnight Massacre" of 1976, when the New York Mets traded Tom Seaver to the Cincinnati Reds for Pat Zachry, Doug Flynn, Steve Henderson, and Dan Norman. But trading a Rookie of the Year with each of his season's better than the last was a big deal. A nine-player deal. On January 8, 2001, the Kansas City Royals, Tampa Bay Devil Rays, and the Oakland A's made a deal ultimately landing the second pick of the 1994 draft with Tampa Bay.

The Royals eventually acquired A. J. Hinch and Angel Berroa from Oakland, and Roberto Hernandez from Tampa Bay. The A's received Corey Lidle from Tampa Bay; and Johnny Damon, Mark Ellis, and a player to be named later from Kansas City. The Devil Rays received Grieve and a player to be named or cash from Oakland.

The key cogs of the trade were Johnny Damon to the A's, a year before free agency, Grieve to the Devil Rays, and Roberto Hernandez to the Royals.

Johnny Damon ended up playing only one year in Oakland, scoring 108 runs in 2001, before signing a four-year, $31 million free agent deal with the Boston Red Sox. Hernandez, a prior two-time All-Star, played the 2001 and 2002 seasons for the Royals. He was not as dominant for the Kansas City team and left as a free agent to the Atlanta Braves in 2004. The Oakland A's included Angel Berroa to the Kansas City Royals in the trade. Berroa, a shortstop, won the AL Rookie of the Year in 2003.

Grieve didn't know that he was going to be traded, and he still does not like that he was traded from the team that drafted him and that was now at the window of potential World Series runs. "Maybe not at the time, but now looking back I can see why they made the trade. I understand it, and they got back really good players," explained Grieve.

The A's were about to go on a run of several seasons in the postseason, even winning 102 games in 2001. It would be hard for Grieve to look across the field at his friends and former teammates and not miss wearing the Oakland A's uniform. "I remember the next year they rolled into Tampa, I was looking over at them, everything about the team was fun, even their stretching was fun. The strength coach, Bob Alejo, was great at just keeping everyone loose, I couldn't help but to think, damn that was fun and how much I missed it," explained Grieve on the first time facing his old team.

The batting lineup of the 2001 Oakland A's was headlined by Jason Giambi, and the rapidly emerging Miguel Tejada could place fear in the heart of any starting pitcher. The Oakland A's starting rotation with the three-headed monster of Mark Mulder, Tim Hudson, and Barry Zito were at the top of their game and expected to dominate baseball for years. The trio won twenty-one, eighteen, and seventeen games respectively, and the pitcher brought in during the Grieve trade from Tampa Bay chipped in as Corey Lidle won thirteen of his own.

"It was hard to play against them. Going against that staff in a three-game series of Mulder, Zito, and Hudson, with two of them being lefty was brutal. I preferred playing with them rather than facing them," said Grieve on facing the Oakland A's formidable pitching aces.

In fact, the Oakland trio wreaked havoc as a unit from 2000 to 2004, with each player selected for two All-Star games, each winning or placing second in the Cy Young Award for the league's best pitcher at least once during that time period. The Oakland trio was disbanded after the 2004 season with Mulder traded to the Saint Louis Cardinals and Hudson to the Atlanta Braves. Both were traded by the A's to the National League where the A's would not have to routinely face them. These trades firmly established that the general manager, Billy Beane, was willing to trade away players still performing at a high level before the chance to keep them in Free Agency would be too costly for the small market.

Grieve was now on a 2001 Tampa Bay Devil Rays team looking for an identity. The franchise was established in 1998 and in the middle of ten straight losing seasons. The team finished fifth in the five-team AL East Division nine of the ten years with only the 2004-year improvement of a fourth-place finish.

The 2001 Rays fired their one and only manager, Larry Rothschild, and hired Hal McRae, a former All-Star player for the Kansas City Royals in the 1980s, and later had a stint managing the Royals that is still remembered infamously because of a temper tantrum for the ages.

After a loss early in 1993 against the Detroit Tigers, Hal McRae was conducting a press conference. One of the reporters asked about a decision to not bat one of McRae's old teammates, Hall of Famer George Brett, in a key situation. McRae responded with, "a** F***ing question," and stood up screaming and throwing whatever was within reach, most notably his telephone, which hit a reporter in the face hard enough to cause bleeding. The event was topped off with McRae chasing the reporters from the office, following them down the hall, and delivering the classic parting line, "Put that in your f***ing pipe and smoke it!!"

It was about to become complicated for Grieve in Tampa with the selection of McRae as manager. At first, the Tampa Bay Devil Rays responded in much the same way to McRae as to Rothschild, finishing the remaining games at 58-90. They finished with one hundred or more losses for the first two consecutive seasons with McRae as manager.

Grieve did what he could to keep the 2001 team afloat, but the Devil Rays were not a team built like the A's, and for Grieve, he seemed out of place as the player expected to help turn the losing team around.

The end of year numbers for Grieve for the 2001 season may have been disappointing for baseball fans expecting to see bigger numbers for the same Grieve who was protected in the lineup by Giambi, Tejada, Chavez, and others. It was never wise to pitch around Grieve on those A's teams, but the Devil Rays had a different kind of lineup.

Ben led the team in at-bats, with 548 games played at 154, 30 doubles, 143 base hits, 72 runs scored, 87 walks, .372 OBP, tied for team-high at 210 total bases, and even though not known as a speedster, finished second on the team in triples.

Ben provides some interesting thoughts on the 2001–2004 Tampa Bay Devil Rays and his role with the team. "I definitely felt the pressure in Tampa Bay; they gave up a really good closer in Roberto Hernandez, and the talented Corey Lidle to get me, that also added pressure, I wanted to live up to what they gave up getting me."

"I have a shy personality. I'm not outgoing. I only knew one guy when I walked into the clubhouse for the first time, Steve Cox, we were teammates in the Minor Leagues. A guy like me, walking into spring training made me nervous. I am not sure if it was expected to step into being the team leader and voice in the clubhouse, but I'm not a vocal leader at all," explained Grieve on the start of his days in Tampa Bay.

The 2002 Devil Ray roster did not include Vinny Castilla or Fred McGriff, and Greg Vaughn appeared in only sixty-nine games. It was time for Grieve to step out from the shadows of the more established players. But for the first time, Grieve suffered from injuries, resulting in his playing in just 136 games and 482 at-bats. Ben's dad, Tom, explained, "Ben was off to a really good start in 2002, before a MRSA infection in his hand took him out for a month." Methicillin-resistant Staphylococcus aureus, otherwise known as MRSA, is a virulent infection resistant to antibiotic treatment.

Ben finished the 2002 season with a then career low of 136 games, 482 at-bats, 62 runs, 121 hits, 64 RBI, .251 batting average, .353 OBP, and 208 total bases. Even with the reduced time in the lineup, he was able to smack 30 doubles and 19 home runs. In fact, his 19 home runs were second on the team. A young and exciting rookie, Carl Crawford made his presence known appearing in sixty-three games as an outfielder, and Aubrey Huff replaced Greg Vaughn at designated hitter and hit 23 home runs. The two players were ascending and perhaps Grieve could help lead another franchise building into a contender.

After only two seasons, Hal McRae was let go as manager, and Lou Piniella—a Tampa Bay hometown hero—was brought in to replace McRae. Piniella earned a Rookie of the Year in 1969 with the Kansas City Royals, became an All-Star in 1972, and is perhaps best known for being a New York Yankee fan favorite from 1974 to 1984, helping the Yankees to four World Series appearances, two World Series Championships, and managing the team for the tumultuous, demanding owner George Steinbrenner for 1986 and 1987. Piniella was then pushed into the role of general manager, allowing Billy Martin back to manage in 1988, before Martin was fired again to bring back Piniella during the 1988 season.

After the New York managing roller coaster, Piniella managed the Cincinnati Reds to the 1990 World Series Championship and led the Seattle Mariners to four playoff appearances, including the record setting team of 2001 with the major league record of 116 regular season wins.

Lou Piniella (ironically nicknamed "Sweet Lou") is known for the ferocious, demonstrative, and passionate way he played and managed. For Grieve and his quiet, controlled demeanor, playing for Piniella was expected to be anything but a sweet experience.

If 2002 hit Grieve with the injury bug, 2003 hit him with a sledgehammer. As the season started in April, what first appeared to be a bruised thumb turned into an infection keeping him out of the lineup for nearly a month. The infection was so nasty that it required a stay in the hospital, antibiotics, and surgery before he could swing a bat.

Grieve battled back into the lineup, but a June 26 game against Piniella's former team, the New York Yankees, revealed a chasm between their manager and the player who hoped to lead their franchise forward.

Grieve, pinch-hitting for Carl Crawford, was facing Mariano Rivera. Grieve quickly went down 0 balls and 2 strikes. He took the next couple of borderline pitches, ones that easily could have rung him up as a strike out, before not swinging at the final pitch of the game to strikeout and leaving the tying run at third base. Grieve did not argue; he just walked back to the dugout.

As a player, Lou Piniella would have argued the pitches with the home plate umpire—especially with the game on the line in the ninth inning. It wouldn't matter to Piniella if the arguing made a difference. He loved to see players who could spit fire. But Piniella is not Grieve, and back in the dugout, Piniella had a short interaction with Grieve, causing Piniella to lose his composure and yell in the face of the young player. The whole ordeal was caught by the cameras and blew up across news stations everywhere, making the bad situation even worse.

According to Piniella (as widely reported), Grieve said "that it doesn't matter" when asked why he didn't argue the calls with the home plate umpire. After the game, Grieve went home without having further spoken to Piniella, and the manager went on a tirade to reporters to vent his frustration with Grieve and his perceived lack of caring about winning. A surprised Grieve later turned on the TV to see video of the scolding and the questioning of his caring about the game of baseball.

Ben said he was responding to the question by Piniella of why he (Grieve) didn't argue with the umpire. His answer "[The Umpire] He doesn't care," became "It doesn't matter" to Piniella. This was a huge miscommunication, probably made worse by unsaid frustration with each other. Ears can sometimes hear what they want to hear, and for the Grieve-Piniella relationship, the results were disastrous.

"We were just complete opposites. He was, when he played, an emotional guy, and it continued as a manager. He was probably well liked by his teammates for it, but he was the opposite of me as a player. I kept everything inside. I didn't want people to know how I was feeling. He is more fiery, animated, and emotional than me. So as a manager he probably wanted to see the same from his players. But that wasn't going to come from me," explained Grieve. In fact, his behavior after the strikeout was on brand with how he conducted himself as a player. Ben had grown up in the game, modeling himself after players he saw as even-keeled, not letting the game's emotion, and a good or bad at-bat, throw him off who he was as a baseball player.

"I think in a key situation striking out and coming back to the dugout, I don't want people to think I'm mad, people to be like, oh, stay away from him. I don't want attention drawn to myself. If I hit a home run, I wouldn't flip my bat or slow pace around the bases, because I don't want that extra attention. It's just the way I am," explained Ben. "But do not mistake that with I don't care or that inside I am not mad as hell. I just don't show it."

But Piniella had the credibility of a World Series Champion as a player and manager. The narrative of an uncaring player with a bad attitude was now out there like a ticking time bomb for Grieve. And another issue that could affect his health and career, unbeknownst to Ben, was lurking just skin-deep and could take his life if left untreated.

Ben Grieve first noticed something was wrong during his warm-up swings, just by the sound of the swing. "Usually when I would take my warm-up swings, it would have a certain 'woosh' sound, almost like the sound a box fan could make. My swing didn't have that sound anymore," explained Grieve. It was the only time he could remember not hearing his own swing signature while warming up.

Then in 2003, his bat started to feel heavier. Turning on a 98-mph heater is hard enough, but trying to do that while feeling weaker, a little slower, makes it that much harder. "I kind of thought the weakness was from not lifting weights as much during the season," explained Ben. Remember, he had missed an entire month earlier in the year with a thumb infection requiring surgery. If only the answer were as simple as missing some arm curls during the season . . .

Once the team returned from the West Coast road trip, Ben played one more game at home, before the swelling in his right arm raised enough alarm to have the source investigated by team doctors. "I was in the hospital a couple of nights as doctors were trying to figure out what was happening, it was scary for sure," said Grieve. A blood clot was found under his right armpit. Ben received two rounds of medication and saw some improvement, but there was still some blockage. Tom Grieve noted there was scarring in the blood vessel, meaning the clot may have been there for some time before diagnosis.

Ben does not like to offer excuses for what others may perceive as underperformance, but hesitatingly he admits that the clot may have had something to do with it. "I have no idea how long the blood clot was manifesting before it was diagnosed, but looking back it could have affected my hitting for some time. I am not sure though," explained Ben.

Two key symptoms of the kind of blood clot Grieve had are fatigue and weakness. The clot had to have affected Ben's performance on the field. But for how long?

A 100-mph fastball takes 375–400 milliseconds to reach the plate. This is the time it takes to blink your eye. If you wait the miniscule time, just the blink of an eye, to swing, the fastball is exploding into the catcher's mitt for a strike. You look like a fool and are called a bum by the fans in the stands or those sitting comfortably on a couch watching in high-definition and slow motion. To hit the blazing pitch, there are about 75–100 milliseconds to identify the ball as one to hit. Once the brain gets a yes to swing, the batter has approximately 100–150 milliseconds to do so. The difference between hitting the ball into fair or foul territory is 5–7 milliseconds, approximately the time of a honeybee wing flap. And don't forget the work to have the bat in the right position, at the exact spot where the ball is coming, in a rather large strike zone often from your armpit to the top of your knee.

After his release from a Tampa hospital with clot-dissolving medication, Ben went to Dallas to meet with a vascular surgeon to discuss the best plan for his health. The decision was made to undergo surgery to remove his first rib to ease the blood clot near his right armpit. The surgery was successful, but recovery ended Grieve's 2003 Tampa Bay Devil Rays season. Then in October 2003, the team did not offer a contract to Grieve, and he hit the open free agent market for the first time in his career.

Grieve's year-end statistics for 2003 were abysmal for what he, the Devil Rays, and other MLB teams expected from the once healthy player. Grieve only appeared in fifty-five games, 165 at-bats, hitting 4 home runs, bringing home 17 runners, and hitting a paltry .230. Remember, in 2000, Grieve and the A's had signed a four-year contract extension designed to bring him to the brink of free agency to cash-in after he hit the seven-year MLB service time milestone. Instead of a nice, long-term contract, Grieve was left looking for a job, any chance to play in the major leagues. It was a shocking fall for the once All-Star and Rookie of the Year.

As a baseball free agent for the 2004 season, he was free to sign with any team that wanted him. "I met with the Texas Rangers, we had mutual interest, they wanted to sign me, but they were going hard at Manny Ramirez first and wanted to see how that would go," said Grieve. "In the meantime, as I was waiting, the Milwaukee Brewers offered me a contract, so I took it." (Manny Ramirez did not end up signing with the Rangers either.)

Ben Grieve signed a one-year, $700,000 "prove-it" deal with the Brewers, hopefully to reestablish his market value for the next year closer to the $5,500,000 he made in 2003 during the last year of his contract extension. Ben served as a reserve outfielder and a key bat off the bench for the Brewers appearing in 108 games, starting sixty-five games in right field with forty-two as a pinch hitter, and one game as a designated hitter. He hit 7 home runs, drove in 29, hitting .261, with a .364 OBP in only 234 at-bats for the Brewers before a trade deadline deal shipped Grieve to the 2003 National League pennant-winning Chicago Cubs as they attempted to make the post-season. Grieve was replacing the 1996 NL Rookie of the Year, the left-handed swinging outfielder Todd Hollandsworth.

Grieve had 4 hits in 16 at-bats, with 1 home run mostly in a pinch-hitting role as the Cubs faltered at the end of the year, finishing third in the division, failing to make the playoffs. But then on September 17, Grieve reminded everyone what he was still capable of doing as he came into the game as a pinch hitter during the eighth inning. He smacked a 0-2 pitch to deep center field for a double. Coming up in the ninth inning, he drove a ball deep to right field for a home run against Todd Van Poppel during a 12-4 Cubs victory. This victory allowed the Cubs to briefly hold the Wild Card lead for the playoffs. Ben's home run against his fellow James W. Martin High School

Baseball alum, Van Poppel, ended up being Grieve's last MLB home run.

Playing for the Cubs and being at Wrigley Field left a long-lasting positive impression on Grieve. You can hear the hints of the romance of a baseball fan as he almost seems whimsical when discussing the field and his time playing for the Chicago Cubs. "Even though I wasn't there that long, the Cubs were my favorite stop as a ballplayer. When the Cubs are good, there's nothing like being on that team in that park. I'm sure Yankee Stadium and certain parks may be similar for home team players. But I've never had that experience in Oakland with the fans, or in Tampa with the fans. Although in Milwaukee, the fans were really good, there was just something different about Wrigley Field," explained Grieve. "I really wish I had a baseball card as a Cubs player, but I was never with the team in spring training when baseball cards are usually taken by the card companies."

Grieve was released at the end of the 2004 season and signed a free agent deal with the Pittsburgh Pirates to go to 2005 spring training and try to make the team. "I was cut by the Pirates late in spring training that year. They even tried me at first base to find more ways to try and use me, but I never played there before and it was clear I couldn't do so on the major league level," said Grieve of his 2005 Pittsburgh Pirates spring training. "I was cut pretty quick after the first base audition."

After being released by the Pittsburgh Pirates, Grieve thought he was done. However, his agent called asking him to take a minor league deal for the AAA Cubs team in Des Moines, Iowa, and the chance to be called up during the season to the Cubs. Grieve accepted the chance, splitting time shuttling between AAA and the Cubs. His total for the Cubs that year was 20 at-bats over twenty-three games with all but one game as a pinch hitter. The last game of the 2005 Cubs season was also the last game of Ben Grieve's career.

The player making Major League Baseball look so easy as a youngster, tearing up the minor leagues, and being heralded as the next great player had one last at-bat in him. It was the top of the ninth against All-Star closer Brad Lidge of the Astros. Grieve stepped in with the tying run on base. But he struck out. I am not sure if Lou Piniella smiled that Grieve didn't take strike three but went down swinging.

Now in retirement, Grieve is taking the time to connect with baseball and the fans again. He goes to baseball card shows and signs autographs. "The fans going wanting my autograph are diehard collectors, and a lot of them are collecting for a specific Rookie of the Year. They're great people. And I love talking to the fans. If you're there wanting my autograph, you must love baseball," explained the always humble Grieve.

The long-running line on Grieve is still as an MLB disappointment, an all-time bust, a mistake to have been selected so high in the draft, and to have been forecasted as a superstar. Interpretations such as he failed to live up to his potential because he didn't care, had bad practice habits, had a bad attitude, felt entitled, and didn't love being a baseball player are all still there. He just wasn't a good player when compared to the players during his era. Even in retirement Grieve hears all of this. His father gets ticked off when people think it. "My hair stands up as if on fire when I hear it," said Tom. "Why would Ben feel nothing but pride in his baseball career?"

Looking back all these years later, Ben wants everyone to know that he loves baseball, grew up on it, was built for it, and internally had the same emotional highs and lows as any other player. But he can understand how someone could think those negative thoughts if they weren't giving him a fair chance. "Maybe if I watched old clips of myself, I would be able to see it too. I could see how people may think I didn't care," said Grieve. "But it is simply not true. I did care. But my teammates who knew me didn't think it, and that is what mattered to me most. Fans would think things I couldn't control," countered Grieve.

Grieve sees a player who tried and produced. "The thing is in Oakland, or anywhere for that matter, I produced. When I was producing what people expected, they didn't have those thoughts about me. Everyone loves you. When I couldn't meet their rising expectations, people found reasons to say whatever they wanted and pointed out anything as to why I wasn't hitting 30 home runs or hitting .300," explained Grieve on expectations from teams, fans, and media.

As a former general manager and as a broadcaster, Tom saw firsthand the typical arc of fans, media, and the love-hate relationship of players coming through a baseball clubhouse. Monty Fariss, Donald Harris, and Daniel Smith were all drafted, becoming big-time prospects, but somehow didn't perform to the expectations of fans for the Rangers, and Tom saw it. "You can't get rid of people's expectations. That's one of the fun things about baseball and sports. When we would get a young player, as a Ranger fan, you see the names and envision them as stars on your team, being All Stars and going to the World Series. You envision and you hope it's going to happen. And when it doesn't, as a fan, you're disappointed," said Tom.

But to Tom, a player making the big leagues, however brief, makes them an elite baseball player. "The reality is if you've got a big-league uniform on for one inning of one game, it's hard to say that you're a bum. You rose from Little League to high school, to college, to the minor leagues, and played in the big leagues."

Ben Grieve sees his career differently than merely comparing it to others he played with and against. "After I was done playing, I looked back and realized how much better my career would look if it was compared across an even playing field without steroid use," explained Ben. It is easy to imagine the players who played baseball clean, never resorting to steroids or other performance-enhancing drugs, being resentful of the players who did. Especially when all the players, steroid users or not, are scrutinized.

"I went to my last spring training in Tucson with the White Sox. It was basically the end of my career for me in 2006. A White Sox player was talking about steroids or something. I wasn't really listening. And then one of the other guys said something, 'I know all you boys in Oakland did steroids.' I just kind of laughed at it, then I asked, 'What do you mean?' He's like, 'Oh, we know.' 'I don't know what you heard, but not all of us were taking steroids,'" replied Grieve.

He does have an idea of who did steroids during his playing days, but unlike Jose Canseco, Ben won't throw a name directly into the steroid bonfire of unprovable accusations. "I don't know how many people were taking steroids, but it was the steroid era. One of the things I can look back on, and not show any remorse on, is the fact I didn't take steroids. When I hit those 28 homes runs that year, it was all me. There were a bunch of different players to hit more than 28 home runs in a season back then, and not all of them can say it was without the benefit of steroids. To have people suddenly go hitting those big numbers all the way up to 70 home runs is literally ridiculous," explained Grieve.

Tom, as a general manager for the Texas Rangers from 1984 to 1994, certainly signed, drafted, or traded for players he suspected were involved in steroid use. But Tom bristles that a team could have stopped it without the parameters of approved testing by the Major League Baseball Players Association, and the Baseball Commissioner's office. "We certainly suspected some players, but we were helpless to do anything about it. We could not force a player to be tested, and short of a player being caught with a needle sticking out of their arm, we couldn't prove that a player was doing it or dare to take disciplinary action," explained Tom.

Baseball now has a written league-wide policy forbidding steroids with an escalating penalty of eighty-one games for the first offense, 162 games for a second, and a lifetime ban for a third. It is important to note that PEDs can still be used for a valid medical reason and filed with the MLB Commissioner's office.

For players at the time, like Ben, it was playing against a stacked deck, but he is still proud of his career. "I had a seven-, eight-year major league career. I was hoping it would last at least ten or fifteen years, some people even thought I could be in the Hall of Fame one day. It didn't work out obviously, but when I look back it was a good career."

Tom put this in a way that baseball civilians can understand: "I know a lot of lawyers, rock stars that would trade their careers to play in the big leagues." Tom knows fans pay thousands of dollars to go to MLB fantasy camps in Florida or Arizona and wear big league uniforms playing alongside retired Major League Baseball players for a few days, just to feel like a major league player. "That tells you all you need to know right there," said Tom.

 CALE IORG, DETROIT TIGERS AND BALTIMORE ORIOLES, 2007–2013

Positions: shortstop, second baseman, and leftfielder

Bats right, throws right

Drafted by the Tampa Bay Devil Rays in the sixteenth round of the 2004 MLB June Amateur Draft and the Detroit Tigers in the sixth round of the 2007 MLB June Amateur Draft from Karns High School, Knoxville, Tennessee, and University of Alabama, Tuscaloosa, Alabama. Signed August 14, 2007.

Released by the Tigers on March 29, 2013

Signed by the Baltimore Orioles on April 10, 2013

Released by the Orioles on June 17, 2013

Minor League Career Totals

AVG	G	AB	R	H	2B	3B	HR	RBI	SLG	OPS
.215	548	2007	237	431	92	14	41	175	.336	.603

Highlights

- Cale Iorg is one of three brothers to be drafted and play professional baseball in the 2000s.
- Cale's father Garth was one of three brothers to be drafted and play professional baseball in the 1970s. Garth had a nine-year MLB career.
- Dane Iorg, Cale's uncle, had an eight-year career and was a two-time World Series champion.
- Cale's recognitions include:
  - rated Best Athlete in the Detroit Tigers system in 2008
  - voted Best Defensive SS in the Florida State League in 2008
  - rated Best Athlete in the Detroit Tigers system in 2009
  - rated Best Infield Arm in the Detroit Tigers system in 2009
  - voted Best Defensive SS in the Eastern League in 2009
  - rated Best Infield Arm in the Detroit Tigers system in 2010
  - rated Best Defensive Infielder in the Detroit Tigers system in 2011

CHAPTER 5

Cale Iorg

Good Baseball Player—Better Human Being

Cale Iorg was another kid who loved baseball from his earliest memories. He was born in Toronto, Canada, in 1985 and into a life of Major League Baseball that few people would be lucky to have. Baseball, for Cale, was part of his upbringing. His father Garth played in the major leagues for nine years with the Toronto Blue Jays. His uncle Dane also played in the major leagues for about as long and played on the World Series–winning teams of the 1982 St. Louis Cardinals and the 1985 Kansas City Royals. Uncle Lee played baseball at Brigham Young University (BYU) in Salt Lake City, Utah, from 1971 to 1974 and Minor League Baseball for the Mets. Both Dane and Lee are in the BYU Athletic Hall of Fame. The trio was locally known as the "Baseball Iorg Brothers," and later the major league duo was known as the "Iorg Brothers." So baseball was part of the air that surrounded young Cale.

Dane was the designated hitter for the Cardinals in the 1982 World Series, batting .529 in 17 at-bats. In 1984, the Cardinals traded Dane to the Royals. Then in 1985, Dane played against his brother Garth in the postseason, making history as the first set of brothers to play against each other in the American League Championship Series. The Royals won the ALCS that year, and Dane was back in the World Series. This time he was a utility player for the Royals, with 2 at-bats for 1 hit. This 1 hit saved the team from the brink of elimination, enabling the Royals to survive to a Game 7, and the eventual win of their first World Series title.

Dane came up to bat in a scenario every kid playing baseball dreams about. He was called in off the bench to pinch-hit during the ninth inning, with the Royals down three games to two in the best of seven World Series, and—to make it even more dramatic—this was against Dane's former team, with whom he won the World Series in 1982. So Dane now had two rings. But the game of baseball is fast, nothing is guaranteed; the three Iorg brothers knew that and passed it down to their sons and nephews.

The Iorg family was baseball, and the brothers soon had their own children who also loved baseball and played the sport at high levels. The younger generation grew up understanding the advantages and disadvantages of turning a love of baseball into a profession. Dane has two sons, Seth and Court, who played baseball at BYU; Dane has the World Series rings, but his brother Garth has three sons who went on to play professional baseball.

Cale Iorg, the focus of this chapter, is one of Garth's three baseball-loving sons—Isaac, Eli, and Cale. All three were drafted by a major league team: The eldest, Isaac, was a nineteenth-rounder in 2001 and he played four seasons, reaching as high as AA.

As the 2004 MLB Amateur Draft was approaching, Eli and Cale were being discussed across Major League Baseball. Eli would be selected in 2004 by the Cubs in the fourteenth round. Cale was also being viewed as a first-round talent, but Cale kept telling teams not to waste a pick on him. He would not play if drafted, no matter the pick. He felt that he had a higher calling in the Church of Jesus Christ of Latter-day Saints (LDS), which he believed he should answer, and he also wanted to play a year of college baseball. Amazingly enough, Eli and Cale were going to pass on being Minor League Baseball players in 2004.

Cale was not trying to play coy or create leverage by hoping to make teams shell out more money to get his name on a pro contract. He already knew what he wanted to do, and it was something he wanted to fulfill, a dream he could not and would not put on hold, not even for a chance to play Major League Baseball like his father.

Eli returned to the University of Tennessee. The additional year was well spent as he was selected in the first round of the 2005 draft by the Houston Astros.

The first thing Cale planned to do after graduating from Karns High School in 2004, near Knoxville, Tennessee, was to attend the University of Alabama and play baseball for the Crimson Tide. This probably made for interesting conversation at the Iorg household since his older brother Eli was playing baseball just up the road in

Knoxville for Tennessee. The next thing Cale planned to do, after playing just one year of college ball, was to participate in a rite of passage for his faith. He wanted to be available, at nineteen years old, to receive a "call to serve" as a Mormon missionary to go to any of more than four hundred Mormon Missions worldwide. If selected to serve, he would be told where he was going, become properly trained, and expected to serve a minimum of two years on the mission.

As a high school senior, Cale continued to attract the attention of pro and college scouts, batting .495, slugging 15 home runs, with 57 RBI. Cale also showed elite speed by stealing 34 bases in 36 attempts. The power and speed combination were impressive on their own, but he was more than just good as a batter. The 6'2", 185-pound baseball frame was perfect to build and refine into an elite MLB hitter, and he could also play the other side of the ball field. All that offensive potential was wrapped into a shortstop with defensive skills who was well on the way to becoming MLB-ready.

Cale was telling two huge entities (college and professional baseball) what they did not want to hear. A prospect might put off professional baseball to play in college or put off college by playing professionally first and then attending school as a student after professional baseball. But to possibly do both? For Cale, college baseball was important as was a possible professional career, but his faith and the call to serve meant more, and he would answer if called upon by his church.

"It was a good example of what are the things that are important in life. Sports are fleeting. They come; they go. Maybe it works, maybe it doesn't. I didn't want to sacrifice a life-changing opportunity for something that was never going to be a guarantee," said Cale on his 2004 baseball decision.

In 2004 the Minnesota Twins wanted to draft Cale as one of their two first rounders and were putting their chips on the table to procure the young shortstop. As a Mormon, Cale was not a gambler, nor did he know that the Twins were trying to call his perceived bluff; he was simply steadfast in his priorities for when he turned nineteen.

"The Twins were very, very blunt about it. They said listen; we have multiple first-round draft picks. We're drafting a shortstop. We want it to be you, [but] to do that, we're not going to let you go on your mission," said Cale on the Twins' offer and tactics used to convince him to play. "So that was ultimately the deciding factor. I was very upfront with those organizations that this is something meaning a lot to me, something I'm going to do," continued Cale, declining to change his mission plans.

But the Tampa Bay Rays, a small market team, have always been an organization looking to maximize value, balancing creativity with finding the right formula to create winning teams. The Rays were about to surprise Cale by asking him to consider playing professional baseball *and* do the mission. "I ended up getting drafted anyway in the sixteenth round by the Tampa Bay Rays," said Cale. The team was not just taking a blind shot. They had listened to Iorg before the draft about how important the mission and two-year absence was to Iorg, and the Rays came up with a solution for Cale to sign that summer and play professional baseball, bypassing college baseball, and do his mission as planned the next year. It could have been a win-win, if the offer had arrived earlier and the signing bonus was more in line with his baseball skills, rather than his draft position.

"The Tampa Bay Rays were a unique situation and offer. They drafted me and said to sign and come play with them in the minor leagues. I would be free to go on my mission as originally intended and return after my mission back into their organization. That was interesting, but the numbers and the timing of contract offer didn't really work," said Cale.

Baseball front offices traditionally make their first deals with their highest draft picks, spending most of their allowed signing bonus money. Iorg explained, "They initially drafted me, called me, and then didn't call me back for weeks. The rules were a little bit different in terms of being drafted and when you could sign back then. They waited until literally the day before I was going to attend the University of Alabama to start my freshman year to make their offer to me. By that point I was mentally all-in for at least a year at Alabama."

The Rays had waited too long to present their offer, and Iorg took a pass to pursue a different dream while waiting for something even more important for him to present itself. "I went to Alabama. Had an amazing time my freshman year. I made friends, memories, all that college stuff," said Iorg. He also met the woman he would marry in 2009, his wife, Kristin. "It was awesome to play SEC baseball. We had a good team. It was just fun; I loved my college experience. I don't want to use the word regret, but looking back, you know, one year was great, two more years would have been awesome, right? It would have been a lot of fun. It just didn't happen that way. Alabama was a gift that kept on giving. I met my future wife there, Alabama will always hold a special place in my heart," said Iorg.

Even though college can be a big party scene full of pitfalls, temptations, and possible poor decisions, Iorg managed to remain true to his core LDS faith and upbringing. "I didn't have a hard time fitting in. I've always been a guy that doesn't partake in the party scene, I don't drink. I don't do anything like that; I keep my eyes ahead and my head straight. But that doesn't mean that I'm too good to go and hang out with my buddies. If they want to do those things, that's fine. It is just not what I do," said Cale. "I stayed true to who I was and what my beliefs are. But I went out and did stuff, had a lot of good times, and enjoyed Alabama. I didn't sit in my dorm room every night with scriptures."

Cale took a road not many people would take, forsaking a chance by the Twins to be an MLB first rounder with a guaranteed signing bonus well into the seven figures, the prestige of being a first pick, as well as the rarity of being a fellow first rounder with his brother in the same draft. Iorg took another unexpected swerve turning down the Tampa Bay Rays offer to play professional baseball, then go on his two-year mission, and come right back to professional baseball. He instead chose college baseball, of course unpaid, for what he could only promise as one year with the team.

Cale explains, "I have no regrets at all doing it the way it worked out, college ball, mission, and later becoming a 2007 sixth-round pick. I would have been a first rounder in 2005, but looking at the numbers and how it worked out for me in 2007, it went pretty good. I went to Alabama playing baseball my freshman year, made friends, memories, all that. I went on the mission like I planned to do and ended up being drafted by Detroit in 2007, and ultimately signing for $500,000 more than I would have probably received in 2005."

Cale's brother Eli was a first-rounder in 2005, playing five seasons in the Houston Astros Organization, reaching AAA before injuries ended his career. But the youngest son, Cale, a 6'2" 185-pound shortstop, with a blend of cannon arm, premium defense, and good power, evaded signing and was still looked at as the pick of the litter of the Iorg baseball brothers.

Just as summer was arriving after Cale's freshman year at Alabama, he did indeed receive the news he was waiting for. Cale would be serving his church for two years in Lisbon, Portugal. It would be a long way from the mission where Isaac served in Los Angeles, or where Eli served in Argentina. Portugal was far away from the Iorg family in Tennessee and from Cale's girlfriend in Alabama. But Cale was not going to change his mind.

"I was ready to go. I grew up in the church. It is a common misperception that I had to serve a mission. That's not true. The church expects you to live a life that will make you eligible to serve a mission if you so decide. It was not forced, both my brothers went, and I felt a strong conviction to do so," explained Cale. "There was nothing but excitement and anticipation, just for a great life experience and to do something that I felt was a duty and important to do."

The mission was Cale's focus at this time, but he in no way was forgetting his professional baseball dreams. "I loved the game of baseball ever since I could walk. My memories are baseball; it is an amazing sport. Baseball is absolutely what I wanted to do in life," explained Cale.

Baseball scouts may have believed the mission could push Cale's dreams further away, or that he would not want to return to baseball at all. If that were the case, his family would not point him one way or the other. The next steps would be up to Cale. "In no way did my family try to sway me one way or another, or caution that the mission could hamper my baseball hopes. I am blessed with family and parents who know what the most important thing in life is. And baseball certainly isn't. Baseball was always a constant for me, but baseball cannot be who I am, not my identity. Everything in life just has a way of working out. My life is certainly a testament of that," explained Cale. And there were no second thoughts as he accepted the mission and left for Portugal.

"The hesitations about a decision were the other way. . . . Now that I served and I'm thirty-seven years old, I can absolutely say that had I not served a mission, I would have regretted it the rest of my life," explained Cale.

Cale knew that going away for two years could influence some relationships, and he did what he could to understand how his choices would affect people in his life who were not in the LDS. "I didn't want to bring baseball with me, anything that would take away from the mission. I had a conversation with Kristin; she was not a member of the Church at the time. In my mind, it would be selfish for me to say, hey, I know you're in college, but I want you to wait for me two years and not date or anything," said Cale. "We agreed to break up and if it's meant to be, we would find our way back to each other. We wrote, stayed in contact while I was on the mission, but it was not as my girlfriend," explained Cale on the leap of faith he and his future wife took as he was leaving for Portugal.

Cale Iorg is one of approximately one million missionaries to serve over the course of LDS history since 1837. Other prominent members such as baseball great Dale Murphy, the 2012 Republican Party presidential nominee Mitt Romney, and actor Aaron Eckhart all served as missionaries, helping the church to reach over one million members by performing conversions through teaching LDS beliefs, engaging in humanitarian aid, and providing community service.

LDS missionaries do not receive a salary and must pay their own expenses. From 6:30 a.m. to 10:30 p.m., every minute is strictly accounted for, and these young people must "avoid all forms of wordly entertainment," including radio, television, movies, and Internet.

During Cale's era as a missionary, a phone call would typically be allowed to parents on Christmas Day or Mother's Day, and dating was forbidden. But even with his best of intentions of leaving baseball behind for two years, a small part still found a way through to Cale, who said, "I didn't even bring a baseball or glove with me, but after about a year I cracked."

Another member of the mission had played some baseball, and the allure to at least play catch came back to Cale. "I wrote home to my dad asking for a pair of gloves and a couple of baseballs. We lost one quickly and were down to just one left. I threw the baseball and it hit off the top of my buddy's glove and into the back of one car, before it busted the windshield of another car, before rolling down the hill," said Cale. But the failed brief game of catch left further damage to his wallet. "We never found the ball again, but we had to pay $150 for the broken windshield. I didn't throw a baseball again there, and it was only a handful of times I threw one while in Portugal," continued Cale.

The LDS missionaries were given thirty minutes each morning for exercise, and Cale took advantage of this, ensuring he would go back to America in good shape for an eventual return to baseball. But since there were no gyms or baseball fields, he would have to make do with simple exercises. "I took advantage of the physical exercise time each day. Nothing more than the Herschel Walker plan: push-ups, air squats, pull-ups, a couple resistance band exercises, things like that. I came home way stronger than I was before I left on my mission," explained Cale.

Then just as his time at the mission was nearing an end, the Detroit Tigers made Cale a sixth-round pick, but professional baseball was not a sure thing for him, as he also wanted to explore the college baseball option. Also, Cale was not sure he liked the idea of the Tigers selecting him. "I kind of thought it would be a team like the Cubs or Yankees that would take me in the draft," explained Iorg on the 2007 MLB June Amateur Draft. "Those were the two teams out of high school and through those two years that were kind of in on me. They would contact my dad often, but the Tigers really came out of nowhere and drafted me."

The idea of the Tigers was rough for Cale at first. When he had left the States in 2005, the Tigers were 71-91, and he would have to look all the way back to when he was a seven-year-old kid in 1993, for the last winning record for the franchise. The 2003 Tigers team had the most losses in American League history, finishing 43-119.

On his mission in Portugal, Cale did not have access to ESPN, television, or the Internet to really follow the MLB. If he had had access, he would have seen that the 2006 Tigers broke their thirteen years of losing seasons with ninety-five wins and an AL Wild Card for the playoffs. The Tigers went on a postseason hot streak to beat the AL East Champion Yankees three games to one in the AL Division Series, and sweeping the first place AL West Oakland A's, four games to zero. The Tigers went to the World Series as the favorite to beat the NL Champion, the St. Louis Cardinals. The Cardinals, an eighty-four-win team, found a way to easily win the World Series in just five games.

The 2007 Tigers were again a winning team. "When my dad told me the Tigers drafted me, I was like, 'Oh man, the Tigers are garbage.' When I left on my mission, they just had the most losses ever in the season," explained Cale on his initial reaction to the Tigers. "Then my dad told me they went to the World Series in 2006 and what they had been doing," said Cale.

As he let the unlikely news of the Tigers as a playoff-caliber team sink in, the Tigers became more enticing. Cale explained, "As a young athlete, it was now the Tigers are number one in my mind because they drafted me, they took a chance on me. When you look at the Tigers at the time, it could not have been better for me as a prospect and as a shortstop. The shortstop depth was not deep. The table was really set for me to take advantage and make the big leagues quickly. It just it didn't work out."

Cale committed to Arizona State over Alabama baseball in case the Tigers' signing offer was not a deal he could agree to. Unlike the Tampa Bay Rays in 2005, the Tigers were willing to pay Cale for the first-round talent that many teams thought he possessed. The Tigers gave the sixth-rounder a $1,497,500 signing bonus. Cale was the twentieth shortstop drafted that year, and his bonus was the second highest of all shortstops drafted that year.

Interestingly, of the first twenty shortstops drafted in 2007, eleven of them made the major leagues, but only four of the players were able to get past the 1,000 at-bats in the major leagues, and only one of the twenty shortstops became a full-time starter. Zack Cozart, of the Cincinnati Reds, played for nine years, becoming an All-Star in 2017. For Cale, or any shortstop drafted, it would be a steep climb to make the major leagues at any position, and much less to remain a shortstop into the major leagues. Cale was about to find out exactly how hard it would be, and for him, he was going to have to try with one good shoulder.

Cale is now pushing forty and can barely remember not having pain in his throwing shoulder. He would have to go all the way back to 2002 when he was playing high school football to remember when he first hurt his shoulder—the last time his shoulder was good. "I was playing quarterback for my high school football team, which was garbage. We were trash. And I took a hit, and I remember my shoulder just popped out right then and there," explained Cale on his first shoulder injury.

People who become professional athletes are extreme competitors and will often have to be forced to not play, even if badly injured. The skill of covering up an injury is part of the competition of the players who want to be on the field the most. Cale was no exception. He grinned his way through to the end of the football season, and then went to a doctor to see what was wrong. "I ended up getting an MRI after the football season. The guy was, yeah, you really need surgery. My dad was in the Blue Jays at the time and their team doctor did my surgery," recalls Cale.

Shoulder surgeries are hard to recover from even now, but over twenty years ago, it was more of a "cut and wait" healing process when compared to the more effective physical therapy of today. The labrum, rotator cuff, and other parts of the shoulder joint and biceps are intricate, and often they are not able to return to the full strength, flexibility, and range of motion required for elite athletes.

"I didn't get a throwing program or a sport specific rehab. I had a very pedestrian rehab. It was basically, you're out of the sling, you can move your shoulder, you're good to go," explained Cale about his surgery and recovery as a high school athlete. "I didn't know what I was doing. I just started throwing again. I remember my dad called me during the baseball season and asked, 'What are you doing?'"

Cale was doing what competitive baseball players would try to do. He was playing summer baseball. In Cale's mind it was fine, he was only hitting, not playing the field or throwing. His father, Garth, quickly came down on Cale for even doing that. "He's like, 'You've got like six anchors in your shoulder. You can't swing a bat, what are you thinking?'" said Cale of his dad shutting him down for a bit to heal. "No one ever told me these things, and I can honestly tell you that from my sophomore year after surgery my shoulder hurt, even today. I never had a final surgery to fix everything, So I've had a hurt shoulder for over twenty years at this point. It has never ever been healthy with my shoulder," explained Cale.

Back in the summer of 2007, after completing his LDS mission in Lisbon, Portugal, Cale was ready to play his way onto the Detroit Tigers. Many eyes were on him to see if he was rusty after having barely picked up a baseball or swung a bat for two years. The large bonus he scored added to the tension as Iorg set out to prove he was worth the money and the wait.

His father Garth explained, "When [Cale] first played in 2007, he would have been a junior in college coming out from the draft. He played really well, and people were excited by what he was doing. I was told the Tigers were thinking about calling him straight up from there. He was so close, if that would have happened the whole trajectory of his career would have been different."

Cale still hears the baseball whispers that he didn't make it into Major League Baseball because he was a weak hitting, good defensive shortstop, and it makes the nice, polite Cale hot under the collar. "My whole entire life I was an offensive player. I was also really good at shortstop with my defense. That's because I was just eight to nine years old with the big-league shortstops taking ground balls before Major League Baseball games. But I could always hit too. The narrative that I couldn't hit, to this day, will always bother me," said Cale.

Cale understands that the statistics a player puts down are ultimately what matters. People read the back of the baseball card, and there is not much room for explanations or context. But amplification of perspective from the player can bring nuance and new thoughts to the bottom line of a career often seen as a disappointment and can bring a newly formed respect to what the player achieved.

"From the statistics, of course, I struggled offensively, but it wasn't because I couldn't hit, or I didn't have power. I just lost total confidence, lost total control of the strike zone, no plate discipline during the games. But if you showed up before the game to watch me take batting practice, you would think I was awesome. I could always hit for power, typically high on the team in doubles, hits, with plenty of home runs from the shortstop position," explained Cale.

During his first minor league year, as he was playing well and being looked at for a call-up, Cale was showing maturity and physical ability as part of a five-tool player package. "2007 was my first year back after not playing, and I was an All-Star. I was named both to the Mid-Season All-Star and the end of season All-Star teams, and that was even after suffering an injury that should have been months or even a full year off to recover. I was playing awesome that year. That was even with missing a month with a torn labrum," said Cale.

His father, Garth, was at the game when Cale tore his labrum for the first of several times during his minor league career. Garth knew Cale was hurt, and it was bad. But he can't place the injury recovery decisions solely on the Detroit Tigers. "I was there when he injured it the first time. It's not just a Tigers' fault. It's everybody's fault, because you got a kid, you want to get him going and the kid wants to play as well. Cale was trying to get better to just get back on the field. But he was never right after that injury," said Garth.

"Cale was a dynamic infielder, catcher of the ball, a great glove. But he just never could get his shoulder right," said Garth on son Cale after the labrum tear in 2007. Garth describes the play as an explosion in Cale's shoulder.

"He went back for a ball in the hole, his right arm went out there and he kind of two-handed it out there, which you don't see a lot of people do. But when it is two arms down you know, usually the glove is first down and the throwing arm stays behind it. The throwing arm went down and stuck, becoming extremely hyperextended. His arm, the compression, and force down, you could see that he was hurt, and as a coach and a former infielder, I knew it was a bad injury. But he never went on the disabled list or really stopped playing with it; he just did some extra exercises for rehab, took some games off, and started playing again. His arm was never right again, he had a cannon of an arm before the injury in 2007," said Garth.

The Tigers did not want Cale to have an in-season surgery, and an MRI was not even taken. Looking back, Cale wishes things had been handled differently. "I got back in there right away, and it just boils down to I didn't have anybody there to protect me from myself. What I really needed was for somebody to say, 'We need to sit you down and we have to get you right.' Instead, I was just going to keep playing and keep pushing it," explained Cale.

Cale and the Tigers were pushing his arm and shoulder to points of no return. It was as if Cale were driving his own car with the Tigers urging him to keep moving forward as the low fuel light shined brighter and brighter with each passing gas station, one after the other. Cale was moving further away from a likely major league career as the mile markers ticked away until the Detroit Tigers released him from their 40-man roster and eventually released him outright from the Detroit Tigers.

But what kind of career was Cale slipping further and further away from? After his 2008 season, the general manager of the Detroit Tigers was pushing the narrative that Cale would be an MLB All-Star shortstop, and other scouts claimed he was so good defensively that after the 2009 season—not years down the line—he could have earned a Gold Glove. The go-to publication on baseball prospects even named Iorg as the Tigers' best prospect, top defender, most athletic, and having the best arm. Yes, with all those accolades, no one knew he had a torn labrum and rotator cuff.

Perhaps the Tigers knew cutting into his shoulder could decrease his trade value or be a speedbump in the fast lane to the major leagues, but Cale was going to keep on keeping on, and it was what he was expected to do.

"I did it because I always felt like I was one good series away from my call to the big leagues; since I was a kid, my lifelong dream was to make it to the big leagues. I was so close to being there all the time. The organization's telling me these things, my agent's telling me these things, all I had to do was put my head down, grind it out, get there, and then we'll figure it out," explained Cale on the pressures he felt to keep playing injured, to make the Tigers, and establish himself as an MLB player before digging deeper into the shoulder issue.

"When I would talk with trainers about it, I remember one guy told me specifically in AAA, it's a Pandora's box, you go in there and open it up, and you never know what you're going to find," explained Cale.

During the 2007, 2008, 2009, and 2010 seasons, Cale did not receive an MRI to confirm his worst fears, or have a surgery done. During each season the club urged him to play through the season and address it during the offseason. Each year, his batting statistics suffered and his arm and shoulder ached, but Cale was steadily climbing the minor leagues and appeared to be on the verge of the major leagues. Iorg climbed as the top prospects often did: Rookie Ball, High-A, AA, and topping off with a 2010 promotion to AAA and a spot for the second consecutive offseason in the prestigious Arizona Fall League.

Ending the 2010 minor league season with almost 500 at-bats, his bat showed good power for a Gold Glove caliber shortstop with 11 home runs and 28 doubles. He was second in home runs, doubles, and runs, and third in base hits, total bases, and stolen bases in AA before playing his last sixteen games just one level short of the Detroit Tigers with AAA Toledo. Iorg and his 28 doubles in just 126 games easily outpaced the 23 doubles hit by the four shortstops over 162 games for the 2010 Detroit Tigers.

Cale was fighting hard to become a major leaguer, and he simply stroked it in the 2010 Arizona Fall League. Iorg batted .304, slugged .500 for second on the team, with an .881 OPS placing third on the team, first on the team in triples, and showed good speed placing fourth in stolen bases. All this while placing twelfth in at-bats and sharing shortstop with the eighteenth pick of the first round in the 2007 draft, future major leaguer for parts of nine seasons, Pete Kozma.

"The 2010 Arizona Fall League was the first time in quite a while playing baseball that I felt like me. I felt relaxed, I could take a deep breath and exhale. There was no pressure, just six weeks of fun in the Fall League. It was a fun bunch of guys, and the coaching staff was great. It really helped me," recalled Iorg.

High expectations are part of the life of a baseball prospect earning a large signing bonus. Such expectations made it difficult for Cale to meet the cynical eyes of fans and an organization quick to use his two-year break from baseball first as the reason for what was seen as rust to his game, and then later placing the blame on Cale for not meeting the expectations held for him as a future MLB All-Star shortstop.

"I was playing anxious and pressing like crazy to get somewhere with the Tigers. Being in the Arizona Fall League that season and to have somebody sing a different tune, gave me a different voice in my ear. Instead of, 'You must get it together.' 'The major leagues are waiting for you.' 'You're going to be the shortstop if you can just do this and that.' I started pressing like crazy and it made it even harder on me. In Arizona it was like, 'Hey buddy you're good, just relax and play,' and I did, I hit well over .300, it was awesome. I didn't strike out like I did before, everything I had before my mission was back, the game just felt natural and easy again. While on the minor league teams with the Tigers, as a pro, I can tell you I had a game or a series now and then where I felt like it was back. But I never had a long period of time where I felt like I was back like during the Arizona Fall League," explained Cale on how he was able to step his game up.

The Tigers noticed the improvements and put Cale on the 40-man roster for the first time. Entering MLB spring training camp, it looked like things were finally coming together for Cale. Despite all the clawing and gritting of his teeth through the pain of injuries affecting him as an offensive and defensive player, it could happen for him. It was time for Cale to achieve his dream of becoming a major leaguer. "All the good from the Arizona Fall League followed me into spring training. Everything continued for me, and I was playing well," recalls Cale.

"Looking back, I don't think I was very close to making the team. It was interesting because I was getting playing time, doing well, and hitting for power, home runs, and doubles, playing a great shortstop. The team at the time had Jhonny Peralta, who honestly that year ended up being one their best players in 2011. Peralta had the history of being a solid player, but not a good 2010 and not doing well in spring training," explained Cale about his 2011 spring training.

Feeling like he was doing everything right—his own eyes and gut felt he was performing as a ready-to-play major league shortstop—Cale was feeling hopeful walking into a meeting with the Tigers manager, Jim Leyland. "When I was called into Jim Leyland's office, my head is like, holy crap, I think I am being called in because I am making the team, that's how good I was playing, how comfortable I was about where I was as a player," said Cale on his 2011 spring training.

But Iorg did not see it coming. Along with the manager, this meeting included the general manager, Dave Dombrowski. "They said to me, 'We're going to send you down to AAA.' They had picked up this kid, Argenis Diaz from the Pirates, and wanted to keep him in big league camp to see what they had in him," explained Cale.

But the departing message was clear to Cale. Between Jim Leyland and Dave Dombrowski, it was "You're doing awesome," explained Cale on his takeaway from the meeting. "I was doing what they were hoping for all along, and to keep doing it, and I was going to be with them real soon," explained Cale of the meeting and how the team was high on his potential for the Tigers.

Argenis Diaz played twenty-two games with the Pittsburgh Pirates in 2010 and did not make the Tigers. He was assigned to the Tigers AAA team, playing third base for Toledo the first half of the season, and then for the next two and a half seasons, he started for the AAA club. Argenis Diaz never again played in the major leagues.

The 2011 season for Cale Iorg continued the good play of his 2010 minor league season, the Arizona Fall League, and big-league training camp. But the "real soon" was not occurring as he had imagined it would play out.

"I get out there in AAA, I'm the starting shortstop for the first half of the year and I came out doing great. The first month and a half, two months, I'm hitting for a higher batting average than I had since Rookie Ball, .280 or so. I was playing really well again, but this is the point in time my shoulder starts to get really, really bad. It was to the point where I couldn't sleep at night. It just hurt so bad. The longer I tried to play with it that year, my stats kept going down and down," explained Cale. "It is like I know I'm hurt, but again in my mind, I had to keep playing because I was so close to being called up. It was not the time for this to happen. I just had to get it together and come back from the All-Star break ready to pick it up. It is how quickly it can change for a prospect. Suddenly, I go from I had to play every day to a couple weeks later I'm getting sent down to AA," continued Iorg.

"I'm very appreciative of Detroit. But if there's one axe I have to grind with them, it's I said multiple times that my shoulder was killing me. It was just always brushed aside. It was always that they would look at it after this season," explained Cale on the year-to-year discussions of his unrepaired shoulder injuries. "Keep in mind I had shoulder surgery years before. The first year coming back, I was diagnosed with a tear in my labrum. I played with it the entire time and it was now at the point where it was terrible," said Cale.

"I kept getting like, 'We're almost done with the season. Just be a good soldier, soldier on, and we'll get there.' So, I did. I finished my 2011 year in AA, and I was just miserable. Never hated baseball in my life like that year. After the season I finally had an MRI. When I went to the doctor, we're reading the MRI together. Keep in mind this [doctor] is one of the guys that just told me to keep playing the previous years, and now he is telling me we must do this surgery or this surgery, he told me before to wait and now it is a conclusion for surgery. He showed me a torn rotator cuff, a torn labrum. I also had a clavicle that was jacked up and shrinking. I was going in for surgery that offseason and thinking I was also going to have a surgery called biceps tenodesis procedure, the one Curt Schilling made famous when he was in Boston. The surgeon was supposed to relocate the biceps tendon in my shoulder to a different spot because my biceps tendon was always the problem resulting in the shoulder issues for whatever reason," explained Cale.

"The plan was to do that surgery, as well as repair the labrum, and rotator cuff. If you had this surgery, it's understood you don't even touch a baseball for a year. I wake up and the doctor said we ended up not doing it," explained Cale on his expectations for the surgery and the recovery.

It turned out that not everyone was on the same page. Coming out of surgery and the fog of anesthesia, Cale found out his expectations for having the biceps tenodesis procedure would not be met, and the Tigers were just trying to patch him up to play, not really allowing him to have the best chance for long-range recovery.

"I remember being really mad when they told me when I woke up, like really mad. I was going to have to go through rehab for the fixed rotator cuff and labrum, for just the normal surgery, but they wouldn't address the core issue, which was my biceps tendon being in the way, that's why it tore over and over," explained Iorg.

Iorg went through rehab attempting to repair what he suspected was not a truly repaired shoulder to at least try to recover part of his 2012 season. The recovery kept him from participating in spring training, and he was removed from the 40-man roster. "I ended up missing the first half of the year. My job was to do a rehab stint for the Lakeland, Florida, team and hook up with the AAA team at the All-Star break," said Cale.

But just as he was about to jump from the Lakeland team to the AAA team, the familiar occurred again, which Cale knew would happen when the last surgery did not address the condition causing his shoulder to be compromised in the first place. "I'll never forget this play. I'm just getting it back, feeling okay. It was supposed to be my last game there before they shipped me out. The ball hits off my heel and kind of rolls between my legs, I reached behind my legs, wheel around and threw the ball to first. It's hard to describe, but I felt everything just explode in my shoulder," said Cale on the throw and ensuing injuries that ultimately ended his professional baseball career.

Cale Iorg refused to let others see his pain and kept on playing, determined to keep his return to AAA and hopefully the major leagues a possibility for 2012. "I remember thinking the rest of the game, I am playing with all this pain, but I'm leaving tomorrow for AAA," recalled Cale. Looking back now, he knows he was getting in his own way in the long run, and the trajectory of his career was pointing further away from his dream of being a Major League Baseball player.

"This is where pride gets in the way because I'm like, I'll be fine, I'll be fine, but I wasn't fine. I wouldn't play shortstop the second half in AAA. It was the continued road of the last one and a half years of my career, I was now playing left field, shortstop, second base, or center field, being turned into this platoon guy, not a major league everyday shortstop," explained Cale.

He could see the writing on the wall, and he knew he would not be with the Tigers much longer. The self-confidence long faded, Cale no longer wanted to have the ball hit toward him. His baseball world was crumbling all around him. "The Tigers were moving on from me. I just remember being in the field praying with every pitch, please don't hit the ball to me because my shoulder was hurting that bad. The whole thing was awful. Just doing anything, sleeping, was terrible. Eating was miserable. Going to the bathroom hurt my shoulder, and it stayed that way," explained Cale on how the injuries were affecting not only his baseball career, but his life. But there would be no surgery going into the 2013 season.

Cale went back to baseball for 2013 playing in the World Baseball Classic for Canada with his shoulder throbbing the whole time. Then after Team Canada was eliminated, Cale returned to the Tigers late in spring training just to be traded to the Baltimore Orioles near the end of spring training, but the deal did not go through. The Tigers still wanted to clear the roster spot and gave Cale an outright release, meaning he was now a minor league free agent and could sign with any team wanting his services. The Tigers gave up on the player they once looked at as a future All-Star, Gold Glove MLB shortstop.

The Baltimore Orioles signed Iorg as a minor league free agent to see if they could find a way to unlock the mystery of why he was not the player everyone thought he could be. It became clear quickly that on the field, Cale was held together by grit and pride, but he was no longer a baseball player who could play the game. "I wasn't there long, they said I didn't look good, that there was something wrong. I was sent in for an MRI. I had torn my rotator cuff and had a torn labrum, I tore everything again. My career was over. I had not much left in the tank, physically, mentally to give to baseball anymore," said Cale.

The end was there for Cale to see as the doctor and he went through the results of his tests and examinations. The end of his baseball career would be hard, but it also would be a relief and a way for Iorg to return the focus to his young family so often apart as he was playing baseball.

"Sitting in the doctor's office I don't think I heard a word after, 'You've got tears again in your shoulder.' I didn't hear anything, it was like a movie, I just went blank. It was now I have to do something else. I got out of there to call my dad. It was an emotional call, to say I was done, I had nothing left to give to this game anymore. I then called my wife," explained Cale.

Being the player that he was, Cale didn't just clean out his locker and go back home. He still felt the responsibility to play the innings through and joined the team as they were going on a road trip for several games. "I called [my wife] and said we're getting ready to go on a road trip. When we get back, I'm out of here. Baseball was easy to walk away from because I had so many important things waiting for me, and the world doesn't stop because I was out of baseball," explained Cale.

"Baseball just wasn't fun anymore; it was time to move on. That day made it easy for me to know what to do. My wife was always with me where I played, except for the last year and a half when we had our daughter it was not practical anymore to always be there all the time. I could see the writing on the wall for baseball and it was not looking good," continued Cale.

For the Iorg family, Alabama was the backdrop in which Cale had originally met his wife, Kristin, and it would become part of how he found his next career. "After my 2012 season, my wife and I went back to watch a football game in Alabama. My brother-in-law and sister-in-law were still students at Alabama, and they shared an extra ticket with a friend to go to the game. The friend's dad owns the company I work at now," said Cale.

"We all go to the game; my wife and I were talking to him [the friend] the whole time. A week after the game, he texts me because his dad wanted to call me. He owned a mortgage company, knew about my dad and uncle. His dad called and he's like, listen, I love hiring athletes because you guys are competitive, disciplined, and you're motivated. If baseball doesn't work out, I want you to know, you have a job here," explained Cale of the phone call.

At that point, Cale still had his mind on baseball for the foreseeable future, and the thought of a postbaseball career was not creeping in just yet. "After we finished up, my wife wanted to know what it was about, and I said he offered me a job. She was all excited. But I was like, I don't really need a job; I have one right now. But that call led to where I am now, my next career," said Cale.

Several months after that call, right after telling his family he was done as a professional baseball player, Cale was ready to reach out to Pat Flood to see if the job offered during their phone call was still on the table. "When I left that doctor's office, I first called my parents and my wife. My third phone call was to him, and I said, I just got this MRI, I'm done. I'm coming home in a week, is the job still there? He told me to come home, and let's give it a shot. I've been there ten years in July," said Cale, who has already spent more time at that job than the seven seasons he spent in professional baseball with the Tigers and Orioles.

"Our company, the way we try to run business, the way we look and think about business is just so awesome. I went from being a loan officer to a senior loan officer, and I am now running accounts as sales manager for the company. The job is fulfilling and given me the earnings and a lifestyle I didn't know was capable for me outside of sports," explained Cale.

Some people believe that what happens in life is due to fate or is the result of good planning or just plain luck. Cale, however, has a different perspective. "God absolutely takes care of people; he took care of me. I did something that I devoted myself to when I served a mission. I think God took care of me because of that."

But before completely walking away, baseball was going to have another try at keeping Cale. "One of the Baltimore minor league guys asked me if I wanted to coach; he was like, 'I will make you a coach right now.' It just wasn't appealing because at the time I felt like my career was such a failure. How can I go from one day I'm on the team to the next I'm coaching the team? I was still relatively young. The players would just think I couldn't play the game anymore; I just didn't want any part of that. Maybe it could have been different if I had a successful career, but at that point I had bitterness, anger, and frustration toward baseball. I wanted to be as far away from baseball as possible at that point," explained Cale, on turning his back on baseball.

Today, Cale has a slight connection to baseball thanks to his oldest child, Vayda. "I don't watch too much baseball anymore because I think the game is not even close to the same game, it's a frustrating game to watch now. My oldest, my daughter, is the only one that remembers me playing. She likes to go to games, so we have a deal to go to one Braves game a year. I don't necessarily want to watch the game, but I do it because she likes it," explained Cale. "I've devoted so much [of] my life to it. I don't really care to give baseball any more of it. I loved baseball, it just didn't love me back."

Softball is not "girls' baseball," but it is a game that rivals baseball in skill, reaction time, and how enjoyable and seriously it is taken by the players. Cale enjoyed being part of softball as his daughter took to the field with a bat and glove. "My daughter played softball for a couple years. I coached her team, which is the most fun I've ever had, it was incredible to be part of it," explained Cale of his daughter's youth softball team.

Looking back, Cale thinks his baseball career should have unfolded differently. "The only thing, and I'll just reiterate, the only thing that bothers me about my baseball career is it did not happen right. I look back and think what could have been, what if I would have had surgery in 2007 or 2008? That is the part of my career that bothers me the most," explained Cale.

"I had never struggled with confidence in myself, but for the last three, three and a half, four years of my career, I experienced challenges in the mental approach to the game, and being hurt all the time didn't help. Back then nobody talked about the mental side of sports. I was a product of mental warfare each time I went to the baseball field. I was lost in each at-bat, I couldn't tell you the name of the pitcher, I couldn't tell you what the count was, it was just me in my head trying to figure out my swing and becoming further frustrated, and eventually losing my confidence as a hitter," continued Iorg.

He always wanted to do the right thing, which included doing everything and more that the Tigers asked of him. "I developed tons of anxiety as I played. I think everyone with the Tigers working with me had good intentions and were genuinely trying to help me. This is not me badmouthing them; I think it was the wrong way to try to help me. I had extra-hitting drills all the time. I had the hitting coordinator coming in all the time to talk and work with me. We're going to try this, we're going to get wider, stand up taller, do a toe tap, do a little kick, close your stance, try to choke up, close your left eye, put loose change in your right pocket. It was like every single day, every month, every week with all this. It was to the point when I was in the box, I couldn't even remember my natural stance," explained Cale.

Even as he kept drowning in the good intentions thrown at him, Cale didn't feel as if he could take control of his game and stance from the instructors and coaches. "I grew up around baseball and the locker rooms. I heard the coaches talk about the players. This guy's hardheaded, you can't coach him, and he already knows everything. I didn't want to be that guy. I would listen to every single piece of advice and do everything that they told me about in the next game. I should have just said, 'Let me play. You guys drafted me for a reason. Just let me do it,'" said Iorg on how he could have advocated for his own career.

Iorg did have some coaches who saw what he needed to succeed as a player. His father, Garth, wishes that his first minor league manager, Larry Herndon, would have had the opportunity to be with Cale each step up the Tigers ladder. Cale also knew Herndon could get the best out of him on the field. "My first year, Larry Herndon, my favorite human being in the world, let me do that. And my coaching staff in my second stint in the Arizona Fall League let me do that. Those were the places and times I played my best baseball," said Cale on how he felt he played his best.

In retrospect, Cale had a torn labrum and a torn rotator cuff for all but half of one season during his seven-year career. From early in the 2007 season, all the way through 2011, the last half of 2012, and into 2013, he played hurt, and was still amazing scouts, opponents, and Minor League Baseball.

Cale still occasionally wonders how other players were able to recover from injuries so quickly, getting back on the field and ultimately furthering their careers or putting up eye-popping results. Cale didn't have the "cheat code" that some other players were using. Cheat codes change more often than testing, and the policies the MLB uses to catch the cheaters and the chances of being caught may be worth the risk. "Steroids, PEDs [performance-enhancing drugs] with HGHs [human growth hormones], was obviously a big one. I can be naïve. I didn't necessarily witness the actual administration of PEDs. I couldn't tell you one hundred percent definitively which player did it or didn't use them. But players did them and it was pretty hush-hush. I was never approached to try them," explained Cale.

Cale sees a difference between how athletes testing positive for PEDs and those outed as users are perceived when considering if the player did it to help the team by recovering from injuries quicker or did it simply for the player to put up numbers to be noticed. "This may not be a popular belief, but I'll tell you this. I've battled shoulder surgeries and shoulder injuries my entire career going all the way back to high school. A guy like Andy Pettitte did it to help recover from a shoulder injury, and he didn't get in trouble for it," said Cale.

Andy Pettitte was among eighty-five players named in the 2007 Mitchell Report to the MLB Commissioner's Office on the use of steroids and performance-enhancing drugs. After being named in the report, Pettitte admitted to using PEDs for just two days during the 2002 season solely due to feeling pressure and obligation to return from injury as quickly as possible. Pettitte is still considered to have a chance to achieve what Roger Clemens was not able to do, which is to be voted into the Hall of Fame by sportswriters. Clemens, who never admitted to taking steroids or PEDs, was named more than eighty-two times in the Mitchell Report. A year after admitting to using HGH twice, Pettitte testified in a 2008 Congressional deposition to using two more times during the 2004 season.

"It seems like everybody just forgot Andy Pettitte was ever a part of the whole Roger Clemens thing. Melky Cabrera used PEDs, gets suspended for fifty days, and comes back signing for millions of dollars," explained Cale.

As Ben and Tom Grieve discuss in the previous chapter, PEDs were a longstanding issue in baseball. In fact, for as long as baseball has been played, owners, managers, and players have tried to get a leg up on the competition. Back in 1875, the rule for pitching was changed from underhand to overhand because so many pitchers threw that way anyway. Slick baseballs, tacky baseballs, corked bats, sign stealing, altering the playing field, and even adjusting air flows mid-inning to change potential outcomes are examples of types of cheating that still occur today. And of course, there have been amphetamines in use in major league clubhouses since World War II, steroids since at least the 1970s, and HGH since the 1990s. If every player who cheated chemically were caught, suspended, or banned from baseball, the game could not be played at the highest levels that the owners and fans have come to expect. The game would be drastically reduced in entertainment, skill, and highlight reel plays.

Does baseball really want to catch all the PED users? Anabolic steroids were banned in 1991, but the ban did not include any form of drug testing. Then ten years later, players on a major league organizational roster who were NOT on the 40-man team roster could be subject to random testing. The first offense was a fifteen-game suspension, going up fifteen games for each offense, before a permanent ban for a fifth time testing positive during the random testing program.

It was not until 2002 that mandatory drug testing was agreed upon for MLB players. Initially this testing was for informational purposes only, and it was not until 2005 that suspensions started. Amphetamines and other stimulants were not tested for until 2005, and testing for human growth hormone (HGH) came along in 2011.

The perceived risk versus gain scenario for players to use PEDs for whatever reason allowed Cale, who as a Mormon would not even consider having coffee or tea in the morning, to understand the siren song of PED use for MLB players. Cale does not encourage the use of PEDs for a player, but he believes that baseball did not, and still does not, do enough to make the use of PEDs just a footnote in baseball past. "As a minor league player, it's like, why would I not take steroids? Take those things, get my body right, I'll serve my fifty games if I get caught. There is a gain to be had, a reward for doing something wrong. I think that's where baseball drastically messes up," said Cale.

According to Cale, the risk of being caught for PED use could be worth taking for at least a first suspension for reasons such as trying to get back or stay on the field while injured, trying to make the big-league team, or playing for a new contract as a current contract is ending. Improvement in production for players seeking a contract extension or a new contract is prevalent, and this even includes those in the last playing year for MLB draft eligibility. Players like Mark

McGwire and Andy Pettitte claimed it had nothing to do with personal gain through increased production or being on a baseball roster. It was simply because they felt the team needed them to be on the field for the best chance to win games.

"A player can have the time of their life playing better than ever, and then some team is going to reward you with an amazing contract. Get caught once, and then move on. Play well and everybody forgets about it again," said Cale.

Cale knew right from wrong, but he knows not everyone did. The field was not even, and he lost ground to players who made different choices. "Should I have taken something and tried to get better quicker? I never did obviously. But I can't say I never had that thought," said Cale. "There's a lot of guys who perform very well, get caught, and it doesn't hinder future earnings. They end up just signing for more money," continued Cale. "I look back on my career and I'm like, was I stupid? Was I one of the stupid ones that just battled injuries the natural way?"

The answer, "Of course not, you did it the right way," does not have to be told to Cale. He knows this, but it still can make him feel cheated by the weak enforcement of Major League Baseball, and the protection afforded by the teams all the way through the culture of baseball. It is likely that some players like Cale never had their major league career because they followed the rules, while many others who didn't follow the rules went on to have long and successful careers.

Iorg is fine, however, with not getting his call to the big leagues because he stuck to his principles. "At the end of the day, I can look in the mirror, I did it the right way. I didn't keep deserving players [away] from the major leagues that were doing the right thing," he explained.

Cale's dad, Garth, reflects on the legacy of his children and baseball. "I look back on my kids and I think about their decisions between mission service and professional athlete. They ended up doing both and serving Jesus Christ. A baseball career is so short when compared to living the gospel, trying to follow Jesus Christ as a lifelong pursuit," explained Garth Iorg on the hard decisions each of his sons came to on their own.

"Baseball is what I did. It is not who I am. I think my kids are like that too. When we get together as a family it is never about baseball. It is all about family and what we are doing now. We all are into fly-fishing now, that is our passion, our competitive outlet," explained Gath as he sees himself and his boys.

Cale and his brothers did not have long successful Major League Baseball careers, unlike their father and uncle, but the brothers still have much to be proud of. Cale didn't give up his baseball jersey until his injuries practically tore it off his back. Cale knows he always gave more to the game than his body could endure, never allowed the game to cheat him, and never cheated baseball. How many baseball players can say the same?

"I was given a wonderful opportunity that could have worked out great. A couple choices one way or another could have changed things drastically, but it just didn't happen. What I am most proud of with baseball is I was always true to myself, to what I believed in, true to the lifestyle I wanted to live. I can walk away knowing I never embarrassed myself. I never set a bad example for the church and what I believe in," explained Cale.

Cale understands the gift of baseball in his life. The love of baseball is still there somewhere, woven together by the love of his daughter and her refusal to let him quite forget. You never know, an extra ticket could sit you beside a talkative stranger and his daughter. Listen and talk to them, because, you know, baseball and life have a funny way of working and pushing you to new heights.

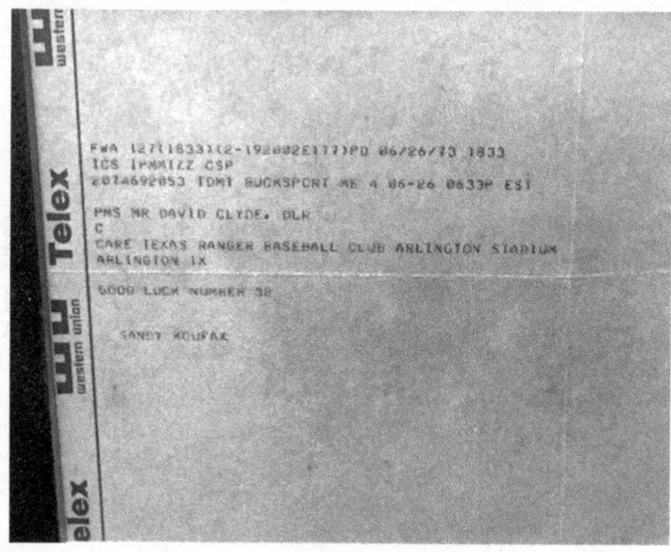

western union Telex

FWA 127(1833)(2-192002E177)PD 06/26/73 1833
ICS IPMMIZZ CSP
2074692053 TDMT BUCKSPORT ME 4 06-26 0633P EST

PMS MR DAVID CLYDE, DLR
C
CARE TEXAS RANGER BASEBALL CLUB ARLINGTON STADIUM
ARLINGTON TX

GOOD LUCK NUMBER 32

SANDY KOUFAX

The great Sandy Koufax was aware of the comparisons between him and David Clyde and sent a telegram to David Clyde wishing him well before his first start. Clyde long idolized Koufax. The telegram is framed and cherished by David Clyde to this day. *Personal photo by David Clyde*

Ben Grieve in the Oakland A's dugout during his Rookie of the Year campaign. *Personal photo provided by Ben Grieve*

Brian Cole as a child growing up in Mississippi learning to love the game of baseball. *Personal photo provided by Greg Cole*

Brian Cole showing off his stroke during Mets Spring Training in 2001 shortly before losing his life in a car accident. Cole was considered to be one of the most electrifying prospects in all of baseball. *Personal photo provided by Greg Cole*

Brian Milner warming up at Exhibition Stadium in 1978. *Personal photo provided by Brian Milner*

Left to right, Pat Gillick, Brian Milner, Bobby Doer at Exhibition Stadium in June of 1978. Gillick was enshrined in the Baseball Hall of Fame in 2011 for his excellence as a baseball executive and general manager. Doer served as the hitting coach for the Blue Jays and was enshrined in the Baseball Hall of Fame in 1986 after a long career with the Boston Red Sox. He was selected for nine All-Star teams as a second baseman. *Personal photo provided by Brian Milner*

Brian Milner sharing a fantastic 1978 Father's Day with his parents at his hometown Arlington Stadium before a game against the Texas Rangers. *Personal photo provided by Brian Milner*

Dan Pasqua showing off the sweet stroke that tempted the Yankees and the fans to hype him to unattainable levels. *Personal photo provided by Dan Pasqua*

 BRIAN MILNER, TORONTO BLUE JAYS, 1978–1982

Position: catcher

Bats right, throws right

Drafted by the Toronto Blue Jays in the seventh round of the 1978 MLB June Amateur Draft from Southwest High School, Fort Worth, Texas

Major League Career Totals

AVG	G	AB	R	H	2B	3B	HR	RBI	SLG	OPS
.444	2	9	3	4	0	1	0	1	.667	1.111

Minor League Career Totals

AVG	G	AB	R	H	2B	3B	HR	RBI	SLG	OPS
.239	362	1274	136	305	12	10	12	164	.321	.621

Highlights

- After being diagnosed with type 1 diabetes at age thirteen, Brian Milner managed the lifelong condition to become an elite athlete.
- Milner is the only drafted high school positional player to make his professional baseball debut at the MLB level.
- Milner is the only catcher to be drafted and make his professional debut at the major league level.

CHAPTER 6

Brian Milner

It Won't Ever Happen Again

Every now and then the beginning of a story is too good to be true, and in the case of Brian Milner's baseball career, it is and it isn't. Brian happily recounts his story with pride, perspective, and gratitude for the game of baseball, which shaped not only his life, but also the lives of his sons.

Eighteen-year-old Milner had no intention of being a professional baseball player for the 1978 season. Rather, he was set to play baseball and football at Arizona State, where the baseball program is one of the titans in the history of NCAA Division I baseball. Milner was looking forward to playing for the legendary baseball coach Jim Brock. Arizona State was headed for an NCAA Championship in 1977, runner-up in 1978, and champion again in 1981. During Jim Brock's twenty-three years of coaching, 175 players went on to play professional baseball. Milner was walking into a wonderful situation both in terms of an education and in continuing his baseball journey.

With an average of eight players per year going from Arizona State baseball to professional baseball during Brock's tenure, Milner was hoping to have the best of both worlds as he wanted a college degree and a professional baseball career. The young catcher from Southwest High School in Fort Worth, Texas, was going to be a tough player to lure away from college baseball if selected in the 1978 MLB June amateur draft, but the 1978 Blue Jays were going to take their best shot.

Brian Milner was born November 17, 1959, in Fort Worth, Texas, as the grandson of sharecroppers on one side of the family and Native American grandparents on the other. Milner was not raised with a silver spoon in his mouth, and he recognized education as important as sports for his future.

"I told everyone up to the draft I was going to go to Arizona State to play baseball and the opportunity to play football. I told teams I would not sign if drafted because education was ingrained in my head from day one. Get your education, it is something nobody can ever take away from you," explained Milner on his mindset going into the 1978 MLB player draft.

Brian is not sure how much his stance to not sign if drafted prevented him from being drafted higher. Milner, who is extremely humble and gracious, does admit that he was a top player in the baseball scouting world leading into the 1978 baseball draft. "Jim Walton put a major league scouting number grade on me that was just phenomenal. He told me that I was the highest grade he put up in years," explained Milner.

The Toronto Blue Jays were a fledgling second-year expansion team ready to take some risks to get the best players they could, as quickly as they could, and the Blue Jays president and general manager decided that young Milner was worth it. The Blue Jays pulled the trigger, making Brian their seventh pick in the draft. (Milner was the 158th pick overall in the MLB draft that year.) Now that he was selected, the Blue Jays were ready to pour on the charm, dollars, and promises. "The Blue Jays took my parents and me up to Toronto. They were respectful of the NCAA rules to ensure I would still be eligible to play college ball if I didn't sign. The Blue Jays were absolutely first class, Peter Bavasi was president, Pat Gillick was the GM, and everyone down the list with them. It was kudos to those people and the organization," said Milner. "It just came down to [the fact that] they brought my parents and me up there and said we really want to sign you and make you part of the organization," explained Milner. "They were putting it all out there on the table."

The Blue Jays offered Milner a $150,000 signing bonus, a major league contract with a spot on the 40-man roster for four years, and even the opportunity to bypass the minor leagues and start his career on the major league level. Brian was about to make the decision of his life, putting in motion what would ultimately lead to so much more for him.

"My parents did what they should do, talked about the positives and negatives of going to the Blue Jays, they weren't going to make me sign, it was my decision. We weren't exactly people of money, but my dad was a CPA and knew it was a good opportunity," explained Brian. "He later told me I would have been crazy if I didn't sign." The $150,000 afforded Milner the means to go to college as opportunities presented, and the Blue Jays agreed to be flexible in allowing him to attend classes during the MLB offseason.

The amount of the signing bonus offered needs to be put in perspective to reflect the esteem and importance the Toronto Blue Jays had for their seventh-round draft gamble:

- The No. 1 pick in the 1978 MLB draft was Bob Horner, drafted from Arizona State and the recipient of the 1978 Golden Spike Award given to the nation's best amateur athlete. Horner went from being Baseball All-American and College World Series Champion direct to the major leagues, the 1978 Rookie of the Year in the National League for the Atlanta Braves, and an All-Star ten-year career. His signing bonus was just over the $150,000 offered to Milner at $162,000.
- Kirk Gibson, Baseball and Football All-American at Michigan State University, was the twelfth pick overall. Gibson became a two-time World Series Champion, All-Star, NL MVP, ALCS MVP, and a Silver Slugger. It took a $150,000 bonus to sign the college gridiron star to baseball. The Detroit Tigers took a leap of faith as Gibson had only played one year of college baseball and was already drafted by the NFL St. Louis Cardinals after setting MSU and big-10 receiving records.
- The Toronto Blue Jays selected Lloyd Moseby (with a $55,000 signing bonus) in the first round as the second pick overall. The speedy centerfielder became an All-Star and one of the franchise's first star players.
- Dave Stieb was also drafted by the Blue Jays in the fifth round as an outfielder signing for a $30,000 bonus. The Blue Jays convinced Stieb to move to pitcher, and he became a seven-time All-Star, pitched a No-Hitter, and was one of MLB's best pitchers of the 1980s.
- Three catchers were taken in the first round that year. Bob Cummings, seventh, by the San Francisco Giants; Nick Hernandez, eighth, by the Milwaukee Brewers; and Bill Hayes, thirteenth, by the Chicago Cubs. The three first-round picks combined for 9 at-bats at the big-league level. The three catchers received a combined total of $162,000 in bonus money, with Hayes at $62,000

> and Hernandez and Cummings at $50,000 each. Only Bill Hayes played at the major league level, batting .222 spread across 1980–1981 for the Chicago Cubs.

"I heard rumors after the draft that I would have gone at the top, at least in the top five picks, but I don't put much stock in rumors after the fact and all that," said Milner. Even with the Blue Jays offering almost as much as the No. 1 pick, three times what they offered their own first-rounder Lloyd Moseby, and five times the amount to sign Dave Stieb, who became a pitcher worthy of the Hall of Fame and the Blue Jay's first pitching Ace, Milner still wanted one more thing before he would agree to sign.

"I told them I would agree to the contract, but I wanted to do one last thing before I would sign a professional contract. I wanted to play in the Texas High School Baseball Coaches Association All-Star Game at the Astrodome," said Milner.

For part of his childhood, Brian Milner lived in the shadow of the Houston Astrodome. He wanted to fulfill his dream playing in the historic stadium. "I could almost see the dome being built from my home. I didn't want to miss the opportunity to play there, I didn't know if I would ever have a chance again," explained Milner on why he wouldn't sign until after the game. (Milner never did play in the Astrodome again, but many years later [in 1999], he was there as a baseball scout during the second to last Astros game ever played there.)

"That night after the Texas High School All-Star Game, I signed my major league contract and reported the next day to the Blue Jays as they played the Texas Rangers in Arlington. It was only twenty miles from our house. Looking back, baseball has been the good, the bad, the ugly, all of it, but it was just wonderful," reflected Milner.

"I didn't know what was going to happen, it was left open-ended, they had a spot to fill, and they were putting me on the team for now," explained Milner. Although open-ended, and without fanfare, Milner set a franchise mark as the youngest Blue Jay player at eighteen years and 218 days. He also became the first high school catcher to go directly from high school to the major leagues. For Milner, it was just one day after his last appearance in a high school game. Both accomplishments still are the marks to beat for the Blue Jays and for Major League Baseball.

On June 23, 1978, the 6'2", 200-pound catcher became the 14,053rd player in major league history and collected his first base hit. Although Milner argues he really should have two knocks that night.

Brian Milner made his professional and MLB debut on the road playing the Cleveland Indians on June 23, 1978. Milner batted ninth, behind Louis Gomez, a light-hitting shortstop barely batting above the Mendoza line with a .210 batting average over his eight years with the Minnesota Twins, Toronto Blue Jays, and Atlanta Braves. The Blue Jays were true to their word and placed Milner in a batting spot with the least pressure attached. The opponent was a hulking 6'3" pitcher and hard thrower, Rick Waits, who was enjoying what would probably be the strongest of his twelve-year career. Waits put up a low 3.24 ERA and thirteen wins. Waits was coming in hot off a complete game shutout his last game pitched, bringing a paltry 2.53 ERA into the Blue Jays and the young Milner. Waits dominated the month of June in 1978, opponents batted .208 against him and were only able to put up a 1.28 ERA against Waits.

The result of the game for the Blue Jays was a loss of 8-3, with Waits throwing another complete game. Milner was the battery mate for a solid righty pitcher, the 6'3" Jesse Jefferson. The pitcher proved to be what the Blue Jays needed as they were finding their legs as a baseball team. He started thirty or more games and tossed two hundred plus innings in 1977 and 1978. Jefferson played for five teams over his nine-year MLB career, and by 1978, he started eighty games from the mound. A veteran pitcher can often be disastrous for a young rookie catcher.

The velocity Milner was seeing in high school was about to be put on hyperdrive—the ball movement from straight with maybe just a little movement, to a baseball that could dart in, slide away, or just fall off the table. As a hitter, it would be formidable, and as a catcher trying to receive the ball cleanly and call the pitches, it was a heroic task. But for Milner it was another fairy-tale step in his baseball journey.

"Jesse was a sinker and a slider pitcher as his two primary pitches. We worked well together. I can't remember him shaking me off any; he went with went I put down," said Brian Milner, on calling the pitches during his first major league game, just days after playing his last high school game. "I always took pride as a catcher and calling the game. My job was to make the pitcher comfortable and confident to throw whatever pitch he had to when we needed it," said Milner.

The Blue Jays trusted Milner to start as the catcher to a pitcher with two primary pitches of sinker and slider. Those two pitches are up there—right with the dreaded knuckleball—for causing the catcher to have to block and cover the ball up as it could bite hard into the dirt.

Milner knew this was a way to set his tone quickly as a catcher, and to make an impression on his teammates, coaches, and the team brass. "A catcher is part psychologist. You're the one calling pitches and moving your shortstop and other fielders over due to approaches to the batter and game situation. A catcher needs to be in total control; they lead, take charge, and use their personality for the right results," said Milner. "All the fielders are looking in at the plate and the catcher. There are sixteen eyes looking at the catcher and he has nowhere to hide. You can't fake it, make it up, everybody sees through that. It's going at the batter and holding your team together," explained Milner.

How would a young Brian Milner come to handle older pitchers not willing to trust the young catcher to call certain pitches for the game? The image of the crusty old catcher going to chew out a young pitcher can be one of the hidden joys of baseball for teammates and fans alike. The catcher, uniform dirty, soaked with sweat from the "tools of ignorance" they wear for safety, is also their badge of honor. The catcher goes out there and usually in a few words, with demonstrative body language, conveys the message to clear up the disconnect.

Johnny Bench was perhaps the best catcher the game ever saw. As a young catcher he was tested by veteran pitchers. "Johnny Bench would take his glove off if the pitcher would shake off to pitch a fastball. He would just catch the fastball with his bare hands; now that is intimidating. I'm a nice guy. I'm nonconfrontational, but I'm competitive. I will run through you to get the run, but don't try to run through me to get to the home plate, it wouldn't end well," explained the 6'2", 210-pound Milner, who would look even bigger with the catcher's gear on.

Milner dug in for his MLB at-bat. He went down quickly 0-2, before grounding out to the shortstop side. Third baseman Buddy Bell took a better angle to the ball, cut in, and came up throwing to nail the speedy Milner in time to rob him of an infield base hit. "I don't care, I count it as a base hit. I beat his throw by at least the whole length of my foot," said Milner. "If that were today it would be overturned to a base hit for sure."

To further illustrate that Milner once possessed the speed to beat the throw of Bell, regarded as one of the best defensive third baseman of the 1970s, to first base, Milner explained just how fast he was back then. "I used to make it a game between the batter and me. On ground balls needing me backing up a throw to first base, I would race the runner down the line attempting to beat them at first base. I beat quite a few runners for sure," explained Milner.

Officially 0-1, he grounded out to the pitcher in the fifth, and was anxious to rip a base hit as Rick Waits held a commanding 6-1 lead. "I already had 2 strikes on me, Waits threw me a changeup, it came out looking like a balloon, I swung and missed badly, I was so early with my swing I could have swung twice. Oh geez, that was ugly," laughed Milner.

In what probably felt like forever to him to achieve his first official MLB base hit, Milner stepped onto the plate with one out, down 8-3 in the ninth. Milner attempted to ignite a rally against Waits with his first MLB base hit. The next batter hit into the pitcher's best friend, and the double play ended the game with a loss to Milner and the Blue Jays.

Every player remembers their first hit. Milner was lucky to secure it in his first game, and his teammates shared his joy. "They congratulated me after I came in the dugout. Later that night I had my big-league initiation. Somebody got a baby bottle and put a full beer in it. I had to chug it," explained Milner. He was not a beer drinker and not even sure what kind of beer was chuggable through a baby nipple, but he enjoyed it. "I do know beer in Canada is so much better than beer down here in the states," clarified Milner.

Milner finished his first game as a starter in the big leagues. He was one of four catchers to start for the 1978 Blue Jays. Alan Ashby and Rick Cerone basically split the year behind the dish with, respectively, eighty and seventy-eight games started. Milner started two games, on June 23 and June 27, and Ernie Whitt squeezed in a start on September 16 for the 148th game. The Blue Jays had two catchers establishing themselves, playing semiregularly for long major league tenures, and Whitt, who would eventually become the best of the catchers for the Blue Jays, was still in the wings lurking as the hot-shot young catcher was given the chance none of them thought could happen to an eighteen-year-old. As Milner explains, "I am sure there was some animosity toward me, especially the catchers already at the big-league level, like Rick Cerone, Alan Ashby, and Ernie Whitt. They were the mainstays, grinded it out in the minors, and I just show up in the majors."

Milner is a gentleman, maybe his memory gets fuzzy from time-to-time, or maybe he does not want to single out a player years after the fact, but he remembers what one of the catchers said to him. "I don't remember who said it, but they said, 'You know your days are coming, enjoy it now, while you can, but your day's coming,' and then likewise to Medicine Hat I went the next day," recalls Milner. "I am sure there was some animosity, resentment there," he explained. "I haven't met a stranger and I'm a Texan, so it is all good," laughed Milner at the comment caught from his catching brethren.

Milner made it straight from high school to the big leagues and then the minor leagues, all the way down to rookie ball, over the span of about two weeks. It would all work out for the "catching firm" of Cerone, Ashby, and Whitt, as each went on to successful long MLB careers.

Rick Cerone was drafted in the first round with the seventh pick of the 1975 MLB draft by the Cleveland Indians. He quickly made the Indians for the first time less than two months later. He appeared in seven games and had 12 at-bats that first year, and he shuttled between the minor leagues and Indians for two years with only 28 at-bats at the major league level before a trade to the Blue Jays in 1977 allowed him to get 100 at-bats in a major league season for the first time. Cerone had played college baseball for Seton Hall University and served minor league time to get his chance. It worked out well for Cerone as he played for eighteen years for eight different teams. After the tragic loss of Thurman Munson during the 1979 season, the Yankees traded for Cerone hoping to stabilize the hole left by the captain. Cerone did an admirable Munson impression hitting career highs in home runs, RBI, and batting average, and he led the league in percentage of base runners caught stealing and finishing seventh in the 1980 AL MVP voting.

At just seventeen years old, Alan Ashby was drafted in the third round of the 1969 June draft. Ashby took 330 games before being called up to the majors in 1973, receiving 29 at-bats. He spent most of his playing time of 1974 in AAA receiving just 7 at-bats. Ashby established himself in 1975 as a major league catcher, and eventually would play 17 seasons, 1,370 games, and ranks 57th on the all-time list with 7,086 putouts as a catcher.

Ernie Whitt was a model of perseverance waiting for his time as a major league catcher, and he was the only catcher to start a game on the 1978 Blue Jays to eventually become an All-Star catcher. Whitt was drafted in the fifteenth round of the 1972 June amateur draft by the Boston Red Sox, from a tiny school in Michigan, Macomb Community College (MCC). The baseball team at the school must have been pretty good at that time because three players made the major leagues from their 1972 team: Art James, Whitt, and the 1981 AL ERA leader, Steve McCatty. The three of them are the only players from MCC to appear in the major leagues as of 2023.

Whitt played each step from A-ball before he received 18 MLB at-bats during his fifth professional season in1976. Whitt came to the Blue Jays in the 1976 expansion draft, and split 1977, 1978, and 1979 between the minor leagues and the Blue Jays, only appearing in twenty-five games at the big-league level. In 1980, at the age of twenty-eight (near the age catchers begin to decline), Whitt received his first regular time with the departure of Rick Cerone. Whitt is sixth on the Blue Jays all-time leaders for games played, tenth for home runs, and he caught the most games in Blue Jays franchise history.

Even as Milner heard the whisper of rookie ball waiting at Medicine Hat, in Alberta, Canada, he was about to endear himself in Toronto to Blue Jay fans of 1978 and beyond. Brian created a magical moment in his last major league game, special enough to last a lifetime.

June 26, 1978 turned out to be the day on which Milner could hang his big-league catching helmet and be proud. On paper, the 1978 Baltimore Orioles with their ninety-plus win team playing against the one-hundred-plus loss 1978 Blue Jays would be an easy victory. The chances of an Orioles victory were additionally inflated with 1978 All-Star pitcher Mike Flanagan on the hill. But as they say in football, "Any given Sunday" happened as the Blue Jays put up a score more traditionally seen in football. The Blue Jays clobbered the Orioles 24-10 and knocked out the future 1979 Cy Young Award Winner, Flanagan, after one inning pitched.

Milner easily could have lost himself in the moment looking out and seeing baseball stars like Mike Flanagan, Eddie Murray, Rick Dempsey, and Ken Singleton as his opponents. "I went from watching these guys on TV and now you find yourself facing them. . . . I look back on it and just say wow. But at that moment I had to focus and do what I had to do," said Milner.

Brian Milner went from watching Flanagan while sitting comfortably in his living room chair to facing Flanagan eye-to-eye in the inhospitable batting box. Milner responded with a single to right field driving in a run for his first MLB RBI giving the Blue Jays a 3-1 lead in the second inning.

Flanagan couldn't get an out in the second inning, forcing a call to the bullpen for Joe Kerrigan. The Blue Jays hit Kerrigan hard to take a

9-1 lead at the end of the second inning. By the third inning Milner had his second hit of the game when he singled to right field off Kerrigan and later scored. The bottom of fourth had Milner facing left-handed reliever, 1983 All-Star Tippy Martinez. Milner drove the pitch to the centerfield wall. "They had me shifted a little bit to the right side and the ball bounced at the centerfield warning track, came up and bounced off the wall. I could run fast, and it turned into a chance for a triple. The ball was all ahead of me, still in the outfield, as I was approaching second base. I knew I could make it. I slid into third base and was safe," explained Milner on his triple against Martinez.

Then what happened next was like a dream to Milner—unfolding all around him with an audible, slow, and steady rise finishing with the tip of a cap. "The next thing you know, I'm standing there dusting off my pants, the third-base coach telling me to tip my hat. I had no idea why, but as I looked up, lo and behold, maybe there's twenty-three thousand people there looking back at me, and they are giving me a standing ovation," explained Milner. "It was an unreal moment of just being in the big leagues, having fun. I was just playing ball and suddenly I am standing on top of third base tipping my hat to the crowd in the middle of a standing ovation. I never thought it could ever happen to me," Milner marveled.

Never had a catcher been drafted and sent right to the big leagues. Here he was, just a kid on third base, but really on top of the world, feeling the adulation of the Major League Baseball crowd. It would never be better for Milner on the field as a player.

During the fifth inning, Milner had the chance to bat twice more as the lineup batted around. He started the inning with a ground out and ended the inning with a fly ball. Then in the seventh inning, Alan Ashby came in the game to replace Milner. It would be the last game for Milner in the major leagues.

The Hall of Fame manager of the Baltimore Orioles, Earl Weaver, noticed the effort of Milner during the 24-10 loss. "I remember Earl Weaver made a comment about me in the paper. I went three for five, and it was the kind of game you wish for as a kid, except for the seventh game of the World Series. Earl Weaver said that they stayed away from me in the draft because I am a type 1 diabetic. The Orioles felt it would be an issue for me down the line," said Milner.

Yes, Brian Milner has type 1 diabetes and was first diagnosed at age thirteen. Under most discrimination laws, including the Americans with Disabilities Act, type 1 diabetes is considered a disability. But

Milner never felt like this illness diminished his skill as a player. Type 1 and diabetes in general are not well understood in relation to sports today, even less so in the 1970s.

Skepticism and questions abound on the risk of signing a player with the genetic disease causing the pancreas to produce little or no insulin. A person with type 1 diabetes can experience symptoms like low blood sugar, fatigue, and blurred vision. When a baseball team must put the future of a franchise on a player with a complicating factor like type 1 diabetes, it is certainly understandable to consider the risk versus gain scenario.

Ron Santo was a Hall of Fame third baseman with the Chicago Cubs and White Sox playing from 1960 to 1974. Santo is not just remembered as the first player to wear an ear-flap batting helmet, but as a gritty player with type 1 diabetes. He kept his fight with diabetes secret until just a few years before he retired. Santos was first diagnosed at eighteen and concealed it for so long because he was afraid of not being given the chance to play baseball, or later being forced into retirement. His fears were valid, but his nine All-Star Game selections proved a player can perform at the highest levels if the illness is managed properly.

Discussing his own experience with diabetes, Milner says, "It didn't cause me an issue on the field, that was just my personal case though. You can ask ten different doctors about it, and probably receive ten different answers about diabetes in athletes." The Blue Jays just accepted Milner the player and were excited to see him develop his game.

Major League Baseball is a fast game that needs to be played slow. Milner was just out of high school and still used to the throws of high school pitchers. The bat was looking good for Milner, but the bat is just a bonus for a catcher. The glove matters too. "I was just back there trying to stop the ball, not really catching as a major league catcher would. I was just hoping to not look like a mess," explained Milner. "I was a freak show," he concluded.

"I was always inching close to the batters when I was catching. I had a catcher's interference call on me, somebody stole a base off me in Cleveland. There was a passed ball for an error at home," revealed Milner on defensive mistakes during his two starts for the Blue Jays. "Things glared out when it came to the finer points of catching, those mistakes shouldn't happen. Looking back, it was probably why I was sent down quickly. I needed to be sent down for more defense. I was just not ready as an overall package for the big leagues," explained Milner.

Similar to the way the Blue Jays convinced Milner to bypass Arizona State and gave him an open-ended first chance in the major leagues and a guaranteed four-year MLB contract with a spot on the 40-man roster, the Blue Jays approached Milner with respect as they were about to demote him to Alberta, Canada, for the rookie league. "They demoted me in a classy way. Peter Bavasi, Gillick, Hartsfield, and Bobby Doerr, the hitting coach, called me in for a meeting. They decided to send me down to Medicine Hat. To an environment, receiving playing time and competing to get better and pay my dues," explained Milner.

"I knew I had to get better defensively. From high school and catching pitches that were slower, and basically straight to the filthy movement and speed in the major leagues was too big of a jump," explained Milner. "It is a whole different level of reaction and instincts that I could not just pick up in the major leagues. It was absolutely the right call for me and the Blue Jays to have me go down," concluded Milner.

So Brian Milner landed in Medicine Hat as a major leaguer sent all the way back to the rookie league with something to prove to himself and to his new teammates. The good bat flashed in the big leagues for a couple of games but deserted him as he began to play in Medicine Hat. "I couldn't buy a base hit in the beginning. I was hitless for my first 25 to 30 at-bats. The guys gave me a pretty hard time about it. I was a guy coming down from the big leagues and couldn't buy a base hit. I am sure there was some jealousy at me, but that is the nature of the beast. They had to scratch and claw for it, and I just started at the top. But generally, everyone was decent about it though. I pretty much felt that pressure at the top and the bottom, and throughout my career," explained Milner.

At Medicine Hat, Milner took the bull by the horns and showed that he was a player to be reckoned with, a gamer, and a genuine young player for the Blue Jays future. "I was basically thrown into the cattle pen, and I was going to have to fight to make it through. Keep working hard to get bigger and better. That is just the way baseball is, you can't just talk a good game, or just look good in baseball pants. There is no politicking, you must go out and keep producing numbers to earn your way to the top and to stay there," explained Milner.

Milner had missed approximately two weeks of the season with his new team and teammates. Including Brian, Medicine Hat had four players who later would play in at least one major league game. Milner and outfielder-first baseman, Paul Hodgson, played a combined twenty-two games at the major league level. Lloyd Moseby, the 1978 Blue Jay first pick, and the catcher sharing time with Milner, Geno Petralli, the 1978 Blue Jay third pick, combined for twenty-four MLB seasons and 2,397 games.

Milner came right in, and even with an atrocious batting slump to begin his year, he still managed to finish third on the team with 4 home runs, 36 RBI, and a .307 batting average, compared to Moseby's 10 home runs, 38 RBI, and a .304 batting average.

Even more importantly, Milner found a mentor to help him become a better catcher ready for the majors. "Johnny McLaren was my manager, and he's an ex-catcher and he was the right guy for me. He walked me through a lot of ways to be a better catcher. I learned a tremendous amount on catching, handling a pitching staff, calling a game, and other finer points of the game," said Milner on his 1978 Medicine Hat catching internship.

Milner did all of this with two significant injuries at the most physically demanding position of catcher on the diamond. "During one of my first games for Medicine Hat, I dove for a baseball, laying out for it like I was laying out for a football and tore my stomach lining straight up to my belly button," said Milner. And even as he was playing through that injury, which would place most players on an injured list, another injury developed that is kryptonite for a catcher. "Each time I threw the ball I experienced pain and numbness from my neck down through my right arm," said Milner.

After gutting through the season and being selected as a Pioneer League All-Star, Milner had hernia surgery in November and another surgery in February to remove bone chips from his right elbow. "Injuries for me started coming pretty quick," explained Brian of what would become a shortened career partially defined by injuries. "I don't think I had more injuries than other players could have had, they were just injuries," he clarified.

"I went down thinking I would possibly be back in September," said Milner. With the injuries and upcoming surgeries—and not knowing for sure if he would receive a call-up for September—Brian decided to get a jump on college and prepare to earn his way back to the Blue Jays. "Not being able to count on a call-up, I chose to go back to school when the minor league season ended in August, and to work hard to build my hitting and catching to make the club out of spring training.

I thought I would make it back to the big leagues, but I never did," Milner said.

After the two surgeries, Milner was not able to make the Blue Jays out of 1979 spring training. He did receive a bump up to Low A-Ball, the Dunedin Blue Jays, in the Florida League, but his season was only thirty-eight games and a low .188 batting average.

The 1980 season improved for Milner. After major league spring training with the Blue Jays, he was assigned to High-A with the Kinston Eagles of the Carolina League. Milner was healthy enough to play in a team-high 124 games of the 135-game season.

The 1981 season started with another major league spring training and not making the team. Milner began the season with a promotion to the AA Knoxville Blue Jays of the Southern League. Brian battled through the season to play 112 games and batted .231. But the two injuries in rookie ball plus another surgery for carpal tunnel syndrome and a knee injury sliding into a base—coupled with the extraordinary wear and tear of being a catcher—were making Milner appear to be shifting from prospect to nonprospect. (Milner will not mention his diabetes as part of his declining game.)

What if there was a way to transform from being a catcher to something different for Brian Milner? Hang with me here. There was once another mega-prospect at catcher, struggling to maintain behind the dish and pull through the nosedive to become a star. I am referring to two-time NL MVP Dale Murphy, who looks like he could be Brian Milner's older brother. They are the same age gap as a senior Murphy to a freshman Milner roaming the halls of the same pretend high school. Put them on a baseball field together, and it would be difficult to see the difference. Murphy at 6'4" and 210 pounds and Brian Milner pushing 6'3" and 205. They possessed the same player tools of young catchers, both great athletes with fast speed—not just for a catcher, but as a baseball player. Comparing the Murphy and Milner rookie baseball cards shows an uncanny resemblance.

Murphy, a two-time MVP, seven-time All-Star, and five-time Gold Glove winner was one of the best hitters and outfielders of the 1980s for the Atlanta Braves, and each year creates a stronger push for Hall of Fame induction. Like Milner, Murphy was supposed to go to Arizona State before being drafted as a catcher. Murphy played his first two seasons in rookie and Low-A, always hitting more than 5 home runs a season or batting higher than .254. Murphy remained healthy his first two years and made his Braves debut in 1976, his third season as a catcher. For 1976 and 1977, he played thirty-seven games for the Braves and hit a combined 2 home runs in 141 at-bats.

In 1978, Murphy started 16 games as a catcher, but then shifted to first base starting 125 games. The difference in production jumped to 23 home runs for the twenty-two-year-old Murphy. In 1979, he started just twenty-seven more games behind the dish, never again playing catcher for the remainder of his fifteen-year career. Murphy averaged 30 home runs and 94 RBI. Not too bad for an athletic catcher released into another position.

Milner, when faced with this question of "What if?," thinks the Murphy template is worth pondering, but he is not ready to put a "could 'a been" MVP on his own mantle. "I remember watching [Murphy's] career. It might have made a difference," admitted Milner. "I have taken notice of changes from a prominent position like catcher or shortstop and have seen a hitting improvement. The intense emphasis on the defensive position may weigh down their hitting."

Milner goes on to explain the rigors of catching that could take away from batting. "Catching is physically and mentally taxing." Those are two of the most talked about factors for catchers, but Milner goes on to explain this from his opinion based on his experience. Look at this from the perspective of a catcher in a crouch 95 percent of his time on the field versus a batting stance for 4 or maybe 5 at-bats per game. "As a catcher, think about how many pitches are coming straight at you. Now stand in as a batter in the box and the pitches come in differently, across your field of vision," reasoned Milner. "Is that detrimental to your offensive success?" asked Milner.

Some great Hall of Fame catchers may answer no, but how many of them also saw their offensive numbers crumble as father time took away their offensive production prematurely, as compared to other positions. Johnny Bench, perhaps the greatest catcher in baseball history, retired at only thirty-five, only starting thirteen games as a catcher during his last three seasons while splitting his games on the infield corners of first and third base. "I know Johnny Bench, Ivan Rodriguez, Jorge Posada, Thurman Munson may debunk the train of thought, but the 'Baseball Gods' love making unique oddities that can be buried in this wonderful game," explained Milner.

Once you compare Murphy and Milner, however, both catchers in the minors for their first four years, it does make us wonder if Milner was stalled by catching and not transitioning like Murphy to a different position. Dale Murphy 48 home runs, Brian Milner 12. Dale

Murphy 232 RBI, Brian Milner 164. Dale Murphy 396 hits, Brian Milner 305. Dale Murphy 74 doubles, Brian Milner 48. Dale Murphy 111 walks, Brian Milner 100. Dale Murphy 434 games, Brian Milner 362. Dale Murphy batted .264, Brian Milner .260.

Murphy in seventy-two more games had slightly better power numbers than Milner, but keep in mind that Murphy hit another gear as a batter while at AAA in 1977 with 22 home runs, 90 RBI, and a .305 batting average as he began to transition to first base. Murphy and his march to stardom launched the next year as he belted 23 home runs for the 1978 Atlanta Braves as their starting first baseman.

By 1982, Milner repeated time at AA as a catcher. He was removed from the 40-man roster for the first time in his career, cleared waivers, and agreed to a minor league contract with the Blue Jays to remain in their organization. Milner appeared in only thirty-seven games, hitting 0 home runs and batting just .148, with a second knee surgery and second carpal tunnel surgery.

Injuries, four surgeries, and stunted growth as a batter reduced the wonderkid to an afterthought as 1983 major league spring training came around. "Each time I went to major league spring training it hurt a little more to not make the major league team. I still had hope and worked hard all off season, and I wanted it to happen, but each spring it wouldn't pan out. Each time, I was thinking I must get back. I want it back. It became more difficult to be sent down each year," said Milner.

In the Spring of 1983, the train was coming down the tracks toward Milner. Even with the warning lights flashing and horn blaring, he was still surprised. "I was out there working, trying to make the team. Larry Hardy was my manager, he turned to me and said, 'You really ought to consider going into coaching. Sometimes your name is on the wall and sometimes it might not be on that wall the next day.'"

Baseball is a game of results and how a player can help the team. It was now apparent that the twenty-three-year-old Milner was out of time. "[Larry Hardy] was hinting in his own way that if I wanted to stick around baseball, it would have to be as a coach and not a player," said Milner. "My pride was not ready to do that."

Hardy was right. Milner soon looked up and his name was no longer on the wall. He was released at the end of 1983 spring training and went home to Texas, spending the next seven years switching between college classes, landscaping, plumbing, carpentry, and working at a grocery store. But Milner's baseball story, legacy, and impact would continue to unfold, almost by chance as he became friendly with a customer who knew exactly who he was.

The customer was Trey Hillman, a former professional baseball player reaching as high as AA before retiring in 1987. Hillman quickly made the transition from a player to becoming a baseball scout for the Cleveland Indians, before starting a thirteen-year career with the New York Yankees as a manager in their minor league system. Hillman eventually became a major league manager with the Kansas City Royals from 2008 to 2010. Hillman goes wherever he can for the best baseball experience. Hillman is the only manager to win the Korean Series and the Japanese Series, equivalent to the MLB World Series in Korea and Japan.

"I was working my tail off and then I met Trey Hillman," said Milner. "We got to knowing each other because he and his father used to watch me play games in high school," explained Milner. According to Milner, the two struck up a friendship, and Hillman offered to set up a meeting for Milner with the New York Yankees, and the meeting went well. Milner explains, "I was soon hired as a minor league catching and hitting coach. It was a great six years. I was able to work with guys like Andy Pettitte, Derek Jeter, Jorge Posada, Mariano Rivera."

Milner worked for the Yankees from 1990 through 1995, with stops at extended spring training in Oneonta, New York, and multiple tours in Greensboro, North Carolina, and Prince William, Virginia. "The players at that level are hungry, energetic, and rambunctious," said Milner. "It was a lot of fun."

Seeing Andy Pettitte and Jorge Posada up close and coaching them gives Milner a clear opinion on Pettitte and Posada's Hall of Fame consideration. "I hope they get in one day. I love Jorge like a son," explained Milner.

Milner readily admits he is not good at keeping in touch with former teammates or players he coached or scouted. "I do not have any social media stuff, but I would love to run into Jorge and catch up with him one day," said Milner. "Look at all the Championships those guys had, it was a special crew, Mariano Rivera is one of the classiest and best individuals I've ever met. I was part of their development and helped them along the way," said Milner.

The not-so-old ex-catcher, Brian Milner, helped Posada develop into a catcher after playing exclusively as an infielder through his college and early days in the minor leagues. The Yankees liked the idea of the switch-hitting Posada as a valuable weapon if he could learn how to become a catcher. Milner was one of the coaches to help turn Posada into an All-Star catcher and key leader on the Yankee champion teams of the 1990s and 2000s. "I was Jorge's catching coach for the two years when he was in Greensboro and Prince William. We let him play, allowed him to make mistakes, and guided him along the way," explained Milner. "I cannot take any credit for those guys, we had so many great coaches, instructors, and those players worked so hard to become what they were, it was extraordinary to be even a small part of their journey," explained Milner.

Baseball is not just about how hard you can throw or how hard you can hit. The ability to pull back and know when to keep something in reserve is a large part of the game, and for Andy Pettitte, the former catcher was there to offer the advice that young flamethrowers sometimes need to hear. "[Pettitte] was struggling throwing the ball at 95 or 96 and regularly falling behind in the count," said Milner. Knowing the game is about changing speeds and disrupting the batter, Milner offered simple advice that is hard to follow for a young pitcher. "Pettitte said, 'Millsy, what am I supposed to do?'" Milner was able to explain how to hit a sweet spot, almost like how a NASCAR driver can race to the absolute edge of disaster but hold back just enough to not crash into the wall.

"You got to find that point between the two where it is your speed and movement combined with the ability to harness the pitch putting the ball where it is needed. If that is 92, 93 miles per hour, keep repeating it, soon it will be up to 94 or 95 as your body learns that pitch," said Milner to Pettitte. "Suddenly when you need to reach back and dial it in for a pitch or two at 97 or 98, whatever it may be, you will have it," explained Milner to the future All-Star pitcher. "It is one of the haunting mindsets of the minor leagues, do I go all out, or pull back? It is about finding just the right balance of the two," explained Milner.

As Milner was teaching Jorge Posada the advanced tools of receiving the ball, it would often require physically demonstrating what to do. A catcher needs to be able to catch the pitch and throw pop-ups as a base runner is attempting to steal a base. The technique is called "pop time." Simply defined, this is the time it takes for the ball to hit the catcher's glove and arrive in the second base glove. A catcher needs to (1) combine footwork to be able to get into a throwing position after catching the ball, (2) transfer the ball from glove to throwing hand, and (3) have the strength and accuracy to throw the runner out. An average MLB pop time is 2.01 seconds. The importance of this time is it affords the pitcher 1.3 seconds to deliver the ball to the catcher. The way to understand this timing is the sound of the "pop" of the catcher's glove as the ball strikes to the "pop" of the glove at second base.

In 1992, Milner was still a relatively young man at thirty-two wearing the catcher's gear alongside the twenty-one-year-old Posada. Milner recalls, "Posada was so athletic, and good on his feet, at Greensboro we would challenge each other for throwing times to second base. I could still throw then. We were often deadlocked, days I would beat him and days he would beat me. He was learning the craft, in the end, he got it down and it became off the charts."

The catching coach still looked young and athletic, matching the young prospect who became part of the core of Yankee Championship teams as the catcher. People started to notice Milner, and as the 1994–1995 Major League Baseball strike dragged on with an approaching spring training and 1995 season, the MLB owners did not want to have games cancelled again, like the end of the previous season, which tragically wiped out the 1994 World Series.

Approximately 950 games were cancelled in 1994. By January 1995, the owners agreed to open major league spring training with replacement players, and even play the season with those players if the Major League Players Association and the MLB owners could not strike a deal for the 1995 season.

Active, former, or minor league players were being looked at by the owners to fill spring training camps. Milner felt as if he were about to be put in an awkward position with the New York Yankees and the players he coached. "I guess some people felt I could still play a little bit," said Milner. "It got to me several ways that if the Yankees needed catching help in spring training or the season, that they were going ask me to be one of the replacement players," said Milner. Thankfully it never got to that point for Brian, who shared, "I wouldn't have done it. It is not the right thing to do as a former MLB player to crossover like that."

In fact, Milner never considered making a comeback as time moved forward after the baseball strike. He loved coaching and being able to be home more. "I never really considered playing again once I retired," said Milner. You really need that eye of the tiger to be a player, and by 1991, my son Hoby was born. Being a baseball player is brutal on families," said Milner.

The 1995 season ended for the New York Yankees by losing in an epic American League Divisional Series to the Seattle Mariners. After the season, the Yankees made big changes starting at the top by replacing Manager Buck Showalter with Joe Torre. Former AL MVP and fan favorite Don Mattingly chose to retire. Changes often roll downhill as well. "The Yankees cleaned house after the 1995 season, top to bottom, going different directions, [and] I was one of many not making it back for 1996," said Milner. "I went to the Chicago Cubs as an area amateur baseball scout and later did advance scouting."

Even though he missed out on being part of the Yankees organization as they dominated baseball by winning four World Series in five years and appearing in six World Series from 1996 to 2003, Milner is happy with how things worked out for the Yankees, his former players, and himself. "When I look back at baseball, the first thing I think about is time away from my family. As a scout I was able to be home more and make it back when I needed to be there. It was a lot of fun doing different things for the Cubs. As a coach I was putting everything I had to place the players I worked with to be a major league player," said Milner.

Being a scout is skill. It can also come down to being the first to spot a player, or just trusting what you see and being an advocate for the right player. Eric Hinske, the 1992 AL Rookie of the Year, was a player like that for Milner. "I had some pretty good luck as a scout. Spotting a player with baseball skill is easy, Grandma can see the tools, but for me it was about the whole player makeup, proper frame of mind, off the field stuff, work ethic, everything that brings the tools together," said Brian.

"I signed Eric Hinske to the Cubs. I loved him, thought he could be a fourth-round pick in the 1998 draft. I told Jim Henry, the scouting director, don't let him slip past the eighth round. We ended up taking him in the seventeenth round. I was just appalled he lasted that long, but you know, that's the game and it is the business," explained Milner. "He had the right player make-up, he played in the World Series three times," concluded Milner.

Milner attained a lifelong goal he had once placed on hold to play professional baseball for the Toronto Blue Jays. When he informed Arizona State in 1978 that he would not be attending, he never imagined it would take just over thirty years to finally get his degree. "It only took to age forty-nine, but I did it," explained Milner.

As a Yankees coach, Milner blended coaching, mentoring, and teaching, and starting in 2008, he did the same back home in Texas. "I taught eight years at Poly High School in Fort Worth, which is inner city, coached baseball, taught World Geography, and I was a Special Education teacher. I then taught Special Ed at an inner-city elementary school. I couldn't wait to get to school each morning, I loved it," said Brian.

Professional baseball seems to follow Milner, as two of his boys play professional baseball. His son Hoby Milner is a major league player, whose MLB debut was in 2017, and his stepson Collin Hetzler is the hitting coach for the AAA Syracuse Mets. "I am proud of both the kids. They're good kids and focused on what they need to do to get where they want to be," explained Milner. He has been able to see Hoby in-person pitch in the major leagues. He is witnessing Collin climb each step of professional baseball and now knock on the major league door as a hitting instructor. The only thing missing may be that Milner's parents were not able to be there to see him play for the Blue Jays at the major league level.

As Brian Milner looks back across his fairy-tale baseball career, he knows he is the answer to a few great trivia questions:

1. Who is the only catcher to be drafted and go straight to the major leagues?
2. Who is the only position player to be drafted from high school and go directly to the major leagues?
3. Who is the youngest Blue Jay player of all time?

Yes, all Brian Milner.

"It has been a good life. I wouldn't change it; I made the right decision all those years ago signing with the Blue Jays," said Brian. "The game of baseball has been wonderful for me and family."

The joy of baseball all these years later for Milner is not just memories of the big time like receiving an unexpected standing ovation in his second and last major league game; or getting a hit off the next year's AL Cy Young Award winner, Mike Flanagan. It is also more the romance of baseball, reminiscent of a bygone era resembling a Norman Rockwell illustration, images no longer part of professional baseball. "It was a joy to play in some of those old minor league stadiums, sometimes they had candles and coffee cans for lights; it was atrocious, but that was the life," ended Milner.

 RON NECCIAI, PITTSBURGH PIRATES, 1950–1955

Position: pitcher

Bats right, throws right

High School: Monongahela High School, Monongahela, Pennsylvania

Major League Career Totals

W	L	IP	SO	WHIP	ERA
1	6	54.2	31	1.738	7.08

Minor League Totals (incomplete)

W	L	IP	SO	WHIP	ERA
17	19	220	UNK	UNK	UNK

Highlights

- Ron Necciai's professional baseball career was put on hold to serve in the US Army.
- Necciai set the unbreakable professional baseball record of 27 strikeouts in a game.
- He served as the team bus driver and team pitcher for parts of his MiLB career.
- Necciai is considered to have one of the top-ten curveballs of all time.
- Hall of Fame General Manager Branch Rickey considered Ron Necciai as a generational pitching talent.

CHAPTER 7

Ron Necciai

Pure Gas and Class

Every now and then we read or hear something that seems impossible to believe. One such case involves the unlikeliest of pitchers, Ronald Necciai, who set the 1952 baseball world upside down with his nasty curveballs and overpowering fastball. Then it disappeared. He was the man who did something nobody had done before, and it is nearly impossible to believe it could ever happen again.

On May 13, 1952, Necciai struck out twenty-seven batters against the Welch Miners. The game pitched was a no-hitter, with Necciai recording every out of the nine-inning game by strikeout. Four Miners batters did reach base in the 7-0 Bristol Twins victory as a walk, an error, a hit batsman, and a dropped third strike to spoil the perfect game bid.

This game was far from perfect, but never in the history of professional baseball had a player dominated the competition with as many strikeouts in a nine-inning game. There have been thousands of no-hit games and dozens of perfect games, but only one time in professional baseball history and the hundreds of thousands of games played, has all 27 outs of a regulation nine-inning game occurred via strikeout.

Hard-throwing fastball pitchers, such as Nolan Ryan and Justin Verlander, often rise above the game and become household names. Home run hitters, like Barry Bonds and Mike Trout, can make headlines, but the sound of the shotgun blast of a fastball exploding into the catcher's mitt, doubled with the visual of a burly slugger going to his knees swinging in vain for a fastball already past him, is almost enough to overload the senses of a baseball fan.

The game of baseball in all its splendor comes down to a pitcher and a batter. Each has an opposite goal—the pitcher to send the batter back to the dugout swinging, the batter to hit the ball over the wall for a home run—both perfect but opposite and true outcomes, nothing but pure performance. Imagine the overpowering fastball and grit of Bob Gibson against the patience, strength, and stubbornness of Lou Gehrig for an at-bat. It never happened, but what if it had? Baseball is the sport where parallels and time boundaries blur and the imagination can soar.

Pitchers like Nolan Ryan, Roger Clemens, Tom Seaver, and Steve Carlton were strikeout assassins expected to be in that rarified elite for professional baseball, but not Ron Necciai. Who was Necciai?

Ron Necciai was born in Gallatin, Pennsylvania, in 1932. The area was thick with coal mines, factories, and steel mills. Necciai's father died at thirty-one from pneumonia, leaving four children behind. On top of playing baseball, football, basketball, and soccer while at Monongahela High School, Necciai held part-time jobs to help support his family. "The area was known for providing the steel for rebuilding the US Navy after Pearl Harbor, rebuilding the world after World War II, and kids, lots of kids. I was one of those kids running around playing sports there," proudly boasted Necciai of his hometown.

In 1951, Necciai (also known as Kid-K and Rocket Ron) was a skinny nineteen-year-old. An image of the fictional Ichabod Crane could be used to describe the young Necciai. Arms and elbows would stretch around his enormous Adam's apple as his baseball card height of 6'5" struck fear from the mound, and he would unleash a furious fastball at triple digits. The thing was, he was not always sure where the ball would go. Perhaps this variety helped Ron and caused the batter even more unease; they would have to think twice about digging in or crowding the plate.

Necciai, even after seventy-plus years since his 27 strikeout game, is a mixture of reluctance and pride about his magical night in Bristol. "I was not really a pitcher, I just threw the ball, I didn't think much. I threw so many pitches and worked deep into the count all-night. It felt like each at-bat went 3-2, or 2-2," recounts Necciai, almost apologetically.

His pitches were not just strikes. There were lots of balls and off-target pitches, but somehow each time the batter walked away in a strikeout for all the outs. The number of batters walking back into the dugout that night with a strikeout kept going up and up, but Necciai didn't notice or seem to care about the record he was setting. "Nobody was saying a word to me about it as the game was going on, and I didn't notice because I was just trying to pitch to each guy. It started as just another game, like everybody else I was just trying to make the big leagues," said Necciai. "I had to throw at least two hundred pitches that night, a lot of balls, there is no way they would ever leave in a young pitcher like that today," continued Ron. Most pitchers would have a dead arm the next start, but not Ron Necciai.

When did he realize there was something special going on as he pitched that night? "I didn't even realize what was happening after the game," said Necciai. His manager George Detore and catcher Harry Dunlop had to tell him that he had 27 strikeouts. Necciai's response could go down as one of the strangest in baseball history. "So what? What's the big deal? This game has been played for over a hundred years, it had to be done before," explained Necciai. He was wrong; it had never happened before. In fact, it had never happened before *or since,* in the hundreds of thousands of professional baseball games played from the dawn of professional baseball in the 1800s until today.

Along with Cy Young's record of 511 wins, the 27 strikeout in a regulation nine-inning baseball game is amongst the unbreakable records in baseball history. Modern pitchers do not go as deep into games as pitchers did one hundred years ago, nor do they pitch as often, making five hundred wins impossible, four hundred wins unlikely, and even the finish line of three hundred wins is not likely for a young pitcher making their debut in this baseball era. Necciai's record cannot be broken. It is a perfect 27 outs on strikeouts and can only be tied.

The funny thing is that Necciai didn't want to be a pitcher. He was initially signed as a first baseman with little power or bat control. His baseball road would have been much shorter, but the Pittsburgh Pirates saw something special. They recommended that he move to the pitcher's mound because he had a strong throwing arm. But he was hardly a refined or highly trained pitcher. Necciai did have some pitching experience, but he was uncomfortable pitching after his fastball broke the ribs of a player during high school. Now, however, it was about being a professional baseball player and not going back to his hometown to work in the steel mill or factory for the rest of his life.

As an eighteen-year-old pitcher, the tall but skinny 160-pound Necciai pitched in just four games in the first couple of weeks before growing frustrated and deciding to call it quits anyway to go back to Pennsylvania. "I went back. Worked in a factory and living back at home, but

I started to realize that playing baseball was a much better way to make a living," said Necciai. "Playing baseball was a lot better than the $25 dollars a week I was getting." And the Pirates must have seen something they liked during his rough first season because they took Necciai back and even took him to 1951 spring training. Fate and Branch Rickey intervened to put Necciai square on the path to the major leagues.

The Hall of Fame general manager of the Pittsburgh Pirates was Rickey, the same man who in 1945 had had the courage to sign several African American baseball players to ultimately bring African Americans back into Major League Baseball after an 1887 "Gentleman's Agreement" set the precedent to not issue contracts for Black players. This was a bold step by Rickey, and a courageous one for Rickey and the players to reestablish Black participation in Major League Baseball and their affiliated teams.

Bud Fowler is widely recognized as the first Black professional baseball player in 1878, and Moses Fleetwood Walker is recognized as the first African American major league player with his debut in 1884. Fowler was elected to the Baseball Hall of Fame in 2022. Jackie Robinson broke the MLB color barrier in 1947 to become the first Black ballplayer in over sixty years. Robinson was quickly followed by other great African American players to Major League Baseball, such as Roy Campanella, Don Newcombe, Larry Doby, Satchel Page, and many others. Branch Rickey was a lifelong baseball man who saw all the great players for the better part of the twentieth century.

In 1951, Necciai made an impression on Rickey during spring training. Rickey assigned George Detore to coach Necciai with the instructions to drop his arm-angle to a side-arm delivery and to further develop him. As the 1951 season went on and with more difficult results for Necciai, he wanted to go home again, but this time Necciai was convinced to stay by Detore, with the promise of an extra $90 dollars a month to double as the team's bus driver.

Detore and Necciai worked on velocity, encouraging Necciai to throw the ball harder, and refining a biting curveball. The results looked dismal with a 4-9 win-loss record and a 4.84 ERA for Necciai's 1951 minor league season. The ERA and win-loss record do not suggest a pitcher on the rise, or even being much of a prospect.

A deeper look into the numbers, however, shows a different story, with breathtaking velocity, and a swing-and-miss pitching arsenal that translated into 106 innings pitched, only allowing 91 hits, striking out 111 batters, and allowing 0 home runs. The Pirates saw the tantalizing potential again and invited Necciai to their 1952 spring training.

Rickey believed in the overpowering talent of his skinny beanpole of a pitcher. As recounted in Andrew O'Toole's *Branch Rickey in Pittsburgh*, Rickey once said, "I've seen a lot of baseball in my time. There have been only two young pitchers I was certain were destined for greatness, simply because they had the meanest fastball a batter can face. One of those boys was Dizzy Dean. The other is Ron Necciai. And Necciai is harder to hit."

Necciai was on his way to making the team following spring training in 1952, before stomach ulcers began to wear him down. He suffered from ulcers his whole life, always managing them to a certain degree, but he was now losing the battle just as his grip on the major leagues seemed a reality. But as Necciai's weight dwindled to about 150 pounds, his strength and speed on his fastball withered, and he was not able to break camp with the Pirates to make his major league debut as planned. Yet.

This time he wouldn't retreat home but went back to the minor leagues to recover and reunite with his baseball mentor. "The Pirates wanted me to go down to the minors to gain my strength back, and come back once I was fully recovered," said Necciai. "They wanted to send me to the higher-level New Orleans team, but I wanted to play for my first coach at Bristol, George Detore. He kind of became a father figure for me, and I trusted him," explained Necciai.

The 1952 baseball season began for Necciai, and he worked through the pain of the ulcers to gut out dominating performance after dominating performance for his team, the Bristol Twins. The pitching statistics for each game looked even more unlikely than the last, for example, striking out twenty during a start and nineteen in another. Then following up a few days later from the bullpen with the bases loaded and no outs, Necciai struck out the side and struck out eleven of twelve batters faced. This was all unlikely and simply dominating, leading up to the evening of May 13, 1952. This was supposed to be just another Tuesday game under the lights. Necciai said, "I was feeling terrible all day. I had nothing in the bullpen before the game. My catcher said just go out there and throw one pitch at a time, and that's all I did."

Once Necciai set the record at 26 strikeouts, he recorded one more, bringing the total to 27 and winning the game. He doesn't credit or discredit the night with thoughts such as the game was played under what could be considered inferior field lighting by today's standards, or that his strikeout total may have been helped by a foul ball lost in the lights, or that he struck out batters who just wanted to bunt to make contact with a ball. "The park was a good park, especially by the day's standards," said Necciai. "I didn't know or care how many strikeouts I was getting during the game, I was just throwing the ball and trying to get outs."

If strikeouts happen and dozens of news reporters are not there to witness, does it even happen at all? The fact that 9 innings were pitched with 27 strikeouts was slow to pick up steam in the media, but once it was verified as real, Necciai became national news. He went out his next game and threw 24 more strikeouts in 9 innings, and Necciai was now the buzz of baseball. He was being looked at for the big leagues, but could he keep it up against more seasoned players?

Necciai moved up from the Appalachian League (a D-league) after posting perhaps the most dominating stretch in baseball history, a 4-0 win-loss record, a miniscule 0.42 ERA, and a mind blowing 109 strikeouts in only 43 innings against just 10 hits. That is an average of 22.8 strikeouts against only 2.1 hits given up per 9 innings.

Necciai proved it was not a fluke as he carved up the more experienced players in the Carolina League (a B-league), with a tiny 1.28 ERA in 126 innings played, allowing only 73 base hits while playing for the Burlington-Graham Pirates. Necciai, at only twenty years old, was the baby of the group as the average age on the team was twenty-five. He completed his 1952 minor league season with 281 strikeouts in 169 innings, and that August the Pirates made the call to bring the young pitcher onto the big-league team.

The expectations from the Pirates were high for the young player walking into a Major League Baseball clubhouse for the first time. The newspapers were writing about him, fans expected "Kid-K" each at-bat. Not surprisingly he felt the pressure at the start and throughout the remainder of the year with the Pirates. "Too much pressure, just too much of it. It seemed like everyone expected me to come in and just strike everyone out. Even the other ballplayers were expecting it, but I was just like them, two arms, two legs, with some good days and bad days," explained Necciai of big-league expectations placed on him.

Necciai stood out from a roster with the average age of twenty-eight, but the locker room was open and friendly to the young hurler. "I had no problems with the older players or veterans like some rookies would have had at that time with other teams. The players knew me from spring training, and we had just really good guys. Hall of Famer Ralph Kiner was still there, and he always treated me great, and that probably helped," said Necciai.

By August 1952, the Pirates were well into having one of the worst records in Major League Baseball history finishing with 42 wins and 112 losses. The opening day roster had thirteen rookies; it would have been fourteen had Necciai's ulcers not sidetracked him.

Branch Rickey's "Operation Peach Fuzz" team was eliminated for postseason play by August 6. The only team to finish with a worse winning percentage is the 2003 Detroit Tigers. A well-used anecdote about the 1952 Pirates team was coined by catcher and future broadcaster Joe Garagiola: "They talk about Pearl Harbor being something, they should have seen the 1952 Pittsburgh Pirates."

"The team had a lot of newer ballplayers. We were pretty bad. Branch Rickey had the team in a rebuild, but some of those guys stayed on the club when the Pirates went to the World Series in 1958," explained Necciai.

Young pitchers can sometimes forget themselves on the mound and need to be reined in by their catcher. Necciai was no different during a game against the Cubs in his 1952 season, and unfortunately for Necciai, the catcher was an All-Star, World War II veteran, and not to be trifled with. "Our catcher was Clyde McCullough. I shook him off a third time for a pitch, he walked to the mound, looked hard into my eyes, and said, 'I've been here sixteen years and you've been here sixteen days, are we going to have a problem?'" said Necciai. "I shook my head, he said good, turned around and walked away. That was all it took. After that whatever he put down I threw it. I was more afraid of him than I was of giving up a hit. He looked like Atlas holding the world up, that's how strong he was," explained Necciai of the catcher who went on to make another All-Star team in 1953.

Necciai was not able to dominate at the major league level as he had just weeks earlier in the minor leagues. In twelve games pitched his record was 1 win and 6 losses with a 7.08 ERA in 54.2 innings pitched. It was just a cup of coffee in the bigs for the expected future ace of the team, but his major league career was put on hold. Shortly after the 1952 season, Necciai was drafted into the US Army for Korean War service.

Like it was for many other Americans, the military war draft was a reality and a commitment. Necciai was able to serve less than a year before being medically discharged for ulcers in 1953. "I was just trying to get back into physical shape after the Army and was only able to pitch in one minor league game in 1953. I probably pushed too fast and too hard, I began to feel shoulder pain, I just couldn't throw," explained Necciai.

The Pirates were as concerned as Necciai and sent him to specialist after specialist at some of the most respected hospitals in the country. Experts at the University of California, Duke, and Baylor all physically examined him and put him through test after test. Throughout 1954 and into the 1955 season, Necciai could not throw without pain. He was still young and could be a star pitcher if he were able to get through this patch. Was this a phantom pain or was it real? The Pirates and Necciai himself needed answers, which were finally provided by Johns Hopkins in Baltimore. "Dr. Bennett at Johns Hopkins told me I had a torn rotator cuff," said Necciai.

With today's treatment, a pitcher could recover with a combination of surgery and physical therapy. For Necciai all those years ago, the answer to a potential recovery was final and direct from the doctor. "I looked at him and asked him will I be able to play again? He just looked at me and said to go home and buy a gas station. 'We just do not know what they really are or how to fix them. We have tried to pin them, stitch them, we have tried everything, but nothing works. Son, you are never going to pitch again,'" said Necciai recalling the doctor's grim words. At only twenty-three, Ron Necciai's baseball dreams evaporated.

Branch Rickey had once compared Ron Necciai to Hall of Famer Dizzy Dean in terms of their talent on the mound, and now they would both have their careers ended by a tear in the posterior glenoid.

It was over for Necciai; would he be okay losing his baseball career with so much left undone? "Maybe I could've been a 'has been' or a 'never was.' I am just a 'might have been,'" said Necciai. "It was hard for a few years after I retired, but I decided to myself I wasn't going to think like that, but it did take me over twenty years to go see a baseball game in person though."

Questions of overuse and what if he hadn't torn his rotator cuff do not seem to lurk in the background all these years later. "I don't see any good reason to look back on my baseball days with regret, it won't change anything. Life goes on. I had a wonderful time in 1952, I was able to pitch in the big leagues, get a major league victory, strike out batters, and even got a base hit. I made some wonderful lifelong friends through baseball, not too bad," said Necciai.

How good does he think he could have been, if only, what if, he could have kept pitching? "I am not sure, but I know Sandy started out a lot like me, a great fastball, a big curveball. He struggled for a long time in the major leagues, and then it all just came together for him," said Necciai, stopping just short of saying he could have been a Hall of Famer like Sandy Koufax. "We both had great curveballs. *Baseball*

Digest once put a list of the top-ten 'curveballs of all time,' and he was number one, I was number six," continued Necciai proudly.

Over ninety years old now, still married after sixty-seven years and with three children, Necciai is long retired from his playing days and a sporting goods career that took him all over the world. But he is still remembered for his 27-strikeout game. "Surprisingly, seventy years later, people know my name. I still get mail from places like Japan, Italy, Poland, and Germany asking for autographs," explained Necciai. And even at his age, he writes or sends back the autographed baseball cards to the senders. "If they can take the trouble to write and ask me, the least I should do is write back," said Necciai.

Baseball has changed a lot since the 1950s. The game is faster, more specialized, and exhaustingly analyzed. Necciai does not always agree with what Major League Baseball has become, but he respects and appreciates the players just the same. He watches the pitchers today and is baffled by the way they are handled. "I believe the more a pitcher can throw, steadily building up the arm, and strengthening the legs the better off the pitcher will be. I cannot understand starting pitchers today being pulled after 80-85 pitches," says Necciai.

As a fan he marvels at players like Aaron Judge of the Yankees and O'Neil Cruz of the Pirates. Judge and O'Neil, both 6'7", tower over other players. "I still watch the Pirates, and the O'Neil kid is incredible. So talented and playing shortstop at that size, they should maybe think about having him pitch as well," said Necciai.

The idea of pitching to Aaron Judge with Necciai's Kid-K 100-mph fastball and knee-buster curve will never happen for Necciai, but how would he have gone at Aaron Judge back in the day? "It always comes down to just the pitcher and the batter, I would throw my fastball as hard as I could up in his eyes and hope he couldn't turn on it, but he shouldn't be able to at that speed," said Necciai. Even after all these years, Kid-K, Rocket Ron has the flamethrower mindset of a man who once struck out a mythical twenty-seven batters in a professional baseball game.

Ron Necciai has often said that he had two lives, his baseball life and after-baseball life. In September of 1952, at the age of twenty, he walked off the mound for the last time in the major leagues after striking out Jim Greengrass, the final batter he would face, to end the seventh inning down 2-0 to the Cincinnati Reds. His second life—now in the tenth decade—is spent doing crossword puzzles, shopping with his wife, and watching baseball on TV. Necciai concludes, "I have everything to be thankful for, no regrets, I have a fantastic family and friends."

DAN PASQUA, NEW YORK YANKEES AND CHICAGO WHITE SOX, 1985–1994

Positions: outfielder and first baseman

Bats left, throws left

Drafted by the New York Yankees in the third round of the 1982 MLB June Amateur Draft from William Paterson University in Wayne, New Jersey

Traded by the Yankees to the Chicago White Sox, November 12, 1987

Signed as a Free Agent with the Chicago White Sox, December 4, 1991

Granted Free Agency October 26, 1994

Major League Career Totals

AVG	G	AB	R	H	2B	3B	HR	RBI	SLG	OPS
.244	905	2620	341	638	129	15	117	390	.438	.768

Minor League Career Totals

AVG	G	AB	R	H	2B	3B	HR	RBI	SLG	OPS
.279	472	1671	302	466	75	23	100	346	.531	.971

Highlights

- Dan Pasqua started his professional baseball career with NFL Hall of Fame Quarterback John Elway as a teammate, and ended his career with NBA legend Michael Jordan as teammate while on a rehabilitation assignment with the AA White Sox team.
- Pasqua played baseball with Heisman Trophy winner, AL All-Star MVP, NFL Pro Bowl Running Back Bo Jackson as a member of the Chicago White Sox.
- Pasqua was voted as the1985 MVP International League Rookie of the Year and Most Valuable Player.
- During the 1985 offseason, the New York Yankees turned down an offer of future Hall of Fame outfielder Andre Dawson of the Montreal Expos for Pasqua.
- Pasqua had one 20 home run season in 1998.
- Pasqua works as a community representative for the White Sox.

CHAPTER 8

Dan Pasqua

A Baseball Paul Bunyan

Dan Pasqua is not a name remembered by many baseball fans born after 1980, but for many 1980s Yankee fans, it is a name that can bring a quick smile and a shake of the head for what almost was.

Pasqua was the local boy who had a chance to live the dream, patrolling the hallowed outfield grass of Yankee Stadium. The year 1961 was a magical one for baseball, and Pasqua was born in Yonkers, New York, on October 16 of that golden year. This was the time when Mickey Mantle and Roger Maris of the Yankees chased the mythical Babe Ruth and the All-Time Season-Record of 60 home runs. Maris hit his 61st home run in 1961, and the Yankees won the 1961 World Series in five games over the Cincinnati Reds. The Los Angeles Dodgers and San Francisco Giants were located on the West Coast, and the New York Mets were not yet a franchise. The Yankees were king of New York and the center of the baseball universe.

In 1962 the New York Mets were born to replace the Giants and Dodgers, who earlier had flown off to the West Coast. The Mets won the World Series in 1969, and they won the pennant again in 1973. By the 1980s, the baseball landscape had changed, and the New York Yankees were looking for their next great player just to compete with the Mets on the back page of the NYC newspapers. The Mets already had a young franchise-shaping slugger in Daryl Strawberry, and the mid-1980s Yankees fans had their answer: Dan Pasqua flashed the left-handed power of Babe Ruth and the good looks and power of Micky Mantle, while great Yankees player Don Mattingly had the humbleness of Roger Maris. Pasqua displayed a tailor-made stroke for the 310-foot away short porch in right field of Yankees Stadium. Pasqua was poised for greatness, and he was one of them—a New York kid ready to take baseball by storm and bring the Yankees its first World Series win since 1978.

The Pasqua family moved from the shadow of Yankee Stadium that living in Yonkers provided, across the Hudson River to the nearby suburb of Old Tappan, New Jersey, and Pasqua brought his Yankees love with him. In all fairness, New Jersey was always a stronghold for Yankees fans, so much so that the Yankees considered moving to the Meadowlands of New Jersey several times over the years.

As a youngster, Pasqua was a Yankees fan and loved to go to the games as often as he could with family and friends. "I was a good high school player in New Jersey, I even made All-County, but teams were not interested in me," Pasqua explained. As a high school senior, he topped out at 5'10" and 175 pounds. Disappointed, but not deterred, Pasqua went off to William Patterson University for an education and to play baseball. "New Jersey had a lot of overlooked high school baseball talent at the time, most of us ended up going to Montclair State or William Patterson," said Pasqua.

Pasqua put his 1981 and 1982 college baseball seasons to good use as he physically matured to a 6-foot, 200-pound baseball machine. Both years, he was a Baseball All-American and capped off 1982 as the New Jersey Athletic Conference Player of the Year.

The player who couldn't attract attention a couple years before was now turning heads across baseball. The team closest to his heart and home was the Yankees, and they selected him in the third round of the 1982 Major League Baseball draft. (Before taking Pasqua, the Yankees took a chance on a player who many consider to be the best all-around athlete since Jim Thorpe. Vincent "Bo" Jackson was taken as their second-round pick as a shortstop. But Jackson did the unthinkable. He turned down the New York Yankees and went on to become the talk of college football.)

By 1985, Pasqua had the Yankees thinking that they had lightning in a bottle. The thoughts were of a lefty slugger ready to be the next link in the long line of Yankee legends leading a ticker tape parade and a World Series trophy through the famous "Canyon of Heroes" in downtown New York City.

How did it go wrong? How did Pasqua go from a "can't miss" player to a Yankees organizational footnote? Pressure, expectations, and impatience from Pasqua himself, the fans, and the New York Yankees organization.

Dan Pasqua was no Mickey Mantle, but unfortunately for Pasqua, he LOOKED like Mantle with a similar body type, size, and weight. Both players had huge expectations unfairly placed upon them. When Mantle was trying to cut his big-league teeth in 1951, he was given the number 6 by the Yankees. This matters because it was the next number after the great Yankee center fielder Joe DiMaggio. "Joltin' Joe DiMaggio" was given the number 5 as a direct link to Lou Gehrig, whose number 4 linked to Babe Ruth with number 3. The pressure of trying to be as good as DiMaggio was perhaps what caused Mantle to slump badly during the beginning of his rookie year; it took a trip back to the minor leagues before being promoted again to the big club later in the year with a new number of 7 to give Mantle some relief from the pressure. Playing center field for the New York Yankees is one of the elite positions in sports, and Pasqua was positioned as a minor league center fielder envisioned to become the next Yankees legend.

"I was definitely being groomed by the Yankees, each step of the way, but I was not thinking about being the center fielder of the Yankees, I just wanted to play in their outfield. It wasn't until after I made the Yankees did the media and fans start with the expectations of being the next great center fielder like DiMaggio, Mantle, or Bobby Murcer," explained Pasqua. "I was just excited about the opportunity to one day play in the Yankees outfield."

In defense of Yankees fans and the hyper-driven New York sports media, Pasqua showed greatness playing up the Yankees minor league ladder by hitting tape-measure home runs, driving in runs, making minor league All-Star teams, and showing the grace of a future Yankee. Then on May 30, 1985, Dan Pasqua became the 15,034th player in MLB history. Wearing number 21 on the back of his pinstriped home jersey, Pasqua made a long-awaited loud grand entrance to the New York Yankees and their highly anticipating fans.

What else could happen to make fans and media lose their collective minds? A home run deep into the right field short porch by Pasqua in the bottom of the fifth for his first major league hit helped to secure a tight 3-1 win over the Reggie Jackson-led California Angels. The New York Yankees threw Pasqua under the bright New York lights, batting sixth in a packed lineup, and starting in the outfield with two of baseball's greatest players, Rickey Henderson and Dave Winfield, who both became Hall of Famers. For Pasqua, being on the field that night was a dream come true.

"I remember as a kid going to many games at the old stadium. My friend's dad had great seats right off the on-deck circle. It was an awesome view. That night changed and my view was now playing in the outfield with Rickey Henderson in center field, Dave Winfield in left, and Don Mattingly at first base," explained Pasqua. So what went wrong?

The owner of the New York Yankees at that time was George Steinbrenner. He brought the Yankees back to greatness after the dynasty began to crumble from the mid-1960s until the mid-1970s. The early 1970s Yankees were an embarrassment to the proud New York Yankees fans, and Steinbrenner designed, paid for, and generally forced the Yankees to greatness with playoff teams and World Series in 1976, 1977, 1978, and 1981. When Pasqua made his major league debut, the Yankees were in the early stages of a playoff drought from 1982 until the 1995 team finally made the playoffs. Steinbrenner wanted to win, and he would often buy the best players he could. Having the patience for his own minor league players to develop was not a Steinbrenner strength. Talented young players were called-up and demoted back to the AAA team so often that the trip was called the "Columbus Shuttle," as a nod to the journey back and forth between the AAA home city and the big-league club.

Pasqua only spoke with Steinbrenner a few times, but when Pasqua was called up in 1985 to make his major league debut, Steinbrenner brought the young rookie to his Yankee Stadium office to make a point. "I had one closed door meeting with George Steinbrenner in my life and it was him calling me in to remind me he was eating a million dollars by releasing Omar Moreno to make room on the major league roster for me, so I better not mess it up," explained Pasqua. "Talk about no pressure."

Moreno was a good player, a key part of the 1979 World Series Champion Pittsburgh Pirates and a two-time stolen base leader in the National League. However, the gauntlet to succeed had been thrown—from Steinbrenner to Pasqua—and the rookie promptly delivered with a home run in his first major league game. But the weight became too much for even the muscle of Pasqua.

The 1985 season was up and down for Pasqua with flashes of big-time talent and some inconsistency balanced between the big leagues and winning the MVP of the AAA-level International League. Pasqua's power stroke and potential fueled an offseason full of hype as he was on every team's general manager's wish list to acquire in a trade. Under Steinbrenner's tenure, and especially during the mid-1980s, "The Boss" had an "itchy trade finger," and in an act of surprising restraint, he passed on an opportunity to fit a future Hall of Famer outfielder into pinstripes. Andre Dawson was offered to the Yankees from the Montreal Expos straight up in a trade proposal for Pasqua. The Yankees thought they had their own Dawson, and better yet, he was a local kid, and the fans were going to love him. Dawson went on to hit 49 home runs and win the National League MVP in 1987.

Pasqua was not the first young hitting prospect to be promoted to the hometown fans and the starved Metro-NY media machine by the Yankees. In the early 1960s, the Yankees had a Rookie of the Year at shortstop in Tom Tresh and a cornerstone at first base in Joe Pepitone. Tresh and Pepitone were expected to carry on the excellence of the Yankees as the playing of Yogi Berra, Mickey Mantle, and Roger Maris was expected to decline. Tresh or Pepitone made good on their early promise by making All-Star teams or earning Gold Glove Awards for fielding in 1961, 1962, 1963, 1964, 1965, 1966, and 1969. The years of 1961, 1962, 1963, and 1964 brought World Series appearances to the Yankees with back-to-back championships in 1961 and 1962.

For Pepitone, his first Yankee years were particularly hard. Born and raised in Brooklyn, he had large expectations thrust on him, like Pasqua would feel years later. As the Yankees won, and with superior talent around Pepitone and Tresh, they were able to play as valuable cogs in the Yankees machine deferring to legends like Mantle, Maris, Berra, Elston Howard, and Whitey Ford. As we know, Father Time is undefeated, and even those stellar players could not produce the numbers from the back of their baseball cards. The Yankees decline started with four straight losing seasons from 1965 to 1968, and Pepitone and Tresh couldn't keep the Yankees afloat at the top of the American League.

For New York Yankees fans it was particularly difficult to watch as Pepitone, the New York City kid, was unable to step out from under the pressure and walk in the steps of the Yankee greats of years past. The year 1969 was the last year in Yankees pinstripes for Tresh and Pepitone, two young fresh-faced baseball stars, burned up and out of the Yankees just as they were going into their baseball prime of thirty years old. Tresh was traded mid-season to the Detroit Tigers and retired right after the season. Pepitone was traded to the Houston Astros that offseason and never found a home again playing for four different MLB teams during the next five seasons. In 1973, Joe Pepitone was finished as an MLB player by the relatively young age of thirty-two. He tried to reclaim his baseball glory by playing professional baseball in Japan during 1973, and his time there was short but impactful. In Japan, a term now used to signify "goofing off" is called "pulling a Pepitone." In many ways, Pepitone is the cautionary tale for today's older Yankees fans in how it does not always work out for the local kid.

And another: The New York Yankees once had a sweet left-handed swinger from New York City as the Robin to Babe Ruth's Batman. This young player was signed after two years playing for Columbia University where he played on both the football and baseball teams. That young player also had enormous pressure on him, as he was signed to be the "next" Babe Ruth. The player did not disappoint and performed as well as Ruth, and only a debilitating disease took him from the playing field at thirty-five and ultimately led to his death at thirty-seven. Yes, Lou Gehrig was a local kid, perhaps one of the best players of all time, but that was over fifty years before Pasqua. Baseball fans possess both extraordinarily long and short memories. Pasqua hitting bombs in the 1980s created pressure and expectations for him to succeed. The positivity of expectations for Gehrig, for Mantle hung in the air, and the negative whispers of "be better than Tresh and don't be a Pepitone" could be heard as well. Pasqua noticed and perhaps started to grip the bat tighter.

"At first I wasn't putting any pressure on myself to be a Yankees great or anything like that, but it changed when I was called up and people started talking about how I could do it," said Pasqua on rising expectations to be the next great hometown Yankee.

As noted earlier, when Pasqua was on the Yankees major league roster, he would start off hitting home runs, and it was off to the races for fans and media. When Pasqua was hitting well he was loved, but as most power hitters go, he was a streaky hitter and could go long spells not hitting the ball well. For Pasqua it was hard to find consistency as he was shuttled between the minor leagues and major leagues during the 1985, 1986, and 1987 seasons. A pattern of Pasqua the future star, and Pasqua the bum blurred for fans and management alike. Pasqua recalls, "It was hard when the Yankees get on you. The fan expectations are known, I was one, they start bullying you because you're not doing what you're supposed to do, what they thought you were going to do. Boos are tough, hard to hear when you're out there. I heard the boos and criticisms at the time."

"I knew of a lot of Yankee players who had a tough time back then; Steve Trout, suddenly, he couldn't find the strike zone, Ed Whitson, they had a tough time. I saw it happening, but it's not something we really talked about, at that time. Andre Robertson had his stuff with the boss and Bobby Meacham got treated pretty rough for sure. Steve Sax came in a year or two later, came in and, you know, got the yips again from second base. It seems like players respond differently to the pressure of New York."

The great expectations from the team, fans, and media began to change how Pasqua saw what he should be to the Yankees. Instead of working hard and being content to be a valued part of a Major League Baseball team that could contend for the playoffs each year, the pressure to be another star in the Yankees galaxy began to make Pasqua push himself to be that star in an already star-driven locker room. The Yankees had players who were future Hall of Famers and All-Stars like Henderson, Winfield, Mattingly, Dave Righetti, Phil Niekro, Ron Guidry, and Willie Randolph.

The year 1987 was lining up to be a big year for Pasqua and the Yankees. *Sports Illustrated* predicted big things for Righetti, Mattingly, and Pasqua in their Baseball Season Preview. Righetti was predicted to be the best closer in the American League, Mattingly to win the American League MVP and take the RBI crown, and

Pasqua was predicted to win the home run crown for the American League. But 1987 was a rough year for those predictions, and none of the three were able to deliver on those predictions. The Yankees player predictions were not the only ones to fall short as *Sports Illustrated* also infamously predicted the Cleveland Indians to win their first World Series since 1948. The Indians were in fact terrible in 1987, losing 101 games.

Some believe there is a hex of sorts on that team as the now-named Cleveland Guardians still have not won a World Series since 1948, although they were in the World Series in 1954, 1995, 1997, and 2016, losing each. The drought is even harder to take for Cleveland fans since the Chicago Cubs broke their 108-year World Series drought against the Cleveland franchise in 2016. As of 2023, the seventy-four-year gap is the longest between Championships in Major League Baseball. The Cardinals NFL franchise holds the record with the then Chicago Cardinals last winning a Championship in 1947.

In 1987, Don Mattingly was the man, the star, the top dog on the Yankees. He was coming off three seasons in a row of placing in the top five of the American Most Valuable Player Award, and Pasqua was being mentioned right alongside him. When Mattingly showed his first signs of a back injury that would ultimately curtail his career prematurely, the Yankees looked to Pasqua to step in for him at his position.

"Don was a great guy, everybody liked Don. He is a humble, soft-spoken guy and a great ballplayer. He was beginning to have his back issue, and they looked around down the bench asking if anyone played first base, no one said anything, then they looked at me," said Pasqua. "Sure, I'll give it a shot. It was a nice change from the outfield. You feel like you're really, really into the game more when you're in the infield," he explained. But "I think things went wrong for me when I began to envision myself as a star for the Yankees instead of just letting Henderson, Winfield, and Mattingly be the stars and ride the coattails. I wanted to be part of that stardom."

Trying to play bigger than he was at that early stage of his career ultimately, and unintentionally, had harmful implications. "I should have sat back and done what I could do on the field, but I don't really think it was a mistake on my part, it was normal I guess. I was young, full of enthusiasm, and talking myself up to a point. I easily could have played within myself, hit 15-20 home runs a year with 60-70 Run Batted In, and being a complement to the lineup instead of putting more and more pressure on myself to be what other people believed I could be," said Pasqua.

Then his last at-bat for the 1987 season teased Yankee fans. The last game of the Yankees season was in front of 25,101, including me and my mother. I was just a sixteen-year-old kid thrilled to see one of my favorite Yankees come off the bench and pinch-hit off the Baltimore Orioles in the ninth inning. It was no outs, and the Yankees were down 4-1. Henry Cotto played left field for the Yankees that day and went 0-3 with 2 strikeouts. Cotto hit a flyball in the bottom of the sixth during his last at-bat, and maybe Pasqua could create something off the bench to lead off the bottom of the ninth.

Pasqua didn't disappoint as he hit a rocket over one of the longest center-field walls in baseball for a home run. The frozen rope jolted and reminded the crowd of the Pasqua power and what an exciting piece of the team he could be in 1988. Pasqua set his then career-high for home runs in 1987 at seventeen. He was still ascending. In that last game in 1987, Pasqua was part of a major league record-setting performance as the Yankees sent five straight pinchhitters to the plate against the Orioles.

Despite the last game of the Yankees 1987 season, the overall season had been a disappointment to Pasqua and the Yankees. The Yankees finished fourth in the American League East, and Pasqua finished 32 home runs behind Mark McGwire of the Oakland A's. *Sports Illustrated* had to be as disappointed as the many Yankees fans after expectations fell short.

The home run by Pasqua to end his 1987 season helped to cause a trade from the New York Yankees. "I was pretty frustrated. I was feeling pretty good about hitting that ninth-inning pinch hit home run. I said things to reporters, basically saying if the Yankees were not going to play me full-time, then they should trade me and give me the chance to play somewhere else," explained Pasqua. "They traded me quick when the offseason began."

The 1980s New York Yankees were a very good franchise, with the best winning percentage in baseball for the 1980s, but they couldn't get to the postseason for the remainder of the 80s following their 1981 World Series loss to the Dodgers. They were never able to string together the proper blend of players. Uninspired, injured, and just unlucky players shuffled through alongside great players, creating hope and disappointment. For each Don Mattingly, Dave Winfield, and Rickey Henderson, the likes of Steve Kemp, Ed Whitson, Roy Smalley, and Dave Collins came in with lavish press conferences and to lofty expectations only to be shuffled through the clubhouse door in short order. Now Pasqua wanted out, and the Yankees were happy to quickly trade a player who grew frustrated and was inconsistent in his game.

For Pasqua, playing for the Yankees was a dream come true, but playing so close to home also came with little room to navigate difficulties. "Once I made the Yankees, I was definitely looked at differently at home, it was uncomfortable and weird at times. I was still me, but people just treated me differently because I was a Yankee," explained Pasqua.

The trade to the Chicago White Sox right after the MLB 1987 year concluded alleviated some of the pressure on Pasqua, but his tantalizing power potential still brought lofty expectations. With this trade, Pasqua felt he was still looked at as being a big thumper in the lineup, but he at least knew he was going to get a chance for playing time.

"I couldn't live up to what the White Sox hoped from me either, but unlike the Yankees, they gave me more of a chance to work through some of my up and downs. They understood I was a streaky player. If I was in a slump with the Yankees, they would sit me or send me down to the minors. I had my chance, but injuries were what held me back," explained Pasqua.

Although he was still not able to get the 500 at-bats really needed to feel like he played a complete season, Pasqua once again hit a career-high in home runs, this time topping it off at twenty. During his first four years in the major leagues, he set an increasing career high of home runs each year—with 9 home runs in 1985, 16 in 1986, 17 in 1987, and 20 in 1988. The home runs, power numbers, and at-bats were going up each year. Dan Pasqua was slowly and steadily building into the player he thought he could be, until injury reared its ugly head for the first time in his MLB career.

Pasqua broke his wrist during the first game of the 1989 season, missing significant time. Ankle and hamstring injuries also contributed, but it was ultimately lingering knee injuries that kept him from the greatness predicted early in his career. The next few years fell short of expectations, but he settled into being a productive player, a member of the team, and not expected to be the face and voice of the team with less media pressure.

In 1990, the Chicago White Sox played their final season at their stadium in Comiskey Park. Dan Pasqua, not known for his legs as injuries began to slow him down, hit a triple to bring home future Hall of Famer Frank Thomas and what would be the last RBI hit in the proud old stadium.

Pasqua only managed to play a few games into the 1994 season before knee surgery kept him out for the rest of the year and ultimately ended his career. "I couldn't even walk on it after that one," said Pasqua of the 1994 knee surgery. Then in 1995, Pasqua gave one last shot to be out on the field during a free-agent camp. "I was hitting great. When it was time to go into the outfield and run sprints, I couldn't do it, I was hobbling around. I knew it was time to retire."

As of the time of writing this book, Pasqua is still involved with baseball as an advisor with the Chicago White Sox, running youth baseball clinics, and serving as a baseball instructor in the community. According to Pasqua, the game has changed and evolved, and he tries to blend yesterday's principles with parts of today's game. "Everything is about swing angle, it is all the kids want to do, but it can get them in trouble. Things like analytics and launch angle are kind of controversial, but only because they are easily misunderstood. I try to teach a purposeful swing, and not just hitting home runs."

It is easy to wonder what Pasqua and his lefty stroke could do in today's game of swing big for home runs, go for extra base hits without fearing a low batting average, and a high strikeout rate not adversely affecting playing time. "If I was allowed to hit in the low .200s like today, I would have 20–30 home runs each year. I don't think I ever tried to hit a home run. If I hit it hard, got a hold of the ball, it was going to go," explained Pasqua of the way he played the game.

Pasqua opened eyes with his breathtaking bombs, All-Star selections, Rookie of the Year, and MVPs during his rapid climb of the New York Yankees minor league ladder. The promise and potential of his first game—homering for his first major league hit, sharing the hallowed outfield grass of Yankee Stadium with the great Dave Winfield and Rickey Henderson—ended with a whimper against the Tigers in Detroit.

On May 1, 1994, at just thirty-two years old (the same age as Joe Pepitone), Pasqua stepped in as a pinch hitter for catcher Ron Karkovice against Mike Henneman with the bases loaded and two outs in the top of the eighth inning. This was the kind of spot a young and healthy Pasqua had lived for. But with his right knee aching and all his other injuries piled up, his playing career ended with a groundball to the second baseman for an easy out, the end of the inning, and ultimately the end of his ten-year MLB career.

Pasqua has many great memories from the baseball playing field, but his connection to three athletes is an unlikely feather in his cap: (1) Perhaps the best athlete of the twentieth century, (2) an NFL Hall of Fame quarterback, and (3) arguably the best basketball player of all-time were teammates of Pasqua. Remember, he started his career by being drafted by the Yankees behind future NFL and MLB star Bo Jackson, and Pasqua later played with Jackson on the Chicago White Sox. Pasqua played with NFL quarterback John Elway in the minors for the New York Yankees in 1982 (for Oneonta of the NY-Penn league), and in 1994 while trying to rehabilitate his injured knee at AA Birmingham, Pasqua played with the phenomenal Michael Jordan.

In 1992, sportswriter Paul Ladewski wrote in *Inside Sports*, "Dan's average of one extra base hit per 7.6 at-bats ranked ahead of more celebrated southpaw swingers Ken Griffey Jr., Kent Hrbek, Fred McGriff, and Dave Parker. Equally overlooked was his capable glovework. Yet Pasqua has never had as many as 500 at-bats in any one season, and at 29, he may never know what might have been."

Pasqua was the image of the ultimate power hitter, six foot and muscular, weight on his back foot as taught by the great batting coach, Charlie Lau. Pasqua displayed a George Brett stance along with brute power. But pressure, unrealistic expectations, impatience by the player and team management, and injuries all rolled into a perfect storm to curtail his performance and make us wonder "what if?" about Dan Pasqua. What if he had been drafted to another team without the pressure and impatience from the New York Yankees and their fans? What if Pasqua had just let the game come to him instead of wearing his at-bats on his sleeve? Mostly, what if he could have stayed consistent enough and avoided the nagging injuries that ultimately drained away the player he could have been?

 BRIEN TAYLOR, NEW YORK YANKEES, CLEVELAND INDIANS, 1992–2000

Position: starting pitcher

Bats left, throws left

Drafted by the New York Yankees in the first round (first pick overall) of the 1991 MLB June Amateur Draft from East Carteret High School, Beaufort, North Carolina

Minor League Career Totals

W	L	IP	SO	WHIP	ERA
22	30	435.2	425	1.738	5.12

Highlights

- Brien Taylor was thought to be the most sought-after pitching prodigy since David Clyde, with the skills to be the next Sandy Koufax.
- Taylor fanned 476 batters in 239 innings during high school.
- Taylor signed for a record signing bonus of $1.55 million from the New York Yankees.
- Taylor dominated during his first two years of professional baseball.
- A still unexplained incident caused what would be career-ending injuries.
- Taylor's ERA was 3.02 in 324.1 innings pre-injury, and 11.24 after his injury.
- As a first overall MLB draft pick, Taylor is only the second such player to not appear in an MLB game.
- Taylor was sentenced to fifty months of prison time on federal drug charges in 2012.

CHAPTER 9

Brien Taylor

A December Night Detour to Greatness

Brien Taylor was born on the day after Christmas in 1971 in Beaufort, North Carolina, a town with a population of nearly five thousand. The infamous Blackbeard and the legend of Brien Taylor are part of the fabric of this small town—each of these men capable of striking fear in the hearts of people. The sight of Blackbeard's ship spewing smoke and making way toward a defenseless vessel invoked fear, and a player in the batter's box facing the smoldering heat or the knee-buckling curve of Taylor felt the same.

Blackbeard met his end at the hands of Lt. Maynard at Beaufort Inlet in 1718. In 1993, Taylor essentially met his own end as his injured shoulder separated him from his Major League Baseball dream. His potential to be among the greatest pitchers in the game ended swiftly even as he tried to pick himself up after December 18, 1993. He continued a slow and painful comeback, but he was just the slightest shadow of his former self.

The exact circumstances leading up to the demise of Taylor are as murky as the low country water Taylor calls home, but the results were immediate and permanent even as he still had the courage to go out there to compete, to be seen and judged in an ultimately heartbreaking display of how much was missing and never to return to the one-time pitching prodigy.

The left-handed pitcher stood an intimidating 6'3" and 220 pounds on the mound. A man among boys with hands as big as the Dodgers great Sandy Koufax, capable of spinning baseballs so beautifully that they lulled batters to sleep, only to be rudely awaken by the smack of the catcher's mitt and the umpire yell of "strike three!"

(As a writer, I am being only slightly dramatic. By the time Taylor finished East Carteret High School, he had struck out 213 batters in just 88 innings pitched. It was simply David versus Goliath with Goliath winning every time.)

It seems like every great young pitching prospect, especially a left-hander throwing heat, is compared to Koufax. This is so from David Clyde (featured in another chapter in this book) all the way to Brien Taylor, and this will probably continue long into the baseball future. But Yankee talent evaluators like Brian Cashman and Gene Michael also brought up more contemporary pitchers of the late 1980s and early 2000s, like Randy Johnson and Pedro Martinez, to describe what Taylor could become.

Brian Sabean is considered one of the top talent evaluators in baseball history. Sabean helped build the 1990s and early 2000s Yankees dynasty, went to the West Coast with the San Francisco Giants as the general manager and won multiple World Series rings, and as of 2023, he was back home with the New York Yankees to bring them more rings. On a spring day over the phone as the Yankees are about to embark on spring training, Sabean is looking back on perhaps the best high school pitching prospect he ever saw.

"We tracked every start of the spring his senior year. Brien Taylor was a man-child amongst boys, so to speak. The size, strength, athletic ability, baseball talent was just uncommon for any high school athlete, in any sport or position, not just a starting pitcher. Looking back, he's easily the best high school pitcher I scouted in person. It is not even close," said Sabean.

Taylor was certainly a pitching prospect before his senior year in 1991, but he found height and more on his fastball from his junior to his senior year. According to Taylor, by the time he was a freshman he could throw 90 mph, and he thought he might be drafted after high school. As a junior he could throw 92 mph or so. "I was maybe 5'10" or 5'11" maybe 160 pounds as a junior. I shot all the way up to 6'3", 200 or so pounds when I pitched as a senior. I always had a good fastball, but now it was even harder. I was throwing gas in the high 90s, maybe even higher sometimes as a senior," said Taylor looking back thirty-plus years at his younger self.

Taylor came from a family that was not financially well-off. He did not have the grades affording him the option to play D1 college baseball and use that as leverage with the New York Yankees. Brien was the second of four children; his mother Bettie worked at a seafood facility picking crabs, while his father Willie did masonry work. The Taylor family lived in a double-wide trailer with just one light bulb.

The young man had his mother handle the contract negotiations for the first-round pick. He didn't even have an agent, and a young, inexperienced Scott Boras was his advisor. "I am sure the Yankees felt as if my mom, with no education, would be easy to push around, [but] they quickly learned different," said Taylor.

The Yankees came in with what they thought was a fair signing bonus of $300,000 for the high school pitcher. But after talking to Boras, Bettie Taylor did not like the number. The goal was to get at least what the 1990 best high school pitcher got. Todd Van Poppel received $1.2 million to sign with the Oakland A's, and that was as a fourteenth-round pick. But Taylor didn't have the leverage of a waiting baseball scholarship at the University of Texas that Van Poppel had.

"Boras told my mom and me that it was not often the New York Yankees had the top pick in the draft, and to use that to help us get a better deal," said Brien Taylor. The situation was that Taylor had an advisor looking to make a splash in the baseball world, and a mother who wanted to ensure her son was not going to be overlooked or taken advantage of because of their perceived limited options. Sabean quickly figured it would not be a quick and neat signing.

"We thought she was really committed to not having him sign. She said they knew what Brien was, that we had our head in the sand on it, he was a number 1 pick and wouldn't just sign. What came along was a tough negotiation. The more we talked to him, the more we understood that he was willing to gamble on himself and enter the draft again next year," explained Sabean.

Then nearby Louisburg College in North Carolina became the leverage that Taylor needed to force the New York Yankees to consider opening their checkbook. "My mother would not budge for the New York Yankees, even with a briefcase of cash. I enrolled in a nearby junior college, and the Yankees had to do something or lose me," said Taylor. "George Steinbrenner was officially banned from running the Yankees at the time, but once we saw in the paper that he said, 'The Yankees front office should be shot' if they didn't sign me, we knew it could work," explained Brien.

Even though the owner was not allowed to run the team, it is clear that his voice still had a strong unofficial role with the team, and his voice reverberated to the Yankees brain trust. "That era, that was the height of Mr. Steinbrenner's ownership, and that would have been Mr. Steinbrenner's style. No matter who the pick was, we were going to sign the number 1 pick in the country. I never thought of it any other way," explained Sabean.

Brien and his family were waiting until the bitter end and forcing the Yankees into their best possible deal. "There is so much gamesmanship. We didn't want to give up anything in our leverage, just like they wanted to gain everything possible from being the No. 1 pick. Time was on their side. They used the clock as a strategy. We just got to the position where the result was too hard for both parties to walk away," said Sabean of the waning days of the contract negotiation.

A deal was signed the day before college classes were starting. For Brien, the pushback led to setting the record for highest contract of a draft pick of all-time. The $1.55 million dollar deal easily outpaced the Todd Van Poppel deal of $1.2 million. "We knew they had to budge. George would have killed them if they let me go. I got the call from my mom of the offer; I got back as quick as I could to sign that deal before they changed their minds," said Taylor.

First contracts for any player can be overwhelming, and Taylor was lucky to have Scott Boras go through the original contract language as he was about to sign. "It was buried in the fine print, but it was there. Scott Boras found language that would have made me give money back if I was hurt under certain conditions. It was a good thing he is what he is because he had that changed quick. The whole thing was a real eye-opening experience of how much baseball was a business," said Taylor.

With the 1991 minor league season over, the Yankees sent Brien to instructional camp that fall to prepare for the 1992 minor league season in Fort Lauderdale for the High-A team. "We started him high up in 1992. Making the Fort Lauderdale team as a high school draft pitcher taken in the previous year speaks for itself on his talent and what we thought he could do. He was that good, jumping straight to that level is almost unheard of. He was also named the top prospect by Baseball America going into the 1992 season," said Sabean. "Those were the kind of prevailing winds around Brien Taylor."

In 1984 a young Dwight Gooden set the baseball world on fire as "K-Korner" mania took over each time the nineteen-year-old hurler took the mound. Gooden jumped from High-A ball straight to the major leagues with the Mets and a 98-mph fastball leading the NL in strikeouts, making the All-Star team, and winning the NL Rookie of the Year Award. Gooden followed up with one of the most dominant seasons in Major League Baseball history in 1985. He won the Triple Crown of pitching by leading the league with 24 wins, 268 strikeouts, and a 1.53 ERA.

But by the time Gooden was just twenty-one, he began to show signs of slipping as his ERA almost doubled and his strikeouts dipped to 200 from 276 and 268. The 1986 Mets still won the World Series, but when he couldn't find his way to the World Series ticker tape parade down the Canyon of Heroes stretching from the Battery to City Hall, it signaled something was wrong with Gooden and that his career had already peaked at just twenty years old.

No matter how good Brien Taylor and the Yankees believed Taylor was going to be, he was going to have to develop fully—emotionally and physically—before facing the rigors and demands of playing in New York City for the Yankees. Taylor was moving fast, but the Yankees wanted to be more cautious with player development than the Mets had been with Dwight Gooden. "Our style back then was more understated than that. We all knew his upside, and we agreed he was going to earn his way up, but we also knew he was a powerful pitcher and would come up quickly," explained Sabean on the Yankees approach to Brien Taylor's development.

Yankee fans wanted to have their answer to young slugger Daryl Strawberry and pitching ace Dwight Gooden. But the Yankees didn't see the need to counterpunch what the crosstown Mets were doing. The Yankees were going to do it their way—the Yankee Way. "That was not the way we develop players and pitchers," Sabean explained about the New York Yankees and how they want to groom their future stars. "We don't try to hype our prospects, it is better to overdeliver versus underdelivering, and part of that is protecting the prospect or the player," explained Sabean.

"Taylor needed some minor league experience, earn his way up, and to be further polished as a young pitcher. He also needed better command of the strike zone. His fastball was so big, intimidating, a legitimate breaking ball, and the makings of a change-up. Strikeout totals are one thing, but he was throwing a lot of pitches per at-bat, and that is something he needed to cut down as you come up through the minor leagues," explained Sabean on his assessment of the young 1992 Taylor.

Taylor had a great season in 1992 High-A ball. He went 6-8, with 187 strike outs in 161.1 innings and had a tiny 2.57 ERA. His next stop was going to be AA for the 1993 season. He was succeeding as a player and as a teammate. "Everyone just gravitated toward Brien, coaches, players, fans, everyone. He had such a magnetic personality, so talented, and humble," said Sabean on how Taylor was perceived as a player and person. "I didn't win a lot of games, but I had a good ERA, and struck a whole bunch of guys out. It was a good season for me," explained Taylor on his first professional season of 1992.

Taylor was always a hard worker on the baseball field, and he wanted to be even better for the upcoming season at AA Albany, New York. It would hard to be better than he already was as the No. 2 prospect in Minor League Baseball, just behind future Hall of Famer Chipper Jones, heading into the 1993 season, but Taylor tried anyway. "No matter how good people told me I was, I always tried to make myself even better. There was always a way to improve my game. I am a humble person and wanted to make sure I could be the pitcher people expected to see," explained Taylor.

Taylor excelled as a twenty-one-year-old in AA going 13-7, with 150 strikeouts in 163 innings and a 3.48 ERA. Andy Pettitte, a 1990 draft pick out of Deer Park High School in Texas, also twenty-one years old, appeared in one game after being promoted from A-Ball. Jorge Posada, twenty-two years old, appeared in seven games. Derek Jeter, twenty years old, and Mariano Rivera, twenty-four years old, were just behind making their 1994 AA debut. Core members of the future Yankees championship teams were climbing the minor league ranks, and Brien Taylor was lining up to be the first one to make the big-league team.

Taylor was expected to be promoted to AAA for the 1994 season. The No. 18 overall prospect in baseball would now be just one level below the Yankees and the strong 1994 playoff-contending team.

But Taylor was about to hit a roadblock on his highway to the Yankees and MLB greatness. Nobody saw it coming and when it happened, it was in the blink of an eye, and Taylor is still not ready to say what happened to him.

There are many rumors about what happened the night of December 18, 1993. Bottom line is that Taylor suffered an injury drastically altering his career and his life, ultimately ending a future in the major leagues with a loss of potentially hundreds of millions of dollars in contracts and endorsements.

So what happened? Did Taylor hurt himself in a bar fight? Did he hurt his shoulder shooting pool? Did he simply slip and fall? Some say he was picked up and body slammed. Was it during a fight outside a trailer? Was he the victim or instigator? Did Taylor try to block an attack with his left arm, which bent his arm and shoulder back too far? Was it a missed Taylor haymaker of such force that it destroyed his shoulder? Was the altercation over drugs, a woman, money? Was he cited with a misdemeanor assault? Does it matter? Was Brien Taylor a "bad kid" and something like this was bound to happen? Nobody really knows, except maybe a few people including Taylor, and they have kept the secret as safe as Blackbeard's rumored treasure buried near Beaufort Inlet.

The most repeated version of events is that Brien's brother Brendan had a fight with a man, and Brien became upset that his brother was beaten up. A relative and Brien went to confront this man at his residence. A scuffle ensued leaving Brien injured with what was ultimately diagnosed as a torn labrum of the left shoulder.

Even thirty years later, Taylor is not ready to say what happened that night. He is not sure why he should have to explain or even how to explain exactly what happened to him. It is a personal matter. "I went somewhere, something happened and hurt my shoulder. Everyone has it wrong about what happened, the why it happened, the who was there, where, everything. It is my story to tell, and I am not ready to share it just yet," explained Taylor.

Even as his labrum tore with such force that it looked like he had been in a major car accident, his agent Scott Boras first called it a bruise to reporters once the rumors quickly made their way out of North Carolina. The Yankees wanted a closer look at the shoulder of the player they expected to be a keystone in their franchise. It was definitely not just a bruise, a long way from it, and Taylor underwent surgery a week later.

Boras has fueled the curiosity and intrigue of events surrounding Taylor by sharing with reporters, even years later, the description the surgeon gave him of the shoulder injury. "It was one of the worst injuries the surgeon ever saw; he described the injury of the shoulder as unnatural," according to Boras on the injury. Brien's arm had to be driven with extreme force over his head to cause that type of damage.

On December 28, 1993, just two days after his twenty-second birthday, Brien had surgery on his left shoulder capsule and labrum to try to fix the shattered shoulder of a can't-miss prospect who was ultimately going to miss out on his Major League Baseball dreams.

Derek Jeter, one of the most respected and loved Yankees of all time, focuses on how someone can have it all in front of them, and then it is gone. "We [Brien Taylor and I] were roommates in spring training in 1994. He was a good dude. He was a nice guy, sort of shy from North Carolina. Sometimes one thing goes right, one thing goes wrong, and it can change the course of a career. Unfortunately, for him—and for us as well—he got hurt," explained Jeter.

"Derek Jeter has had the chance to really pile on me over the years if he wanted to. But he never did. Although we don't keep in touch, I respect the guy so much and appreciate him," said Taylor.

Taylor was the 1991 Yankees first-round pick, Jeter was the 1992 Yankees first-round pick, and the two of them were supposed to be generational baseball talents making the rise together. Now Taylor was taking a full year to rehab his arm and trying to come back as strong as ever for 1995. If it would only have been that simple . . .

The Brien Taylor who in 1992 was able to bypass rookie ball entirely was a Gulf Coast Yankee. His pitching line of 2-5, with 38 strikeouts in 40 innings pitched and a hefty 6.08 ERA, was not encouraging for the now twenty-three-year-old rookie making his rookie league debut. His fastball was nothing like the Brien Taylor fastball drafted in 1991. An easy 98 was now about 88 mph. His curveball was not able to go over for a strike, and he couldn't find the strike zone. "My fastball was gone; I couldn't control the baseball anymore. I was just getting back and trying to dig myself out, I was working to get better, and make it come back," explained Taylor.

Looking through his 1995 statistics, there were some horrifying numbers. He was not even close to what he was able to do preinjury. Taylor's command of the strike zone and walks had always been a mild reason for concern. His walks per 9 innings went from 3.7 in 1992, to 5.6 in the much tougher and more selective hitters in AA, and against the youngest and least disciplined rookie ball players, it ballooned to 12.2. Taylor also hit ten batters with a pitch. It took him four times as many innings to approach ten hit batsman than in either of his previous seasons. Simply put, his fastball was more pedestrian, he lost his curveball, and his change-up didn't develop.

But there were signs of hope for the Yankees and Taylor. His strikeouts per 9 innings pitched of 8.6 strikeouts showed his fastball could still miss bats, and he only allowed 29 hits in the 40 innings pitched for a career low 6.5 hits per 9 innings. He was causing batters to swing through the ball, and they were not able to hit—even if this was smoke and mirrors by Taylor. If his command and curveball could return as well as gaining a few mph on his fastball as his shoulder improved, he may make it back after all. There were a lot of ifs, but it could happen. So the Yankees took a shot to see how the new Taylor would do a level up in A-Ball for the Greensboro Bats.

The average age of the 1996 Greensboro Bats pitching staff was 21.3 years old. Young Taylor, who always seemed to be playing against the older guys, was now one of the old guys on the young team. The year 1995 had been different. Taylor was recovering from his injury and was playing to get the work in, to show enough for the Yankees to move him forward, which they did. However, the results for Taylor in 1996 were, as former Yankees Manager Joe Girardi would say, "not what you want."

Taylor racked up a 0-5 record, with 11 strikeouts, 43 walks in 16 innings pitched, and an 18.73 ERA. Not only were his innings pitched down, but his walks per 9 innings went from 12.2 to 23.7 and hits from 6.5 to 11.6. Brien Taylor was not himself; the Yankees knew it, but more importantly, Brien knew it too. "I was not me anymore, I couldn't be myself and do what I used to as a pitcher," explained Taylor.

The Yankees kept him in Greensboro for 1997 and 1998, as Taylor kept working hard, hoping to rebound back to form. He was only healthy enough to be out there for a combined 52.1 innings pitched with an ERA in the double digits. "Sometimes after I hurt my shoulder, I could feel it start to come back from time-to-time, but then it would be gone. Some days I felt as if I never even held a baseball before in my life. I couldn't get a pitch near the plate," explained Taylor of his postsurgery struggles.

After the 1998 season, the New York Yankees gave up on Taylor. This was not a surprise, but Taylor was not ready to give up his love for baseball and his comeback. "I signed with the Seattle Mariners in 1999. I was working in extended spring training when they released me, I wasn't healthy enough to compete," explained Taylor. "I used to strike everyone out, now I was just a pitcher hoping to get a ground ball for an out."

Taylor took the rest of 1999 off from baseball. The next year, he attempted another comeback, this time for the Columbus RedStixx, in Columbus, Georgia, for the Cleveland Indians A-Ball affiliate. This led to a sad ending for Taylor as he appeared in only five games for 2.2 innings, walking nine batters, and produced seven wild pitches. Taylor was done as a professional baseball player at the age of twenty-eight. He packed it all up and went back home to North Carolina.

The player who signed with the Yankees for $1.55 million was about to become another person trying to get by and pay his bills. "I didn't go crazy when I first signed. I bought my parents a house, and I purchased a Mustang GT, those were the only big things at the time," said Taylor. But it was now close to ten years later, and the money of Major League Baseball did not happen.

To pay the bills, Taylor, father of five, worked as a UPS driver, then as a beer distributor, and even helped his father as a brick layer. As hard as that would be for Brien at only the age of twenty-nine, he was hit with another curveball he hadn't seen coming. "I couldn't breathe, always winded, couldn't walk very far. I was diagnosed with CHF (congestive heart failure)," explained Taylor. "I was really sick."

For Taylor, that was the final nail in the coffin of his professional baseball career. "The Yankees reached out to me to see if I wanted to give baseball another shot in 2001. I knew I couldn't do it, I had CHF, I am sure the Yankees didn't know," said Taylor.

Taylor didn't really miss parts of professional baseball anyway. "Working hard for money was fine by me. My parents raised me to be hardworking and humble, I always was going to do what I had to do," said Taylor. "I didn't have money before, became a millionaire, and back to not having it, I was the same person the whole time."

For many people back in North Carolina, seeing Taylor in an older car and working blue-collar jobs seemed like it would have been a mighty blow to the ego of the former baseball player who had left to take his shot with the Yankees and received a huge amount of money to do so. According to Taylor, even now some feel sorry for him and how his life panned out, while others are happy it didn't go as planned. "I am still a legend back home to some people, but there were also others who were happy as hell to see me fail. I don't care about those people, I wouldn't be able to convince them anyways," said Taylor.

It would be a rough road for Taylor over the next ten years or so after retiring as a player, culminating with an August 2012 federal sentence for cocaine trafficking. The man who had his picture proudly displayed on baseball cards was now the face in a mugshot. It was a shocking fall for the player his teammates and coaches described as shy, quiet, and a good guy.

Taylor was sentenced to thirty-eight months in prison and was released in September 2015, with three years of supervised release.

A combined two-county undercover narcotics team worked for several months in 2011 on the case resulting in various narcotics charges against Taylor. In the end, he pleaded guilty to distributing twenty-eight grams or more of crack-cocaine. "It was a horrible thing for me to do getting involved in all that. It just snowballed on me. I was trying to make a whole bunch of money back, got caught up with the wrong people, made bad decisions," said a remorseful Taylor years later in 2023. "But a lot more of it was made of it, because I was Brien Taylor, they really came at me, building it up, playing me along and making it even worse than it had to be."

During testimony in the case, several surprising factors emerged: Taylor had dealt drugs in 2003, 2004, and again in 2011. The US Attorney's Office said that Taylor was responsible for 208 grams of crack and 100 grams of cocaine trafficked. US District Court Judge Louise Flanagan had several things to say about Taylor during sentencing. "He seemed completely unprepared for a life after baseball, which he was confronted with almost immediately," said Flanagan to Taylor's defense lawyer. And speaking directly to Taylor, the judge continued, "You were viewed by many in your community as a hero because of your baseball career. A hero dealing drugs is a very dangerous person."

Taylor made sure to apologize to the community and his five daughters, four of whom he was raising on his own. "I just want to say I'm sorry for all the harm I caused to individuals and their families, I am sorry to my children for letting them down," said an apologetic Taylor in federal court.

These days, Taylor is a long way from the mistakes and troubles of his past. With his daughters and the rest of the family, he stays busy and is a Yankees fan. "They are my team, they gave me an amazing opportunity, it didn't work out, but it was nothing the New York Yankees did that stopped me from making it," explained Taylor.

Taylor is not sure if he is interested in coaching baseball, but he wants to make a difference to some of the young players coming up. Many of the minor leaguers today were born after he hurt his shoulder in 2003, but he feels that his story—including the pitfalls and what ifs—can be an important lesson and have a big impact. "I would love to find a way to be a guest speaker in baseball, maybe with the New York Yankees, minor leaguers, rookies, all of them. I once could have had it all, then the opportunity was gone. It can all disappear. I know what happened to me, maybe one of them can avoid what happened to me," explained Taylor.

Brian Sabean, one of the best baseball minds today, shares his thoughts on Taylor the baseball player and how he compares favorably to another left-handed pitcher, Vida Blue. Blue made his MLB debut at nineteen years old and pitched until he was thirty-eight, earning top honors and accomplishments like MVP, CY Young, and three consecutive World Series Championships, winning at least twenty games in a season three times, and appearing in six All-Star games. "Brien had such a repeatable and natural fluid arm movement. I can't remember anyone having any concerns about his delivery. Every team in baseball loved his talent level. Our opinion of him was the industry standard of him. He was a world-class athlete, his strength, his endurance. Comparing anyone to Sandy Koufax is never fair, but I would say Taylor was more like Vida Blue and had that type of athletic presence on the mound. Brian was that dynamic and explosive," summed up Sabean on what Taylor might have developed into as a pitcher if not for his injury.

Sabean is a baseball man, one who knows what a cold business baseball can be, and how players can come and go and be easily replaced on the roster or in an organization's plans. Taylor was a baseball player whom Sabean developed for a short time with the Yankees. All these years later, as I was working on this book, Sabean asked me how Taylor is doing and asked me to give his phone number to Taylor so the two of them could catch up. I passed the message and number to Taylor, and I hope they do talk all these years later.

I am not sure that Sabean tries to reach out to many players more than thirty years after their paths only slightly crossed, but Taylor was a player who once had the Yankees and the baseball world buzzing with dreams of what he could do. So the haunting question remains, what could Brien have become if only he had not hurt his shoulder that December night?

CHAPTER 10

Other Incredible "What If" Players

Joe Bauman, 1B, Minor League Baseball Player, 1941–1956*

**with three years removed for WWII service and three more years missed playing semiprofessional baseball*

Joe Bauman is truly the Babe Ruth meets Crash Davis of Minor League Baseball. After making his professional baseball debut for a Brooklyn Dodgers minor league team in 1941 at the age of nineteen, he returned after service in World War II at twenty-four years old to bash 48 home runs, drive in 159 RBI, and hit over .300 for a minor league team in 1946.

Bauman reached AAA for the Boston Braves in 1948, but after the season, he did not want to be reassigned to a lower classified team and walked away to play semiprofessional baseball and earn more money than he would have made as a major league player for the 1949–1951 seasons.

At the age of thirty, he returned to the minor leagues and was stalled at a low classification for four years despite hitting 50, 53, 72, and 46 home runs those years. His RBI totals those years were 157, 141, 224, and 132. Bauman had perhaps the best offensive season of any player, in any league, in the history of baseball in 1954. He more than doubled the home runs hit by his nearest finisher, Jim Zapp, who hit 32.

Bauman hit .400, slugged 72 home runs with 224 RBI, and had a 1.451 OPS over 138 games for the 1954 minor league season, setting a professional baseball record for home runs that stood until 2001.

The minor league team was the nonaffiliated Roswell Rockets of the Class C Longhorn League, in the same New Mexico town made famous by the 1947 Roswell Incident of the recovery of debris in the desert. Even more perplexing is how Bauman, playing in the minor leagues, had not been signed to a major league team to play for an affiliated team since he had walked away from the Boston Braves in 1948.

Bauman batted .337 with a cyclical 337 home runs and drove in 1,057 RBIs. He made it as high as AAA, but he was never on an MLB roster. Bauman retired at age thirty-four to live in Roswell until his death in 2005 at eighty-three years old. The legacy of Bauman and his prowess of home runs lives on with the Minor League Baseball Home Run leader award, aptly named the Joe Bauman Home Run Award.

Lyman Bostock, OF, Major League Baseball Player, Minnesota Twins, 1975–1977 and California Angels, 1978

The story of Lyman Bostock is the saddest tale of them all, not just because of the talent he possessed, but also for the way he was perceived as the best of the best of people. He was murdered in his prime, at age twenty-seven, and in what may be the biggest mystery of all, it is not known if he was the target or just in the wrong place at the time.

The man who shot Bostock, Leonard Smith, was ultimately found not guilty by reason of insanity. Seven months after being committed to a mental health facility, Smith was found to no longer be mentally ill and released. The Indiana insanity laws were subsequently changed so that those with mental illness could be found legally guilty, turned over to a mental health facility for treatment, and then could be sent to prison if released from psychiatric treatment.

Bostock played Major League Baseball for four years, batting .311 for the Minnesota Twins and California Angels. After signing a free agent contract for millions with the Angels, he started off in a slump and believed he did not earn his first monthly check. Attempts to return it were rebuffed, so he donated the salary to charity. Bostock was shot and killed in his hometown of Gary, Indiana, after playing a game at Chicago's Comiskey Park near the end of the 1978 baseball season.

Following his 1980 release, Leonard Smith did not talk or give interviews about the death of Bostock before passing away in 2010.

Steve Dalkowski, P, Baltimore Orioles, Pittsburgh Pirates, and California Angels, 1957–1965

Steve Dalkowski would squint with his glasses on, then rear back to throw a mighty fastball from his left arm to hopefully arrive somewhere in the area of the catcher's mitt, and quite often between the batter's boxes, and more than just occasionally, the ball would hit the batter. In fact, some say Dalkowski's fastball was the best in the history of baseball, but his lack of control of his pitches was just as legendary. Neither pitcher nor catcher would know the precise location of the intended pitch until it was caught or picked up after it stopped rolling.

Dalkowski had an astonishing 1,324 strikeouts in just 956 innings pitched, with almost as many walks (1,236). The hard-partying, undisciplined pitcher was the model for the "Nuke LaLoosh" character in *Bull Durham* and possibly also Charlie Sheen's classic spectacled Rick "Wild Thing" Vaughn in the movie *Major League*. He played in nine different minor leagues during his nine-year career. On the cusp of making the major league roster for the Baltimore Orioles, he hurt his arm in 1964 before finally retiring in 1966 due to injuries. Dalkowski died in 2020 at the age of eighty in New Britain, Connecticut.

Mark Fidrych, SP, Major League Baseball Player, Detroit Tigers, 1976–1980

Mark Fidrych was a national phenomenon in 1976 for the Detroit Tigers and Major League Baseball. With an average fastball, but impeccable control, Fidrych went from a spring training nonroster invitee to the American League's All-Star starting pitcher in Veterans Stadium in Philadelphia in 1976, the year of our Bicentennial. No big deal, right?

Fidrych was nicknamed "The Bird," and baseball fell in love with him and his unusual baseball superstitions and odd behaviors, such as strutting around the mound after an out, talking to the baseball like a friend, or even like a foe. Fidrych would even toss the ball to the umpire if he felt the baseball was going to result in a base hit.

Fidrych appeared on the covers of *Sports Illustrated, Rolling Stone,* and the *Sporting News*. The *Rolling Stone* cover is still the only cover devoted to a baseball player by the music magazine.

Fidrych led the major leagues in ERA, won the 1976 AL Rookie of the Year Award, and finished second to Hall of Fame pitcher Jim Palmer in the AL Cy Young Award for Best Pitcher that year. And much Like David Clyde before him, The Bird starts became national events on TV and resulted in sold out ballparks. The Tigers averaged over twenty thousand additional fans for games in which Fidrych was on the bump at home.

Fidrych was an All-Star in both 1976 and 1977, winning twenty-five of his twenty-nine career wins those two years, before his career was curtailed by injuries to his knee and pitching shoulder. He retired at age twenty-nine. Then a bizarre accident in 2009 ended his life at age fifty-four. The Bird was found dead beneath his ten-wheel dump truck after his clothes became caught in a spinning shift of the truck, causing Fidrych to suffocate while he was working on his truck.

Sidd Finch, P, New York Mets Free Agent Signee, 1985*

**Infamous April Fool's Day joke by legendary writer George Plimpton for the late 1985 March issue of* Sports Illustrated

The 1985 New York Mets discovered the best prospect in the history of the game in Old Orchard Beach, Maine. Sidd Finch was going to be Cy Young, Sandy Koufax, and Tom Seaver combined. Finch could easily throw a fastball at 168 mph without even the need of warming up. Raised in an English orphanage, Finch went to Harvard and used yoga to refine his pitching skills. Finch was, in fact, the whole package.

Sports Illustrated blew the cover on the Mets' amazing prospect who they had quietly been working under wraps in spring training and were about to unleash on baseball. Mets fans were excited, and other major league teams were not sure what to think.

Finch was 6'4" and wore a size 14 shoe. He had an assigned locker wedged between Daryl Strawberry and George Foster for what was expected to be the unveiling of Sidd Finch to the media by the Mets on the day after April Fool's Day. On April 2, 1985, the Mets held a press conference with major networks for what would turn out to be the retirement of Finch from Major League Baseball. Sadly, he walked away from baseball before ever appearing in an MLB game, all for a music career with the French horn.

It is not for certain, but it can be speculated that Finch was afraid to be shown up by the up-and-coming 1985 version of Dwight "Doc" Gooden. The young hurler did his own "Sidd Finch" impersonation that year to soften the departure of the original. But for Gooden, it was not an April Fool's joke on the league with his season of 24-4, 268 Ks, and a 1.53 ERA to lead Major League Baseball in those categories to win the Triple Crown of pitchers.

Perhaps Finch saw the baseball future and figured the New York Mets pitching staff would be just fine without him.

Danny Goodwin, C, Major League Baseball Player, California Angels, 1975, 1977–1978; Minnesota Twins, 1979–1981; and Oakland Athletics, 1982

Considered to be the next Johnny Bench, Danny Goodwin is the only player to be drafted as the No. 1 overall pick in two separate years. First drafted by the Chicago White Sox out of high school, Goodwin opted for college and became a three-time All-American and a College Player of the Year Award recipient. Goodwin was selected by the California Angels in 1975 with a record setting bonus to sign.

The Angels rushed him into the major leagues that same year. Over his nine-year MLB career, Goodwin only spent one full year on a major league roster. He also played a year in Japan. Goodwin is the first player from an Historically Black University to be inducted into the National College Baseball Hall of Fame.

Matt Harrington, SP, 2000 First-Round Selection by the Colorado Rockies, 2001 Second-Round Selection by the San Diego Padres, 2002 Thirteenth-Round Selection by the Tampa Bay Devil Rays, 2003 Twenty-Fourth-Round Selection by the Cincinnati Reds, and 2004 Thirty-Sixth-Round Selection by the New York Yankees

Matt Harrington has perhaps the strangest draft saga of any player in history. He was the Baseball America and *USA TODAY* High School Player of the Year in 2000, but he was not selected until No. 7 overall due to teams being afraid that he would go to college and not sign. Harrington was selected by the Colorado Rockies, but his agent and the team could not agree on a contract. Ultimately Harrington turned down $4 million. Then in 2001, he was selected in the second round by the Padres, who offered Harrington $1.2 million and were also turned down.

The Rays, Reds, and Yankees all took turns drafting and not reaching a deal with Harrington. In 2007, he was not drafted but was signed by the Chicago Cubs and attended spring training, before ultimately being released before the season. Harrington is the only player to be drafted five times by five different teams. He never signed with a team that drafted him, and ultimately, Harrington chose to play baseball in Independent Leagues for seven years with his last baseball game played in 2007. Matt Harrington keeps a low profile and lives in California.

Gregg Jefferies, 2B, Major League Baseball Player, with the New York Mets, Kansas City Royals, Saint Louis Cardinals, Anaheim Angels, and Detroit Tigers, 1987–2000

Gregg Jefferies was a good major league player with parts of fourteen MLB seasons including two All-Star game selections. But as a two-time Baseball America Minor League Player of the Year coming up in New York City with a championship caliber Mets team, he could never truly be the player the media and scouts foretold. Jefferies was so talented that he was compared to the mighty trio of Mickey Mantle, Wade Boggs, and Joe Morgan, each of whom had a Hall of Fame career.

The Mantle power for home runs, Boggs master bat control for gap power and average, and Morgan speed and ability to stabilize the infield, were supposed to be rolled up into the 5'10" 175-pound Jefferies baseball machine. He became the player he was with an eight-hour daily workout six times a week as a youngster, designed by his high school baseball coach father.

Some of the workouts led to confused looks about his unconventional baseball drills, such as taking his bat in the swimming pool for swing practice underwater to increase his bat speed. Jefferies was also particular about his bats, which were all custom crafted for him and kept in separate bags. These were not allowed to be kept with the other players' bats, or even to have another bat touch them. After games, he would clean each bat with rubbing alcohol to keep them their cleanest, even if the bats were not used during that game.

Jefferies was also a new breed of player, who clashed with the veteran and surly New York players as well as the media, front office, and fans. Despite a .289 career batting average, Jefferies, Major League Baseball, and the fans always wanted to see much better numbers. Jefferies retired in 2000 at the young baseball age of thirty-two. In 2001, he turned down a coaching position on the major league level with the Detroit Tigers. Jefferies lives in Las Vegas, gives batting lessons, and is married with four children.

Kevin Maas, DH and 1B, Major League Baseball Player, with the New York Yankees, 1990–1993, and with the Minnesota Twins, 1995

A 1986 twenty-second-round draft pick by the New York Yankees from the University of California, Berkeley, Kevin Maas was positioned by the Yankees to be heir apparent to Don Mattingly. Maas set an MLB record of fewest at-bats to get to 10 career home runs (72). He also earned the MLB record for the fewest at-bats to 13, and 15 home runs. Maas finished second in the 1990 Rookie of the Year voting to Sandy Alomar, Jr.

A traditional cheer included the "Maas-Tops" in right field. If Maas hit a home run to right field, a group of fans would take off their tops and jump up and down as he completed his trot to home plate. High strikeout rates lead to Maas playing for four MLB organizations as well as a year in professional Japanese baseball.

Kevin Maas now lives in California and works as a financial consultant.

Oscar Taveras, OF, Major League Baseball Player, with the Saint Louis Cardinals, 2014, and Minor League Baseball Player, 2009–2014

Oscar Taveras earned two batting titles during his minor league career. He was also a two-time Major League Baseball All-Star Futures game participant and three-time Minor League All-Star game participant. Taveras was a star in the making already leaving a huge mark for the 2014 St. Louis Cardinals. He played eighty games at the MLB level and hit a game-tying home run in Game 2 of the National League Championship Series.

Shockingly, Taveras died in a car accident in the Dominican Republic less than two weeks after the Cardinals were eliminated in the 2014 playoffs.

Glossary of Baseball Terms

2B: doubles hit (offensive)/allowed (defensive)
3B: triples hit (offensive)/allowed (defensive)
AB: at bats
AVG: batting average
BA: batting average
ERA: earned run average (9 * ER/IP) (9 times earned runs per innings pitched)
G: games played or pitched
H: hits
HR: home runs
IP: innings pitched
K: strikeouts
L: losses
OPS: on-base + slugging percentages
R: runs scored
RBI: runs batted in
SLG: slugging percentage (total bases/at bats or (1B + 2*2B + 3*3B + 4*HR)/AB)
SO: strikeouts
W: wins
WHIP: walks and hits per inning pitched ((BB + H)/IP) (base on balls plus hits per innings pitched)

Index

About the Author

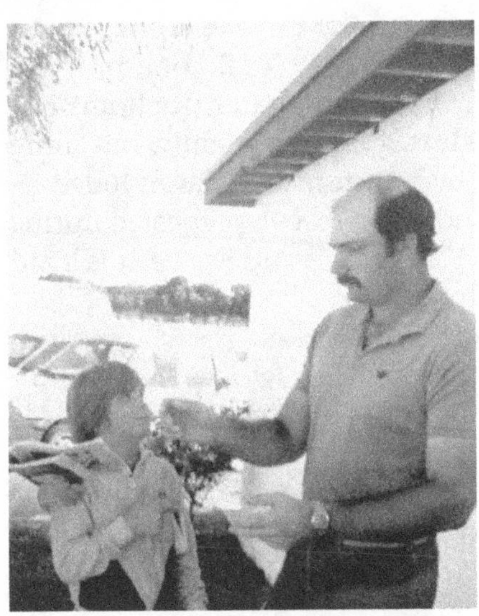

A young Patrick Montgomery, the author, looking up to Steve "Bye-Bye" Balboni during 1984 Spring Training in Florida. This picture sums up the way fans can see their baseball idols. I wanted to meet him even after he was traded by the Yankees in 1983 to the rival Kansas City Royals, and I cheered quietly when Balboni, George Brett, and Frank White won the 1985 World Series. *Personal photo provided by Patrick Montgomery*

Patrick Montgomery is an award-winning writer, screenwriter, and a member of the Screen Actors Guild. His most recent book, *The Baseball Miracle of the Splendid 6*, garnered first place for Sports Book at the 2022 Speak Up Talk Radio Firebird Book Awards and was a winner in the 2022 Hollywood Book Festival. Montgomery is a graduate of the Defense Information School with many qualifications including journalism and crisis communications. During his more than twenty-five years of military, federal, and state service, his articles and photographs appeared in newspapers and magazines internationally, nationally, and locally. Montgomery was the Coast Guard's Author and Photojournalist of the Year. Montgomery served as public affairs officer for the Deepwater Horizon oil spill, Miracle on the Hudson, US Airways Flight 1549, various hurricanes, and DHS National Special Security Events including both Republican and Democratic Conventions, and the Olympics.

Montgomery is a long-time youth softball coach, baseball historian, geek, advocate, and student of the game, including membership in the Society for American Baseball Research (SABR), Internet Baseball Writers Association of America, and the Major League Baseball Players Alumni Association.

Montgomery is married to the wonderful Barbara Montgomery and is the father to his long-suffering daughters, Samantha and Billy Montgomery. The love of baseball runs deep in the Montgomery family. Barbara and Patrick Montgomery were among the Bleacher Creatures and the 49,280 fans witnessing the David Wells perfect game in 1998 at Yankees Stadium, and years later, now with the girls, the four of them were there to watch the Yankees score 29 runs against the Red Sox during the two-game 2019 MLB London Series with the capstone of Samantha snarling a batting practice home run from her favorite player, Brett Gardner. Less importantly, but more shocking, the author was waved at by an astonished Aaron Judge responding to the wave from the author. This feat was repeated during Game 3 of the 2019 ALCS between the Yankees and Astros. It is good to establish relationships and network.

The author may be the only person to be greeted as such by Aaron Judge while he played two different games in two different continents. Major League Baseball probably does not keep official records on such matters, but Team Monty certainly does.

The love of baseball will continue within the Montgomery family, with Billy Montgomery aspiring to one day work in Major League Baseball.

The author can be reached at ptmontgomerybooks@gmail.com. He is happy to hear your thoughts!